Keeping the Faith

Keeping the Faith

RUSSIAN ORTHODOX MONASTICISM IN THE SOVIET UNION, 1917–1939

Jennifer Jean Wynot

TEXAS A&M UNIVERSITY PRESS
COLLEGE STATION

Manufactured in the United States of America

First edition

All photographs by Jennifer J. Wynot

The paper used in this book meets the minimum requirements
of the American National Standard for Permanence
of Paper for Printed Library Materials, z39.48-1984.
Binding materials have been chosen for durability.
∞

LIBRARY OF CONGRESS CATALOGING-IN-PUBLICATION DATA
Wynot, Jennifer Jean, 1971–
Keeping the faith : Russian orthodox monasticism in the Soviet Union, 1917–1939 / Jennifer Jean Wynot.—1st ed.
p. cm.—(Eugenia and Hugh M. Stewart '26 Series on Eastern Europe)
Includes bibliographical references and index.
ISBN 1-58544-332-8 (cloth : alk. paper)
1. Monasticism and religious orders, Orthodox Eastern—Soviet Union—History. 2. Soviet Union—Church history. I. Title. II. Eugenia and Hugh M. Stewart '26 Series on Eastern Europe (College Station, Tex.).
BX581.W96 2004
271′.81947′09041—dc22

2003018573

Contents

LIST OF ILLUSTRATIONS vii
PREFACE ix
ACKNOWLEDGMENTS xvii

CHAPTER 1. *The Church on the Eve of the 1917 Revolution* 3
CHAPTER 2. *Revolution, Civil War, and Famine, 1917–1922* 36
CHAPTER 3. *The New Economic Policy Years, 1921–1928* 80
CHAPTER 4. *The Good Friday of Russian Monasticism, 1928–1934* 114
CHAPTER 5. *The Descent into Hell, 1934–1939* 140
CONCLUSION 170
APPENDIX A. *Decree on Land Nationalization, November 8, 1917* 179
APPENDIX B. *Decree of the Soviet Commissars Concerning the Separation of Church and State and of Schools and Church, January 23, 1918* 181
APPENDIX C. *Sample of Agreement between Believers and Soviet of Workmen-Peasant Deputies* 183

NOTES 187
GLOSSARY 213
BIBLIOGRAPHY 215
INDEX 223

Illustrations

Mother Nektaria, Optina Pustyn Monastery 17
Holy Trinity St. Sergius Lavra, Sergeev Posad 26
Making candles at Optina Pustyn Monastery 29
Relics of Elder Ambrose, Optina Pustyn Monastery 42
Library of St. John's skete, Optina Pustyn Monastery 104
St. John's skete entrance, Optina Pustyn Monastery 105
Bells, Optina Pustyn Monastery 123
Danilov Monastery, Moscow 129
Don Monastery, Moscow 130
Novodevichy Monastery, Moscow 131
All Saints Church and Monastery, Moscow 132
Placing cross on restored church, Optina Pustyn 172
Grave of Elder Makarii, Optina Pustyn 173
Patriarch Alexei II at canonization of Optina Elders 174
Procession at canonization of Optina Elders 175
Author with three Russian nuns 176

Tables

TABLE 1. *Number of Functioning Prayer Buildings, 1936* 148
TABLE 2. *Religious Believers according to the 1937 Census* 152
TABLE 3. *Monasteries of the Orthodox Church Abroad before World War II* 164
TABLE 4. *Monasteries in the Soviet Union by Republic as of 1945* 168

Preface

HISTORICALLY, RUSSIAN ORTHODOX monasteries and convents have had important functions in Russian culture, in both the spiritual and the political realm. As centers of spiritual wisdom, they attracted pilgrims from all walks of life. One of the most famous monasteries in Central Russia, Optina Pustyn, became the site of a religious revival in the nineteenth century. Hundreds of thousands of pilgrims, among them the famous writers Nikolai Gogol and Fyodor Dostoevsky, journeyed to this monastery to receive advice from the elders. Politically, the monasteries played a vital role in the church hierarchy. Two types of priests serve in the Orthodox Church, the "white" clergy and the "black" clergy. The former were married priests who served a parish. The latter were monks. According to Orthodox canon law, bishops, archbishops, metropolitans, and patriarchs cannot marry. Therefore, all of the church hierarchy necessarily came from the monasteries. This fact combined with the conservative character of monasticism made the monasteries potential political rivals in the minds of the Bolsheviks. Additionally, most monasteries owned land and employed peasants. As part of the Bolsheviks' promise to give land to the peasants, they necessarily targeted monasteries.[1]

For women, monasticism offered one of the few opportunities to hold prominent positions in society. Although female monasteries have usually been portrayed as places of exile for former wives of the nobility, women of all classes were drawn to monasticism. Although women could not be ordained as priests, as nuns they could assist in some of the sacraments such as communion. The abbess of a women's monastery also occupied a prominent position in the community. Many laypeople sought out nuns and eldresses for advice and spiritual guidance.

Orthodox monasteries continued to provide spiritual strength throughout the Soviet period, despite severe persecution. This oppression reached its zenith during the period of collectivization in the late 1920s and 1930s and abated with the advent of World War II. Although the Soviets deprived them of citizenship and other basic rights, monks and nuns struggled clandestinely to uphold the traditions of monasticism and the Orthodox Church. Their partial success against heavy odds enabled them to provide a counterculture to the totalitarian Soviet regime. Indeed, of all the pre-1917 institutions, religion proved the most resilient. Why and how it managed to persevere in spite of the enormous hostility against it is a topic that continues to fascinate both the general public and historians. My study of the monasteries should contribute to a fuller understanding of the resiliency of Russian Orthodoxy.

Historiography

My reasons for studying the history of the monasteries during this period are threefold. While many historians of Russian religion have focused on the essentially negative character of this period, specifically the closing and destruction of the monasteries and churches,[2] my aim is to examine ways in which monks and nuns were able to preserve their way of life despite hardship. In other words, although the Soviet authorities closed all of the monasteries and convents by 1930, monasticism as a way of life continued.[3]

Recently, historians have focused on popular resistance to Soviet antireligious propaganda. William Fletcher was one of the earliest historians to do so, but his books, although informative and innovative, were published more than twenty years ago and mainly use secondary sources. More recently, Glennys Young's book examines the methods that both rural clergy and laity used to preserve their faith. The village soviet was often used to keep the churches open, and there are many accounts of parish priests being members of these soviets.[4] The most recent work focusing on religion is William Husband's book on atheism and society in Soviet Russia during the interwar period.[5] However, some of these studies have serious flaws. Despite their excellence in research, they tend to underestimate the depth of religious feeling among the laity, especially peasants. Sheila Fitzpatrick, Moshe Levin, and William Husband in particular dismiss any peasant resistance to government antireligious campaigns as "the desire to defend what was simply familiar and enjoyable."[6] The evidence from petitions and memoirs provides a picture of a laity who often risked their lives to protect monastics and church relics. It is hard to believe that laypeople would risk so much merely in the name of nostalgia.

Historians have thus far almost completely neglected the monasteries' important role in this story. Monks and nuns also displayed the ability to adapt to a new way of life and often used Soviet institutions to survive. Shortly after the Bolshevik Revolution, several antireligious journals reported that monasteries and convents were converting themselves into collective farms.[7] After all of the monasteries were officially closed in 1930, many monks and nuns went back into the world and worked in factories and schools.[8] Many still managed to keep in contact with each other and maintain a sense of monastic community. There were also reports of secret tonsure given to novices.[9]

Aside from the contribution that my work will make to Russian religious history, it will also add to the current body of literature that reexamines Soviet society during the 1920s and 1930s. Due to Soviet propaganda and the unavailability of much archival material, a rather stereotyped view of Stalin's Russia existed until quite recently. Soviet historians portrayed the country as a "workers' paradise," a place where the workers were happy and cared for by the state. Sacrifices were made willingly in the quest to build socialism. Strikes and discontent were unknown. Conversely, Western historians under the influence of the Cold War have depicted the Stalinist era as a time when the population was thoroughly cowed and submissive under the threat of the Great Terror. Recent research shows that Soviet society was more complex. Works by Sarah Davies and Isaac Deutscher provide examples as does Jeffrey Rossman's dissertation on worker resistance under Stalin. Sheila Fitzpatrick and Lynne Viola are among the historians who are reexamining the role of the peasantry under the Stalinist regime.[10]

Much new research also debunks the idea of a monolithic and omnipotent state and demonstrates that Soviet local authorities operated on a fairly autonomous level. Often, central authorities were more likely to be lenient than the local ones. Government action (or lack thereof) in the realm of religious life provides an excellent means of demonstrating this phenomenon.[11] Western historians tended to view the Bolsheviks as having a totally developed sense of government and society from the very beginning. The truth was quite the reverse; Soviet rule proved very experimental, especially during the first two decades. Because Marxism as an ideology never completely described the specific aspects of a truly

Communist society, all Bolshevik leaders, including Lenin, were compelled to improvise to a degree, even after they consolidated their power. They frequently reacted to events rather than managing them.[12]

A third contribution that my book will make is in the realm of European history as a whole. European historians have devoted much attention to monasteries and how they survived under persecution. A study of Russian monasteries under similar and yet far more extreme conditions would serve as a useful foundation for a comparison of Western and Eastern monastic traditions. Moreover, this examination would provide the basis for a comparison between the Orthodox Church and other religions, such as Tibetan Buddhism, which maintained its traditions while under a hostile government.

Methodology

In my research, I focused only on the monasteries under the jurisdiction of the Moscow Patriarchate and not on the Uniate or Catholic monasteries. I chose to exclude these other monasteries for several reasons: There are other works that cover these topics far more extensively than I could, and the Russian Orthodox Church occupied a very central part in the cultural and political life of Russia. As the largest Christian denomination in the country, it naturally had more influence politically and culturally.

A full examination of monasticism in all of Russia is not practically possible, as conditions varied according to geographical location and other factors. Therefore, I compared two provinces, Moscow and Smolensk, where religious life was particularly active. Because historians have paid little or no attention to urban religious life, this book focuses mainly on the Moscow province, using the more rural Smolensk as a basis for comparison. Moscow is an ideal subject. It is both an ancient and a modern city and in many respects is an illustration of how old and new have both coexisted and clashed. For centuries Moscow was the center of Russian religious and political life. The Patriarch of Russia resided in Moscow and frequently played an influential role in statecraft. In 1908 Lev Denisov listed thirty-eight monasteries and twenty-three convents with a total of 2,219 monks and 3,378 nuns in Moscow alone.[13] Some of the most famous monasteries and convents are located in and around Moscow, such as Trinity Sergius Monastery in Zagorsk, Danilov Monastery, and Novo-Devichy Convent. These monasteries faced especially difficult times due to their proximity to the central Soviet authorities, especially the NKVD. For that reason, their techniques of adaptation and resistance differed from those employed by monasteries and convents in the countryside.

Urban life could sometimes prove advantageous as well. Displaced monks and nuns able to escape being sent to prison camps or shot could obtain factory work and also take advantage of communal apartment living to maintain a sense of community. In the early Soviet period, city life also provided some sense of anonymity. This became increasingly difficult after the 1929 laws, which among other things deprived priests, monastics, and their families of the right to work, vote, and live in cities. In the eyes of the state, they became politically disenfranchised, or *lishentsy.* Despite this, many continued to live in the cities and escaped detection.

Smolensk province provides an excellent contrast to Moscow. Located approximately 418 kilometers southwest of Moscow, its population was only 8.8 percent urban in 1925. Although not located in the "breadbasket" regions of the Soviet Union, it was heavily agricultural, specializing mainly in dairy farming and flax.[14] Heavy industry was rare, and even light industry remained scattered. Aside from its rural appearance, the guaranteed access to archival material also influenced me to choose Smolensk as a subject for comparison. During the Second World War, the Germans occupied Smolensk and captured a great many Communist party documents, which were in turn confiscated by the Americans. These papers are now in the National Archives, and microfilms of them are widely available. For this reason other authors as well have used Smolensk for comparative studies. My work serves to complement previous authors' research.[15]

I have organized my chapters chronologically. Chapter 1 provides background material illustrating the position of the monasteries on the eve of the 1917 Revolution. It focuses particularly on the period of the Church reform movement from 1905 to 1907 and the Church *Sobor* (council) in 1917. Chapter 2 discusses the monasteries' role during the Revolution and Civil War (1917–1921) and considers their methods of resistance and adaptation during the period of nationalization.

Chapter 3 examines the period of the New Economic Policy (NEP), 1921–1928, and addresses the uneasy and often contradictory relationship between Church and state. Chapter 4 discusses the last two years of NEP along with the collectivization (1928–1933). The bulk of this section focuses on the schism of 1927 and its effect on monasticism. Chapter 5 examines the period of the Great Retreat and the Purges (1934–1939) and how the monks and nuns were able to maintain their communities in the gulags and in exile.

The purge period provides a natural endpoint to this study. The outbreak of World War II and the Nazi invasion of the Soviet Union in 1941 changed the relationship between Church and state. Stalin recognized the value of the Orthodox Church as a propaganda tool and reopened many churches and monasteries and generally relaxed the prohibitions against religious activities.

When referring to dates, I use both the "old" and "new" calendar systems when they are given in documents. Otherwise, I use the Gregorian calendar. Russia did not adopt the Gregorian calendar, which the west switched to in the sixteenth century, but continued to adhere to the Julian calendar, which is 13 days later. On January 31, 1918, the new Bolshevik government officially changed to the Gregorian calendar. The Russian Orthodox Church, however, still adheres to the Julian calendar.

The interwar period in Russian church history is very controversial for most Russians. Much of what is written about this era, particularly works by Russian émigrés, is colored by the strong feelings produced by the 1927 Declaration. Many members of the "Catacomb Church" and its émigré counterpart, the Russian Orthodox Church Outside of Russia, still consider the Patriarchal Church in Moscow to be a traitor to the faith. Therefore, they tend to classify the behavior of Russian Orthodox during this period as demonstrating either resistance or accommodation. Thus far, much scholarship that covers this period uses this "resistance vs. accommodation" model.[16]

My goal in this book is not to take sides in the dispute concerning which is the True Church, nor do I wish to examine internal Church politics. However, my subject necessitates consideration of this schism and its effect on monastic life. I also demonstrate that the aforementioned resistance vs. accommodation model is not suitable for scholarly investigation. A better method of examining this subject might be to view the actions of many Orthodox as adaptation rather than accommodation. In other words, an individual's or an institution's adaptation to the surroundings is not synonymous with active support of that environment. As stated earlier, many clergy and laity used Soviet institutions as tools to preserve their own faith. The fact that a monastery converted itself into a collective farm does not mean that it upheld the ideals of collectivization.

Although some Russian archival material is now available in the

United States, such as part of the Soviet Communist Party Archives and the Smolensk Communist Party Archives, most of my research took place in Russia. Besides the Central Archives of the Russian Federation (GARF), I also examined the State Archives of Moscow Oblast (GAMO), the Kaluga Oblast Archives (GAKO), the Center for the Preservation and Study of Documents on Recent History (RTsKhIDNI, formerly the Central Archive of the Communist Party), and the Russian State Library (formerly known as the Lenin Library).[17]

In addition to archival research, I also examined local and national newspapers, such as *Bezbozhnik, Antireligioznik, Krasnaia Zvezda, Pravda, Izvestiia,* and *Krestianskaia Pravda* to gain understanding of events. I also conducted interviews with several nuns who survived the interwar period. Unfortunately, there are few living survivors from that period. However, over the past five years the Tikhon Institute in Moscow as well as others have been publishing the memoirs of religious people who suffered persecution during the 1920s and 1930s. Chapters 4 and 5 in particular rely on memoirs, as it is still very difficult to obtain access to the KGB archives. Due to the nature of the purge years and the secrecy that pervaded all aspects of Soviet life, it is difficult to get accurate numbers of how many monks and nuns existed. Unfortunately, researchers have to extrapolate from memoirs and other anecdotal information.

Over the past ten years, Orthodoxy has experienced a revival in Russia, and the monasteries have been in the vanguard. This resurgence has sparked interest within Russia as well as abroad to study the history of these institutions and their role in preserving Orthodoxy in Russia. I believe that my work will enhance the literature already available and benefit Russian as well as non-Russian historians.

Acknowledgments

MANY PEOPLE HELPED to make this project a reality. First and foremost I would like to thank the staff at Texas A&M University Press for their assistance in making this project a reality. I would also like to thank my former advisors at Emory University, Drs. Kermit McKenzie and Matthew Payne. Dr. McKenzie's attention to detail and high expectations challenged me to produce the very best. Our long conversations with Dr. Payne provided unique insights into my work and inspired me to take my research in new directions. Dr. Theofanis Stavrou graciously invited me into his home while I examined the James Cunningham papers in the University of Minnesota library and has acted as a mentor throughout graduate school and beyond.

I am immensely grateful to Emory University for helping to fund this project. Thank you to the history department for providing me with summer funding to do research in Russia and in the United States. The Emory University Fund helped to support my last trip to Russia in 1998.

Dr. Jeffrey Burds and the Russian Summer Archival Program assisted me with obtaining visas and permits for conducting research in Russia, along with valuable archival contacts. Thank you to Father Herman and all of the nuns and monks for the hospitality extended to me at the monastery in Platina, California. I also owe a debt of gratitude to the staff and faculty at St. Vladimir's Seminary in Crestwood, New York, and the Holy Trinity Monastery in Jordanville, New York, for helping me in my research.

This book would not have been completed without the assistance of many people in Russia. Leonid Vaintraub deserves special thanks for introducing me to the archives in Moscow in 1996. Thank you to all of the Russian archivists who helped make my research experience a pleasant one. Father Artemy at All Saints parish church in Moscow introduced me to Mother Serafima, who proved a fountain of information. I am also grateful to Mother Nektaria of California, who allowed me to accompany her to Optina Pustyn for the canonization of the Optina Elders in 1996 and for her help in finding people to interview. A special thank you to Evgeny Shklovsky and his family not only for providing me with a place to stay on both of my trips to Moscow, but also for the affection and friendship they extended throughout my stay.

Last but not least, I owe a special debt of gratitude to my friends and family who have provided me with encouragement throughout this process, from dissertation to book. Words cannot express the gratitude I feel toward them. My grandmother, Jean Gebhart, my brother Gregory and his wife, Amanda, and my mother, Kathy, have all offered unconditional love and support throughout this long process. A special debt to my father, Edward, who not only provided me with paternal love and support but was also my proofreader and gave valuable advice on how to succeed in this profession.

Keeping the Faith

CHAPTER 1

The Church on the Eve of the 1917 Revolution

ALTHOUGH ORTHODOXY is the second largest Christian denomination, Westerners know very little about its history and practices. It is often regarded as simply another form of Catholicism. Although the two do have some common theology and a shared history until the Great Schism in 1054, since then they have evolved into two distinct churches. Like the Catholic Church, the Orthodox Church is hierarchical; that is, there is a head of the Church, the patriarch. The ecumenical patriarch is based in Constantinople. Although he is considered the central head of the Orthodox Church, he is not empowered to make unilateral decisions regarding doctrine. As Orthodoxy spread north of Byzantium, national churches such as those in Romania, Russia, and Bulgaria joined the Orthodox East. Over time, they were granted autonomy from Constantinople and elected their own patriarchs, who administered their own nations' churches. There are now more than twenty of these autocephalous, or independent, Orthodox churches in the world, each with its own patriarch or archbishop. These "divisions" are strictly administrative; the doctrine and liturgical practices remain the same regardless of nationality. The patriarch of Constantinople is considered to be "the first among equals," a term of respect recognizing Constantinople's historic place in Orthodoxy. However, any decisions regarding doctrine or administration are not decided by one person, but rather by a synod, or council, of bishops. The last of these ecumenical councils met in A.D. 787. This system of government differs greatly from the more unified structure of the Catholic Church.[1]

One shared characteristic of both Catholicism and Orthodoxy is monasticism. In both denominations, monasteries have served as the backbone of the faith in their capacities as centers of learning and spirituality. In the Orthodox world, they also play a political role. According to canon law, parish priests (referred to in Russia as the "white clergy") may marry before ordination. However, only monastics (also called the "black clergy") may become bishops, archbishops, and patriarchs. This fact placed the monasteries in a position to influence policy in both Church matters and state affairs. It also contributed to hostile feelings between the white and the black clergy. Aside from this difference, the two forms of monasticism differ structurally. Unlike in the West, eastern monasticism has no fixed rule, and there are no monastic orders. Each monastery has its own constitution, usually drawn up upon its establishment. These constitutions generally fall into two categories: those based on the Egyptian model and those based on the reforms of Basil the Great (A.D. 329–379).

The Egyptian model derived from the traditions of the Desert Fathers, such as Anthony of Egypt, who withdrew from the secular world and went into the wilderness to lead hermetic lives. At first, each hermit led a solitary existence, but as time went on, several hermits gathered together into small groups to provide mutual protection and assist each other in acts of charity. These groups became the basis for what later historians called the *lavra*.[2] These monastic groups never officially organized themselves into distinct communities. They frequently lived by strict ascetic rules, sometimes carried to an extreme. For example, Simon the Stylite had himself walled up in a cistern with no food or water during Lent. Others went into the desert with little food or water for months at a time.[3]

Basil the Great abhorred such extreme asceticism and attempted to impose some order on monastic life. He adopted and greatly modified the *cenobitic* or communal model of another Egyptian ascetic named Pachomius. Under this system, monks and nuns held all property in common and lived and worked together. Ironically, in introducing these reforms, Basil never intended for monasteries to be separate from the rest of the Christian community. However, because of later misinterpretations of Basil's writings, this is exactly what occurred, particularly within the Catholic Church. Basil believed that monks and nuns should live together in communities and at the same time remain part of the larger Christian community; moreover, they should "live lives of perfect communism under the rule of an elected bishop who should command perfect obedience and ... they should work as well as pray."[4] Indeed, in theory at least, monasticism embodies many of the ideals of pure communism. No class consciousness existed, and all monks and nuns had their appointed duties. No exceptions were made on the basis of social class or rank. Monasteries also served as refuges for the elderly and orphans and provided social services such as hospitals and schools. In reality, not all monasteries lived up to this ideal; some merely served as social centers and proved to be as corrupt as lay circles.

Like Catholicism, Orthodox monasticism has various levels. The lowest is the novitiate. In this stage, the novice wears the simple monastic garb, and the only vows are chastity and obedience to the elders. The novitiate is free to leave the monastery at any time. The next stage is called the *rassaphore.* After a period of time, when the novice is ready to fulfill a deeper level of commitment, he or she is fully tonsured into monasticism. During this ceremony, the full *klobuk* (a hat with a veil attached) is given to the monastic, who may then participate in every facet of monastic life. Both monks and nuns wear the same monastic garb. At this stage, one may still leave monasticism but only after deep discussion with the abbot and other elders. The final stage is the *schema.* In the Russian tradition, being tonsured to the schema typically occurs when the monastic is of advanced age or close to death. In the schema, monastics are exempt from all obedience and spend virtually all of their time in prayer. In receiving the schema, the monastics are tonsured again and also receive a new name and new garments—the traditional black robes decorated with white crosses, a skull, and prayers.

Another difference between Catholic and Orthodox monasticism centers on the relationship each has to society. With the increasing secularization that has occurred in the West beginning with the Renaissance, monasteries became relegated to the background. Not so in the Orthodox world, particularly Russia, which did not experience the Renaissance and where the Orthodox church continued to render enormous influence over every aspect of life. The monastery remained the center of spiritual and cultural life. During the eighteenth and nineteenth centuries the institutional church experienced periods of reform and counterreform. Parish priests frequently functioned as petty bureaucrats and often were so overworked that they did not have enough time to devote to the spiritual lives of their congregations. As a result, the laity viewed the monasteries as more remote from the political involvement of the official church and more spiritual than the parish priests. Therefore, in the eyes of many devout Orthodox, the monasteries possessed greater legitimacy than the institutional church.

The Tradition of Starchestvo

The monasteries' position of respect was in large part due to the tradition of *starchestvo,* or eldership, which is unique to the Orthodox world and plays an integral part in Russian spirituality to this day. The Russian religious philosopher G. P. Fedotov defined starchestvo as "an institution which makes a bridge between gifts of the spirit and service to the world."[5] People come to the *starets, or staritsa,* an older monk or nun who is highly regarded for his or her spiritual wisdom, to ask for advice on spiritual and worldly problems. Vladimir Kotelnikov elaborates on the definition of these elders when he writes that "the *starets* touched on the intimate depth of the man something that obliged him to stand absolutely alone before God, to recognize keenly his own personal faults before God and to discern his own personal way of salvation."[6]

Nowhere in Russia was the practice of *starchestvo* more fully articulated than at Optina Pustyn. Located 140 miles southeast of Moscow in Kaluga oblast near the village of Kozelsk, Optina Pustyn occupies a great place in Russia's cultural and spiritual history, perhaps more than any other monastery in the country. Optina's golden age occurred between 1821 and 1891 with its succession of elders. Elder Amvrosii was the first and the most influential. Under his guidance, other monasteries arose in the vicinity. The most famous of these was the women's monastery Shamordino, located in the town of Kaluga.[7]

The popularity of the elders may be partly explained by their emphasis on frequent confession. In the Orthodox Church, confession is considered an important sacrament. However, no absolute rules exist as to how often one needs to confess. The Holy Synod issued a statement declaring that an Orthodox Christian in good standing must go to confession at least once a year. Most clergy and laity interpreted that to mean that they should go to confession only once a year. Therefore, parish priests typically heard confession only during Holy Week. During this time, the number of penitents was so great that the priests were unable to give much time to individual confessions. The elders, however, advocated frequent confessions and made themselves available to the laity. Elder Leonid of Optina (d. 1841) was a popular father confessor because of his ability to elicit detailed accounts of the spiritual lives of his penitents. He also devoted much attention to the spiritual lives of women, whom the parish priests usually neglected.[8]

The bond between the starets and the individual layperson became very important in Russia during the 1930s, when all monasteries were officially closed. The individual starets then came to embody the entire tradition of monasticism. These elders and eldresses became the last living links to Holy Russia, which is why during the 1930s people made pilgrimages even at the risk of losing their lives simply to seek religious truth from them.

Another distinguishing factor between Catholicism and Orthodoxy that has a significant impact on the status of the monasteries is the relationship between Church and state. Beginning with the founding of Byzantium in A.D. 330, Emperor Constantine the Great set the pattern for the emperor's place within the Church life. His duty as head of a Christian empire was to enforce laws, both secular and religious. If a question regarding doctrine arose, the emperor would convene and preside over a council of clerical dignitaries and ensure that its decision was implemented. Despite the emperor's exalted place in Church affairs, general opinion nonetheless perceived that imperial power over the Church was limited.[9]

The authority the emperor had over the Orthodox Church has led to charges of caesaro-papism, defined as complete subservience to the secular ruler. This accusation is not entirely accurate, although in Russia's case it is not totally unfounded. Although the Russians initially followed the Byzantine political tradition of the emperor's extensive involvement in Church life, they later opposed this practice. In the fourteenth century, as Moscow's power grew, the Russian metropolitan objected to the Byzantine emperor interfering in ecclesiastical affairs, stating: "[W]e have a church, but we have no tsar and do not want to have one." The patriarch of Constantinople replied that "It is impossible for Christians not to have a tsar because the Church and state are in close alliance and continuous interaction and it is impossible to separate one from the other."[10] Rather than accepting the role of the Church as a political arm of the state, the early Muscovites interpreted the relationship between Church and state to mean a partnership, or *symphonia,* in which both had equal power and worked together to preserve the empire from foreign and domestic enemies and heresy. In practice, however, this alliance was not evenly balanced; invariably the Church remained dependent on the emperor for protection. However, at various times in Russian history, such as the Mongol conquest and the Time of Troubles, the Church sustained Russia during the years of the temporary collapse of the state. Even in these rare cases, the Orthodox patriarchs never had as much power as the Roman pope.[11]

Early History of Russian Orthodoxy

Since A.D. 988, when Prince Vladimir of Kiev baptized the Russian people, Orthodoxy has played a dominant role in Russian culture and history. Orthodoxy is an important part of Russian identity in that a person who is not baptized in the Orthodox faith is not considered truly Russian. Evidence of this strong identification may be found in the Russian language. The word "peasant" *(krestian)* is derived from the word for "Christian," *khristian.* This strong sense of identity was further enhanced after the fall of Constantinople in 1453, when Russia became the sole independent Orthodox country. This prompted Moscow to refer to itself as "the Third Rome." The first Rome had fallen into heresy before the schism of 1054. The second Rome, Constantinople, had fallen to the infidel Muslims in 1453. Thereafter, as the last remaining non-Muslim-occupied country, Russia had the responsibility and vital destiny to uphold the true faith.

In the early centuries of the Christianization of Russia, the boundaries between Church and state remained virtually invisible. Church and state needed each other, and each contributed to the other's survival. The Church in particular endorsed both the unification of the country and the rise of absolutism. Not until after Constantinople formally granted the Russian church autocephaly in 1589 did the Church begin to lose its independence from the state. So long as Constantinople nominated and consecrated the Russian metropolitans, the Church remained beyond the reach of the Moscow grand princes, although it was many years before the latter fully asserted their power over the Church. The first recorded incident of a secular official removing a metropolitan from office occurred in 1521. Similar arbitrary interferences took place later in the sixteenth century. The most violent and extreme example of state domination of Church occurred during the reign of Ivan IV (1533–1584). Ivan was the first openly absolutist Russian ruler and the first to be crowned *tsar* (caesar). In 1568 he ordered the murder of Philip, Metropolitan of Moscow. This act shocked the people and resulted in Philip's elevation to the status of martyr in the popular imagination. His remains were transferred to the remote White Sea monastery of Solovetsk, which quickly became a famous destination for pilgrims. Philip's murder, combined with the killings of other clergy, signaled the beginning of the deterioration of the previously close relationship between the monasteries and the grand princes.[12]

The Development of Russian Monasticism

Monasticism in Russia began almost at the same time as the conversion of Rus. These early monasteries tended to develop around towns, where the monks and nuns could act as missionaries to the newly Christian Slavs. As time progressed, many monasteries moved to the countryside to get away from the distractions of the secular world.

Traditionally, Orthodoxy placed great emphasis on solitude and contemplation. The tradition of *hesychasm,* or "prayer of the heart," began in Byzantine monasteries and by the fifteenth century was widely practiced in Russian monasteries as well. Hesychasts strove for attaining the apostle Paul's instruction to "pray without ceasing." They did this through coordinating the repetition of the "Jesus prayer" with their heartbeat and breathing.[13] The great Russian monastic and saint Sergius Radonezh is credited with introducing the practice from Mount Athos. The most famous of the Russian hesychasts was Nils Sorskii (1433–1508). Aside from prayer of the heart, Sorskii also stressed the ideal of monastic poverty. It was he who established the first sketes in Russia.[14] However, beginning in the sixteenth century, hesychasm was overshadowed by an emphasis on monasteries accumulating wealth for the purpose of serving the state and society.[15] An idiorythmic pattern developed that differed from Basil's communal model. The word "idiorythmic" means "to live in one's own way." In this type of monastery, the monks and nuns had to pay a fee upon entering and also had to support themselves once inside. They typically lived in private cells that they purchased from the monastery and paid for their own housekeeping and food. Although an elected council supervised the monastery's activities, individuals were not under direct supervision.

The result of this practice was threefold: a reduction in the authority of the abbot or abbess, since everyone remained independent; a decrease in the time that a monk or nun had to be contemplative, since most of the day was taken up with matters of physical survival; and the transformation of the monastery into almost an exclusive enclave for the rich. The monasteries' growing wealth attracted members of the wealthy class, who viewed monasticism as a way to lead an idle life. The fee required to enter the monastery and the necessity of buying a cell outright restricted monasticism to those who had a significant amount of money to invest. Those who could not afford to pay were often turned away or were allowed to stay in exchange for performing the most laborious tasks.[16] In the aftermath of Catherine's reforms in the eighteenth century, supporters justified this way of life by claiming that requiring monastics to provide for their individual expenses reduced dependency on the state, now that the Church was essentially a government-funded institution.

As early as the fifteenth century, the contrast between the idiorythmic and the cenobitic lifestyles led to a split within Russian monasticism between the so-called possessors (those who advocated the idiorythmic pattern) and the nonpossessors (those who favored the cenobitic style). The question of property was not the only division among the two groups. They also differed on the relation of the Church to the state, as well as in their attitudes toward discipline and prayer. The possessors argued in favor of rules and discipline and favored a close relationship with the state, whereas the nonpossessors emphasized personal piety and relationship to God and wanted to prevent the Church from becoming the servant of the state. Many monastics who rejected the dominant idiorythmic model left the monasteries and went to the Russian north to form new communities.

The Reforms of Peter the Great

The reign of Peter I (1682–1725) concluded the process of subordinating the Church to the state. Peter perceived the Church as an impediment to his reforms. He therefore introduced measures designed to weaken the Church's power. The first concerned the monasteries. He ordered the state treasury to expropriate monastic lands, and in 1701 he turned his attention to the monastery department of the Moscow patriarchate. As its name suggests, this department administered men's and women's monasteries. In 1701 Peter placed it under civilian rule, in the process renaming it the College of Economy. He then ordered the monasteries to feed and house army veterans and invalids along with their families. When the Church complained that the monasteries were too poor to accomplish this, Peter abolished the monastery department and returned the land to Church control.[17]

In 1721 Peter proclaimed the Reglament, which abolished the patriarchate and placed the Church directly under government control. All administrative concerns of the Church would be under the direction of the Holy Synod, a council of bishops. The head of this synod was the Ober-Procurator, a layman appointed by the tsar. The Church was divided into sixty-six dioceses, encompassing ten regional districts. Each diocese was further divided into deaneries headed by a *nastaitel* (dean), a member of the parish clergy who was usually in charge of a prominent parish. The

Church could not buy or receive properties without imperial permission. Another part of Peter's new regulation placed the clergy under police supervision and forced them to report certain confessions to the tsar's police. This caused mistrust between priests and their flocks and changed the character of Church-state relations. Instead of the traditional symphonia between Church and state, the new laws did much toward transforming the Church into an organ of the state. The clergy bitterly resented their new status as employees of the state, and, although opposition to Peter's decree began immediately, the Church remained powerless to change the situation. Nevertheless, the quest to recover symphonia continued throughout the nineteenth and early twentieth centuries.[18]

Monasteries faced more pressure under the rule of Peter's daughter Elizabeth. In 1757 she called a joint conference of the senate and the synod, which proposed that monastic and diocesan lands be placed under the control of retired military officers. Villages that were owned by monasteries would be turned over to landed gentry.[19] This suggestion did not come to fruition, and Elizabeth did not broach the subject again. Nevertheless, this illustrates the continued hostility of the Russian government to the position of the Church in general and monasteries in particular.

Catherine the Great

Catherine the Great (1762–1796) reinforced the subordinate position of the Church with her decree of 1764. This announcement officially secularized all Church lands. Approximately two million serfs who had previously belonged to Church lands were effectively placed under state control. Priests and monastics in effect became salaried employees of the state. This meant that the state could limit the number and location of churches and monasteries and the clergy serving them. The monasteries suffered most from Catherine's decree. After 1764 the number of monasteries in Russia decreased by more than half, from 881 to 385.[20] In compensation for their loss, the remaining monasteries were to receive 100 to 150 *desiatinas* of land. (One desiatina equaled approximately 2.7 acres.) Monasteries founded after the decree received no such subsidy. Additionally, monasteries were subjected to a strict budget, and the number of monks and nuns who could be admitted was also severely restricted.

The Beginning of Reform

Although the idiorythmic model dominated Russian monasticism for most of the seventeenth and eighteenth centuries, a reform movement developed that desired a return to Basil's cenobitic model. This movement first appeared among women's monasteries in the late eighteenth century, in direct response to Catherine's 1764 decree. Many women began forming *zhenskie obshchiny* (women's communities). Between 1764 and 1917 they had established more than 220 of these communities in Russia.[21] These informal communities were not monasteries in the official sense but nonetheless conducted themselves as such. They were run on a cenobitic pattern, where all property was held in common and everyone worked together at their appointed task. They were completely self-sufficient and provided peasant women and women of other classes who would have been excluded from official monasteries the opportunity to live a disciplined religious life. Although these societies attracted many women, it was not until the nineteenth century and the tenure of Metropolitan Filaret of Moscow (1821–1867) that a true attempt to reform women's monasteries began. Under his supervision, these obshchiny continued to flourish, and all of them eventually became communally organized monasteries. Filaret's goal was to also convert the older idiorythmic monasteries into cenobitic ones. Here he faced great opposition, mainly because, as Brenda Meehan-Waters observes, he was not an iron-fisted authoritarian but rather a moderate reformer who believed that changes should not be forced, but instead should be appropriate to the spirit of monastic life. By 1917 nearly all of the monasteries in Russia were organized along communal lines.[22]

A contemporary of Metropolitan Filaret who likewise had a great efect on the development of women's monasticism was Bishop Theofan the Recluse (1815–1894). While Metropolitan Filaret concerned himself with restructuring the organization of women's monasteries, Bishop Theofan concerned himself with women's spiritual lives. A gifted preacher who often used folk expressions in his sermons, Bishop Theofan dedicated himself to introducing all people, both monastics and nonmonastics, to asceticism. He viewed young women as being particularly in need of religious education, especially during this period of rapid change and Westernization in Russia. To this end, he established "junior colleges"—diocesan schools for girls. These schools would prepare them to be educated wives of future pastors who could help their husbands on an equal basis—an unusual concept for tsarist Russia. He also took an interest in women's monasticism and was instrumental in establishing new women's monasteries. He delivered a series of sermons to women's monasteries emphasizing the meaning of monasticism and ways in which the women could honor the monastic vows.[23]

Earlier, Paisius Velichovsky (1722–1794) had engaged in similar attempts to reform the male monasteries. He spent nearly twenty years on Mount Athos, Byzantium's most famous monastery, and returned as a revered elder. He helped renew the practice of hesychasm in the monasteries, and his teachings and reforms later played a large role in the monastic revival of the nineteenth century. Perhaps his greatest contribution was the compilation of the *Philokalia,* a collection of mystical, ascetic texts from ancient Christian tradition that contain teachings on prayer of the heart, interior silence, and unseen warfare. Like Metropolitan Filaret, who most likely gained inspiration from his work, Paisius helped establish male cenobitic communities. He laid down the foundations of monastic life, which most monasteries in Russia continue to follow today. In these communities monks individually owned nothing. All property was held in common and was used for the entire community. Responsibility for all aspects of monastery life lay with the abbot. As head of the monastery, he directed every facet of activity, both administrative and spiritual. He was expected to be a man of high morals and to serve as father confessor to the other monks. All monks were required to confess their sins daily to the abbot.

Examining these early attempts at transforming monastic life provides a comparison to the early Soviet period and foreshadows the methods that the monasteries would later use to once again adapt to state interference. In the first place, these efforts demonstrate the monasteries' recognition that in order to preserve their way of life in spite of the state, they would have to strengthen themselves and institute changes from within. In taking the grassroots approach and founding these communities, these men and women profoundly changed the monastic experience in Russia. Some statistics may show their success in rejuvenating monasticism. In 1908, less than 150 years after Catherine's decree, the number of monasteries in Russia had risen from 385 to 1002, the number of monks had grown to 24,444, and the number of nuns had increased to 65,959.[24] The credit for this growth belongs solely to the efforts of the monastics. Like their predecessors, on the eve of the revolution there were monks and nuns who realized that monasticism was under attack from both the

Bolsheviks and the reformist elements within the Church. They recognized that monasticism needed to transform itself before it was too late. Their proposals had an important effect on the character of monasticism under Soviet rule.

Monastic Life

In the cenobitic monastery, life was structured around work and prayer. The day began at one in the morning with individual prayers in the privacy of the monk's cell. Then at five in the morning, the monks gathered in the church to read the matins, or morning prayers. Immediately following matins, they celebrated a divine liturgy. After the service, the monks dispersed to their assigned tasks for the day. While they worked, they were supposed to maintain a rule of silence and pray constantly. After lunch, they worked again until the early evening. At around five o'clock, the monks gathered for evening service in the church. Immediately following the service, which usually lasted for two or more hours, dinner was served. Meals were very simple, usually kasha and vegetables and no meat except fish on feast days. They ate in silence, with one monk reading from the lives of the saints. After dinner, the monks retired to their cells to read or pray. This daily routine never varied, except for occasional feast days and Sundays, when the monks refrained from work.[25]

In addition to the routine of agricultural work and prayer, monastics also had a responsibility to society at large. Many monasteries ran schools for village children and funded hospitals, community kitchens, and orphanages, and all monasteries were required to provide food and shelter to any strangers who sought refuge within their walls. Unlike the Catholic church, where certain orders are involved in charitable work and others are purely contemplative, no Orthodox monasteries are cloistered. They are all expected to be involved in charitable activities in the secular world.

Reform in the Nineteenth Century

During the late nineteenth century, many sectors of society demanded reforms. From the *narodniki* demonstrating on behalf of the peasants to liberal elements pressing for a constitutional monarchy, Russian society recognized that in order to compete on the world scene, it had to make necessary changes. The Orthodox Church was no exception to this sentiment. Many historians such as John Curtiss and George Kline, in writing about the Russian Orthodox Church at the end of the nineteenth and the beginning of the twentieth centuries, portrayed it as stagnant, impotent, and anachronistic, unable or unwilling to keep up with the rest of Russian society, particularly the intelligentsia. The story of the failed reform movement of 1905–1907 is often seen as proof of the Church's inability to make the necessary changes. When the Bolshevik revolution came, the Church could not adapt and was therefore doomed to extinction. This opinion is due partly to the efforts of Soviet historians to justify Bolshevik actions against the Church and partly to the lack of access to archival and other information. However, recent research has greatly undermined this previous approach. Scholars such as James Cunningham and Gregory Freeze demonstrate that certain factions in the Church remained very active in pressing for reforms and made a concerted effort to reach out to the intelligentsia and the emerging urban middle and lower classes. Although admitting that the reforms of 1905 failed, these scholars portray the reasons for this breakdown as the results of more complex causes rather than a case of ineptitude and unconcern on the part of the Church.

The change in attitude was not one-sided. The Church's renewed attempts to reach out to the intelligentsia came at a time when the latter were experiencing a religious renaissance. Nicholas Berdyaev, a reformed Marxist, describes this revival in more detail in his book *The Russian Idea*. He discusses the search among the intelligentsia for true Orthodoxy. To this end, intellectuals established several religious-philosophical societies, the most famous being in Moscow and St. Petersburg, to discuss philosophy and theology. However, this quest for true Orthodoxy did not necessarily lead the intelligentsia to the Orthodox Church. As Christopher Read points out, the intelligentsia mainly defined religiousness as "anti-positivist" or "anti-materialist" rather than belonging to a particular church. Very few members of the intelligentsia were traditionally Orthodox.[26]

Two of the most influential religious thinkers of this period were Sergei Bulgakov (1871–1944) and Nicholas Berdyaev (1874–1948). Although both were former Marxists and at times collaborated on religious journals, their ideas differed radically. Bulgakov retained his Social Democratic outlook and remained more authoritarian. He was drawn to the official Orthodox Church and became a priest in 1918. He believed that the Russian intelligentsia were innately religious and must be involved in politics. He attempted to form a political party, the Christian Political Union, to attack abuses in the Church and the government. In contrast to Bulgakov and his authoritarian outlook, Berdyaev emphasized freedom and individualism. He believed that no power, not even God's, could force or constrain the individual. He also did not share Bulgakov's enthusiasm for the official Orthodox Church and did not attach much importance to the study of theology.[27]

A more conservative sector of the intelligentsia was drawn to the monasteries, particularly Optina Pustyn. These intellectuals came from a wide variety of movements, including Pan-Slavs and Slavophiles. Their main concern was creating a "Russian idea" drawn from the Russian land. They regarded the monasteries as the embodiment of "an unbroken link to the best of Byzantine philosophical and religious tradition."[28] Some of the most famous intellectuals who frequented Optina Pustyn were Fyodor Dostoevsky, Nikolai Gogol, and Lev Tolstoy. Dostoevsky, perhaps the most traditionally Orthodox of the intellectuals, often visited the monastery and consulted with Elder Amvrosii (Ambrose). His novel *The Brothers Karamazov* is semiautobiographical and is set in the town of Kozelsk, located near Optina Pustyn monastery. The character of Father Zossima is based on Elder Amvrosii, and Dostoevsky incorporated many of the elder's direct quotes into the text. One conversation between Amvrosii and Dostoevsky's wife is repeated almost verbatim.

Even Lev Tolstoy, who was excommunicated from the Orthodox Church for his radical beliefs, frequently visited the monastery. Although he held the institutional church in contempt, he nonetheless had great respect for monks and nuns. His sister was a nun in the nearby Shamordino convent, to which he often made a pilgrimage. On his visits, he often consulted with Elder Iosif, who visited the writer as he lay dying. However, Tolstoy's disciples refused to allow him admittance.[29] Of all of the intellectuals to frequent Optina, Konstantin Leont'ev (1831–1891) knew it the most intimately. He was the last major intellectual to be a disciple of Elder Amvrosii. He spent four years at Optina Pustyn, took monastic vows, and later transferred to Holy Trinity Lavra in Sergeev Posad. Leont'ev understood the distance between the average intellectual and the disciplined monastic. He wrote: "Many lay people will listen respectfully to the speech of a good monk who has not had a secular upbringing; they will respect his personal character, will approach for his blessing; but such a monk's intellectual arguments will not carry full weight in their eyes because that exemplary and good monk does not speak the same language that is spoken in secular society."[30]

Despite the Orthodox Church's positive achievements in its mission to the intelligentsia and the high level of learning among the clergy, many

Mother Nektaria in front of house of Elder Ambrose, in the Optina Pustyn Monastery

clergy and laity felt that more improvements to the Church were needed. The dawn of the twentieth century witnessed a renewed call from many members of the hierarchy and clergy to institute reforms within the administration of the Church based on ancient canon law. This pressure for change had three main foci: symphonia, *sobornost,* and spirituality.

The Quest to Recover Symphonia

As mentioned earlier, the word "symphonia" describes a relationship in which Church and government work together in unison and harmony. Although this condition had remained an ideal rather than a reality, many clergy and laity viewed it as a goal worth striving for. Since Peter the Great's Reglament in 1721, the main issue in Church politics involved the quest to restore the Church's position of autonomy, rather than remaining a branch of the government. The debate centered around the question of how best to accomplish this. The traditionalists, who included mainly the hierarchy, favored restoring the patriarchate. The reformers, who were composed mainly of white clergy, disagreed. They resented the monastics' monopoly of hierarchical positions and wanted to change the canon law to allow parish clergy to become bishops and archbishops. They opposed the restoration of the patriarchate on the grounds that, under that system, they had not fared well. The two groups unfortunately never resolved their difference, and the conflict resurfaced with the development of the renovationist movement in the 1920s.

Metropolitans Antonii Vadkovskii and Antonii Khrapovitskii were two of the major proponents of the reform movement. Their desire for a change in the structure of the Church was spurred when the Russian government announced in December, 1904, that it would grant religious liberty to non-Orthodox groups in order to quell disturbances in the southwestern and western provinces. This brought the hierarchy of the Orthodox Church to the realization that their church alone remained under direct state control.[31] Both Vadkovskii and Khrapovitskii were united in their opposition to the procurator of the holy synod, Konstantin Pobedonostsev, and in their support for the separation of Church and state and the restoration of the patriarchate. However, they differed in their ideas as to who would participate in the reformed church government. Khrapovitskii was a conservative who wanted the church to remain under monastic control, whereas Vadovskii was a liberal social reformer who viewed the church as having a broader administration where white clergy and laity, organized into various brotherhoods and other bodies, would have real input into the Church's future.[32]

The movement for Church renewal had an unlikely supporter in the minister of finance, Sergei Witte. He believed that a reformed Church would better support the state and that the current synodal structure encouraged the growth of sectarians and schismatics. Witte foresaw that if the Tsar did not grant the Orthodox Church the same freedoms as other faiths, he would lose the support of the Church at a time when the autocracy could ill afford to have more enemies. Witte also realized that the non-Orthodox groups would quickly seize the opportunity that the 1904 decree offered them and use their new power to proselytize and gain support. The disastrous Russo-Japanese war and the tragedy of Bloody Sunday further persuaded Witte that church reform was necessary. He appealed to Tsar Nicholas to grant immediate autonomy to the Orthodox administration and to call a general sobor (council) to restore the patriarchate.[33]

The revolutionary year 1905 also served to reinvigorate the church reform movement and to deepen the schism between white and black clergy. This was the year of "Bloody Sunday," when the tsar's troops fired on a peaceful procession of workers led by the "revolutionary priest" Father

Georgii Gapon. This event prompted renewed calls for a Church council, such as the letter from a group of priests in St. Petersburg published in the journal of the Petersburg Academy, *Tserkovnyi Vestnik.* This group, known as the "Petersburg thirty-two," asked for the immediate convocation of an all-Russian sobor and the "complete renovation of the administration and inner life of the state church."[34] This letter generated much discussion among both clergy and laity about the status of the Church and the need for reform. Numerous other groups of clergy wrote letters calling for an end to revolutionary violence. Clearly, many clergy sensed the need for reform not only within the Church but also in society at large.

One example of this lobbying may be found in the "Memorandum of Petersburg Priests" (1905). A separate movement from the "Petersburg thirty-two," the authors of the memorandum displayed a more revolutionary tone. After deploring the revolutionaries' disregard of the Church in the liberation movement, the memorandum further states "But the church and its activists, as living forces, cannot remain outside this process, cannot deny their duty to assist in the renewal of the external social order on the basis of truth and love; and hence they must manifest their participation in the construction of a Christian culture, including in this idea the notion of worldly well-being."[35]

The consensus among both clergy and laity was that the current system of the synod under control of the procurator needed to be abolished; disagreement ensued over what the new Church administration would look like. Most laymen generally favored restoration of the patriarchate, whereas the clergy remained divided on this issue between the white parish clergy and the black monastic clergy. This division took a violent turn with the formation of the "Black Hundreds," a catchall term for various extreme right-wing groups that existed between the turn of the century and the 1917 revolution. These associations were protofascist, anti-Semitic, and pro-tsarist in makeup, and although they were not Church organizations per se, they derived much of their support from the clergy. Moreover, several circles were associated with Metropolitan Khrapovitskii's conservative faction. The Black Hundreds, along with the Union of Russian People, harassed priests known for their support of legal, social, and political reforms. These societies received support from several monasteries, as evidenced when Metropolitan Flavian of Kiev and Antonii of Volhynia allowed the Black Hundreds to use the Pecherskaia and Pochaev monasteries as their headquarters and to employ the monastery presses to run off leaflets.[36] Although the synod was embarrassed by the activities of the Black Hundreds, it never officially condemned them. In fact, the synod pursued a contradictory policy: On the one hand, it condemned the activities of the monk Iliodor, who was a driving force behind many Black Hundred actions; on the other hand it simultaneously issued a resolution in 1908 encouraging the bishops to bless the participation of the clergy in the Union of Russian People.[37]

Influenced by Witte, Tsar Nicholas II granted permission for a pre-sobor commission to meet to plan the format of the sobor. The topics of discussion in this pre-sobor commission focused on three main issues: the restoration of the patriarchate, the division of Church administration, and the position of the white clergy. The topic that aroused the most controversy, however, involved the acquisition of property. Since Peter the Great's 1721 Reglament, the Church could not obtain property without the tsar's permission. This prohibited the Church from purchasing property on the open market or from receiving land or other buildings on its own authority. Although originally this restriction applied to all social classes, by the late nineteenth century various reforms had lifted this ban for all social groups except for the Church. By the dawn of the twentieth century, the Church was one of the few organizations that could not act in its own name and for its own advantage. The bishops resented the fact that the October Manifesto granted the freedom to exchange property to all citizens, *including other religious groups* (emphasis added), except for the Orthodox Church. Part of their demand to the government, therefore, included lifting the restriction on property acquisition by the Church.[38]

Despite the pre-sobor committee's work, the sobor never convened. Scholars have put forth various theories to explain the Church's failure to convene a council in 1905. They cite repression from above as the chief reason. Tsar Nicholas II took offense at the determination of the hierarchy to seek administrative independence from the state and therefore never gave permission for the sobor to occur. Other scholars, while acknowledging Nicholas's share in stifling the reform movement, claim that the Church bears far more of the blame for its failure to reach out to all segments of society, particularly the intelligentsia and the fledgling middle class. This criticism may be summarized in one phrase: The Church lacked *sobornost.*[39]

Sobornost is one of those Russian words that defies exact translation, but it can be defined as a total unity of the Church, encompassing all believers, not only the clergy but also the laity. Berdyaev describes it as "the corporate experience of love . . . an organic union of freedom and love, community," and a principle that is opposed to authority.[40] The great religious philosopher Aleksei Stepanovich Khomyakov offers a more explicit definition. He writes that "the unity of the Church is not imaginary or allegorical, but a true and substantial unity, such as is the unity of the many members in a living body."[41] This concept originated with the Slavophiles in the mid-nineteenth century. This group of intellectuals viewed the Orthodox Church as one of the few truly Russian institutions. In their view, sobornost strengthened resistance against the transformation of the Church into an institution of the state. Alexander Bogolepov asserts that the Russian Orthodox Church in the nineteenth century, boosted by this doctrine, reached its apex of development not only in terms of membership but also in terms of the high level of learning among both the clergy and the laity and the interest aroused in the common people and the intelligentsia.[42]

Gregory Freeze elaborates on the charge of the Church's lack of *sobornost.* He states that the Church was "too committed to its supraclass values and mission rather than the larger needs of the nation as a whole." In other words, the Church believed that it needed to remain above specific social classes or political parties and must not favor one group over the other. The Church's interest in the intelligentsia extended no further than acquiring an ally to "help lead the people and resist the state."[43] Aside from a few revolutionary priests, such as Father Georgii Gapon, the Church did not concern itself with the material or spiritual welfare of any particular class, whether it be intelligentsia, peasant, or proletariat. The Church transferred its attention to whichever social class it thought would more strongly support it. This attitude is evident in the way the Church "attempted to superimpose its role and aspirations on the secular idea of *obshchestvennost*—the emerging social identity of the educated, propertied middle strata in the city."[44] The word "obshchestvennost," like sobornost, lacks a precise definition. It is most often translated as "public opinion" or "sociability." However, obshchestvennost referred specifically to the educated middle class, which opposed the authority of the state.

A change in focus provides another reason for the Church's failure to create a true alliance with the intelligentsia. In the wake of the 1905 revolution, the Church began to redirect its attention to the countryside, believing that the peasants provided the key to preserving Orthodoxy in Russia. For the remainder of the prerevolutionary period, the Church placed its priorities in the rural areas. Although it did not totally dismiss the intelligentsia and continued in some measure to reach out to them, the Church ultimately failed to establish an effective urban mission to the middle classes.

Spiritual and moral concerns also played a large role in the reformers' agenda. This was evident mostly in their discussion of the status of the monasteries. Most discussion of monastic reform took place not in the pre-sobor committees but rather in the church journals, especially *Tserkovnyi Vestnik* and *Tserkovnyia Vedomosti.* Chiefly, the accusations involved the immorality of the novices, the hiring of too many outside workers, a general obsession with obtaining money, and a careless attitude regarding the performance of religious duties. Calls for monastic reform found agreement with some people in the hierarchy. The journal *Tserkovnyia Vedomosti* reported that Bishop Arsenii of Pskov had found it necessary to take on the work of straightening out the affairs of the monastic institutions in his diocese. This same journal reprinted a sermon by Antonii of the Kirillo-Belozerskii Monastery to his fellow monks: "From the pulpit we say that God loves labor, that he commanded man to gain his bread by the sweat of his brow; and nevertheless, we amass capital, we forget the slightest self-restraint, and on love of our neighbor we look as an obligation which does not apply to us as monks. . . . If in the West, monasticism is dying from political causes, with us, although unaffected by politics, it is dying as a result of the fact that in spirituality and morality it is continually sinking lower and lower."[45]

The exact magnitude of the problem of monastery corruption is difficult to determine. Judging from the number of articles written by bishops and monks in ecclesiastical journals, the problem definitely needed to be addressed. However, these journals were primarily written by the progressive elements of the Church and therefore reflected a liberal agenda and supported the white clergy's views. These journals' hostility to the synod as well as monasticism is very apparent. Therefore, one needs to read these accounts with a great deal of care.

Reforming the Monasteries

One of the few official discussions involving monasteries may be seen in one subcommittee of the pre-sobor commission in 1906. It decided that the normal authorization for the opening or closing of monasteries should remain in the hands of the diocesan bishop rather than the synod. Only if a monastery needed state subsidies should the central church authorities be involved in its establishment. Under the existing rules, permission for opening and closing monasteries and granting subsidies came not only from the synod but also from the treasury and the ministry of the interior. The representatives wanted the monasteries to be free from the control of the ministry of the interior, which regarded all monastics as parasites and all land in control of the monasteries as wasted. Local bishops should also have the exclusive power to confirm or reject nominations of an *igumen* (superior) to a monastery, with the exception of the lavras.[46]

In the years after the aborted 1905 all-church sobor, monastic reform continued to be discussed, particularly at the Fourth All-Russian Missionary Congress, held at Kiev in 1908. Discussions there were serious enough to persuade the representatives to call a national congress of delegates from monasteries to consider important issues of reform. Chief among the problems discussed were the need for more discipline, a means of returning monks and nuns who engage in immoral behavior to the outside world, and a change in the policy of having female servants and workers on monastery farms, and likewise having male watchmen and doorkeepers at women's monasteries. The congress also called for exact bookkeeping and an end to appointing people who had never served as novices, or indeed had never even lived in a monastery, to the post of abbot or abbess.[47] The preoccupation with matters of morality may indicate that instances of immorality were on the rise. Conversely, it may also indicate the Church's desire to take preventive measures to protect itself from accusations. Although few figures exist to confirm or deny the rumors of monks and nuns breaking their vows of celibacy, the importance of these discussions centers on the monasteries' concern with their image. The ascendancy of Rasputin and stories of his exploits gave rise to tales that all monastics behaved as he did, despite the fact that Rasputin himself was not an ordained monk. The perception of monasteries as places of sin and hypocrisy persisted in the public imagination.

Despite overall condemnation of these abuses and the call for reform, an address in 1912 by one of the participants in the congress, Bishop Nikon of Vologda, demonstrates that four years later the same problems were still being confronted and, if anything, had worsened. He stated: "Of course, there were always weaknesses among the monastics . . . but unfortunately there have now been added to the former weaknesses a sort of spirit of opposition, a spirit of egotism, an unlimited love of honors, and a waywardness, which have agitated those living in the monasteries."[48]

This new "spirit of opposition" may be attributed to remnants of the revolutionary years of 1905 to 1907, when the Church faced both internal and external conflict.

Aside from moral issues, complaints about monasteries also centered around economic affairs, especially concerning the *podvorye,* or diocesan inns. Many of these had shrines inside them which pilgrims would stop and venerate. Ostensibly, the purpose of these hostelries was to provide shelter for pilgrims to the monasteries, usually for a small fee. Although the monasteries oversaw the daily maintenance of these inns, they came under the jurisdictional control of the diocesan bishops. Some of these were located on very valuable land, which brought in considerable income to the bishops, who could spend it as they pleased. In 1908 there were twenty-five of these institutions in St. Petersburg, and the synod and the metropolitanate also had them. Metropolitan Antonii complained that "the chief purpose of the *podvorye* . . . is the financial, economic one—i.e., the gaining of funds for the monasteries in whose names they were built. The *podvorye* degrade the holy work of spiritual and moral inspiration to the satisfying of the religious demands of the local flock by the mere external performances of rituals. The ritual performances in them become a business enterprise for securing funds for institutions outside the boundaries of the diocese." He also objected to these establishments on the grounds that the monks who lived there could not be controlled by the authorities in the capital because they were outside their bishops' jurisdictions. He also protested that those monks hindered the educational and charitable work of the St. Petersburg parishes by diverting income that would have gone to the churches of the capital.[49]

A further economic criticism occurred regarding the perceived capitalistic tendencies of monasteries. As part of the monastic reforms of the nineteenth century, monks and nuns were expected to work the land themselves as part of their obedience to their elders. However, as the century drew to a close, monasteries increasingly relied on hired workers to run their agricultural operations and leased land to peasants for cash payments. These practices allowed critics of the Church to condemn monastics as lazy parasites who exploited the peasants.

Both official and unofficial reports seemed to confirm these accusations. An anonymous article published in 1876 reported that in the period from 1870 to 1874, fifty-nine out of two hundred monasteries surveyed had fewer than 150 desiatinas;[50] the others had holdings ranging from 150 to 66,666 desiatinas, and thirty reported having more than 1,000 desiatinas each. Much of this land was forest, which the monks and nuns were able to turn to a profit by selling timber and firewood. Another official report claimed that the estimated value of the Church's monastery lands in 1890 was as high as 26,595,690 rubles.[51] An auditor for the synod in Smolensk commented that these practices "[give] ground for thinking that the monasteries do not need their lands, as physical labor and work in agriculture are favorite occupations of energetic and healthy monks, and distract them from the lures of vices not proper for monastics." In response to this report, the religious consistory of the Smolensk diocese ordered the abbots of the monasteries to discharge all hired laborers except those who did tasks that the monks themselves were not able to perform.[52]

Most of the complaints centered around men's monasteries, although women's monasteries received their share of criticism. Part of the reason for the relative lack of reproach was the fact that despite the numerical superiority of nuns, their communities were often much poorer than those of their male counterparts. However, enough accusations of impropriety occurred to prompt the synod in 1910 to issue a decree that defined rules for governing women's monasteries. The abbess was instructed to use greater care in selecting novices, simple and modest dress was the rule, and the abbess must ensure that no luxury came into the nuns' cells. The custom of sending nuns and novices out to collect money from wealthy patrons and from donations solicited on the street was now forbidden, as charges of sexual misconduct often resulted. In a final addition to the decree, the synod voted, "with the aim of immediate abolition of disorders in the women's institutions, to entrust to all diocesan bishops the making, through especially trustworthy persons appointed by them, of a careful examination of the inner conditions in the female monasteries (and) of their economy and capital," and declared that these commissions should report their findings to the synod.[53]

Although the years between 1905 and 1917 witnessed sincere attempts at reform, the fall of the Romanovs and the advent of the provisional government in 1917 made it both possible and imperative for the Church to reorganize itself. With the permission of the provisional government, the chief procurator of the synod, V. N. Lvov, announced the calling of a church council. As with the aborted 1905 sobor, a pre-sobor *soviet* took place. It was divided into ten sections. Only the section that reevaluated monasticism and monasteries is discussed here.[54]

From July 16 to July 23, 1917, the All-Russian Congress of Representa-

Holy Trinity St. Sergius Lavra at Sergeev Posad

tives from Monasteries met at the Holy Trinity Sergius Lavra at Sergeev Posad. Its goal was "to draw up a program of transformation of monastery life and the removal of its imperfections."[55] The attendees wanted to place control of the monasteries directly in the hands of the bishops. Previously, the diocesan head or the deans oversaw monastic activity. Now, they called for the establishment of various monastic commissions within each diocese. The chief of these was a special diocesan monastic council that would oversee all aspects of monasteries and monastic life in each diocese. This monastic council would meet at least once a month and assign the bishop to directly supervise all monastery activity. Aside from bishops, who were ex officio members of this council, representatives would include abbots and other representatives from monasteries and convents. Bishops' appointments would account for one-third of the council members, while the rest would be composed of elected representatives. Terms would run four years, with reelection possible after two years, when half of the council's term expired. To prevent financial fraud, a special verification commission would check all monetary accounts and also examine the monastery's use of its agriculture.[56] In addition to the diocesan monastic council, the committee also called for the formation of a separate organization, the diocesan monastic sobor. This group would be composed solely of representatives of monasteries and convents and would meet once a year. The diocesan monastic council would monitor the members of the sobor including (1) the abbots and abbesses of all monasteries of the diocese, (2) the elected representatives from the monastery diocese (the number to be determined by local conditions set by the diocesan monastic council), (3) the members of the diocesan monastic council (who also had the right to vote), and (4) people with experience in the spiritual life of monks (such as elders) by invitation of the diocesan bishop. Only fully tonsured monks, as opposed to novices, could participate in the council. The duties of the diocesan monastic sobor would include the following: (1) discussion of general questions of the life and activities of the monastics and monasteries of the diocese, (2) discussion of the cooperation of monasteries in the diocese regarding spiritual and material matters, (3) examination of the reports of the monastery heads about the needs of the monasteries, and (4) selection of members to the diocesan council and other such organizations.[57]

All of these small local groups were to meet periodically to solve the problems in their own districts and dioceses. For a discussion of monasticism in all of Russia, an all-Russian sobor would convene every three years at the Holy Trinity Sergius Lavra. This ecclesiastical body would be under the watchful eye of its holy synod and would include bishops (by invitation only), representatives from each diocese (elected by the Holy Synod), abbots of the lavras and other prominent monasteries, and very spiritual monks, again by invitation of the all-Russian monastic sobor. This sobor was to discuss general questions concerning the life and activities of Russian monastics and was also to examine the consensus of all monastics in terms of spiritual and material goals.

The proliferation of the number of monastic councils, some of which seem to overlap, poses several questions. Why the need for all of these councils? The answer could be a desire to prove to the critics of monasticism that the monastics were aware of the need for reform and that they were taking responsibility for their own actions and setting up organizations to police their own people. The questions remain, how true to the spirit of reform were these councils, and to what extent did they address the need for change in the monasteries?

The answer to these questions may be partially found in further examination of the declaration of the All-Russian Congress of Representatives of Monasteries. After outlining their plans for the various commissions, the delegates moved on to discuss reforms regarding internal aspects of monastery life. They referred specifically to men's monasteries, although one may assume that these rules apply to women's monasteries as well. The delegates stressed the need for monastic brotherhood councils within each monastery that would consist of the abbot and all other people who occupied positions of authority. This council would meet whenever necessary, but no more than twice a month, to decide all major questions regarding both the internal and the external aspects of monastery life. If the abbot did not agree with the brotherhood council, he could appeal to the diocesan monastic council.[58]

As part of their plan to eliminate abuses, the delegates also urged that greater care be taken in accepting novices into the monastery. They advocated a "weeding-out process" to determine who would be a fit candidate for monastic life. They also established an age limit; a person wishing to be tonsured must be no younger than twenty-five years of age. Younger candidates could be accepted only with a bishop's blessing.[59] A would-be novice would live within the monastery walls, though separate from the brothers, and would remain in secular dress. His sole vow would be obedience to the monk who supervised him in his performance of simple labors. Only experienced monks would be allowed to manage these novices. After several years of living in the monastery and enduring many tests, a candidate would be tonsured to the rank of novice with the permission of the abbot and the brotherhood council.

The declaration also definitely restricted the length of time that outsiders would be allowed to stay within monastery walls. Pilgrims in the hostel could stay no more than three days without the permission of the abbot. Those pilgrims who were perhaps contemplating a monastic lifestyle could stay in the monasteries no more than two years with the blessing of the abbot, who was charged with the responsibility for not only the physical well-being of the pilgrims, but also, more importantly to the representatives, their spiritual well-being. The abbot also had the power to receive or dismiss any lay laborers who worked within the monastery. These new laws were made to prevent instances of laypeople staying at the monasteries indefinitely and also to try to ensure that those pilgrims were there to pray and to gain spiritual wisdom and not merely to take advantage of the monastery's hospitality. Under Orthodox custom, monks or nuns are obligated to provide food and shelter to pilgrims. In return, the pilgrims are expected to do some kind of work, either on the farm or in the kitchen, or cleaning the church. Judging from the thoroughness with which the representatives at this congress addressed the responsibilities of both monastics and laity, there were problems with pilgrims not upholding their end of the bargain.[60]

The author making candles at Optina Pustyn Monastery

The declaration also addressed the problems of transferring monks and nuns from monastery to monastery and the method of handling monastics who had been found guilty of immoral behavior. Frequently these two problems were related and were common complaints for reform. If a monastic was guilty of some indiscretion, many times the abbot or abbess dealt with the problem by transferring the offender to another monastery, often without informing the other monastery of the offender's misdeed. Even if the monks and nuns who transferred to several different monasteries were not guilty of misbehavior, the practice of frequent movement among monastics was contrary to Orthodox custom and disruptive to monastery life. Therefore, the declaration stated that those monastics who had been judged guilty of immoral behavior by an ecclesiastical court would remain in their residences and the abbot or abbess and the other brothers or sisters would guide them in their repentance. The offenders would also be reported to the monastic brotherhood council, which together with the abbot and other monks and nuns would monitor the individuals to ensure that they did not influence the other monastics and the laity to sin. Monks or nuns could be transferred to another monastery only when the abbot and the brotherhood council had determined that they needed to be removed from their original abode. The declaration also emphasized the necessity of monasteries remaining places of spiritual refuge and not places of exile. It was not uncommon for bishops to send parish priests to monasteries for discipline, which did not improve relations between the black and white clergy.[61] Many minor criminals were also sent to monasteries, as well as inconvenient wives and unmarried daughters. This involuntary seclusion aroused resentment and led to abuses in monastic life.[62]

The declaration also offered exhaustive guidelines concerning the daily routine of monastic life. No laity were allowed in the cells of the monastics, and, except for confession and spiritual advice, monks were not allowed to visit the cells of other monks. This was done to avoid any accusation of sexual impropriety. The decor of the cells must be simple and modest. Life revolved around a routine based on work and prayer. To counteract complaints of indolence among monks and the practice of hiring village people to work in the fields, the monasteries were forbidden to hire laymen except to do work that monastics could not.

One common complaint was the frequency with which monks and nuns had left the monasteries either to go on vacation or to collect alms. The delegates sought to correct this by prohibiting monks and nuns from leaving the monastery except in special circumstances, such as illness requiring medical treatment, and then only with the permission of the abbot. Family members could visit the monk or nun at the monastery and stay at the monastery hostel.

The representatives devoted much space and detailed instructions regarding the economy of the monasteries. In this section they explicitly addressed the capitalistic practices of agriculture, including the hiring of laity to work in the fields. They stressed that agriculture should serve as a support to the monastery and not be an end in itself. The pursuit of spiritual perfection—not monetary profit—should be the goal of the monastery. They again stressed the need for all able-bodied monks to work in the fields and listed ways that the monasteries could utilize industry to improve their agricultural output. They also outlined suggestions for monasteries that were situated near each other to pool their resources and collaborate in terms of industry and farming. The abbots would have direct control over individual monasteries' agriculture, while the diocesan bishop and the diocesan monastic council would take responsibility for overseeing the agricultural pursuits of all of the monasteries in their dioceses. All of the profits from farming and industry would be used for building and maintaining educational facilities for the brothers and for financing charitable works (hospitals, schools, etc.).[63]

Turning from reforms focusing on general administrative and moral issues within the monasteries, the delegates addressed their attention to political concerns of the day. At the time of the congress, when this directive was written, the provisional government was still in power. However, relations between the government and the sobor rapidly deteriorated. The first and most serious indication of trouble came with the provisional government's announcement on April 21, 1917, that it was forming land transfer committees. The duties of these councils included surveying properties before generally redistributing land. Estates larger than a certain number of desiatny were scheduled to be expropriated. These lands included monasteries, as well as other Church property.[64]

Another alarming development occurred on August 11, 1917, when the provisional government announced that it would establish a ministry of denominations, which would control all aspects of religious groups. The government obviously viewed granting autonomy to religious organizations as dangerous to public stability.[65] In response, the representatives of the monastery commission discussed methods of adaptation. They gave the responsibility of higher supervision of the monasteries to the holy synod, which would support their interests before government institutions. They charged the synod with defending monastic property from violent seizure and plunder from outsiders as well as from abuses from monastery officials. Realizing that the new regime might dissolve the synod, the representatives voted to petition the provisional government to exempt them from requisition for wartime goods. They argued that land ownership was a necessary part of monasticism, as agricultural work provided both physical subsistence and spiritual discipline. They demanded that the government defend the property rights of monasteries and warned that the government's seizure of monastery land and goods would harm their economic situation to the extent that they would be forced to close. When confronted, the provisional government's head, Alexander Kerensky, replied that these were the consequences of the Church's having gained its freedom.[66]

Another recommendation came from Andrei, bishop of Ufimski and Meizelinski, who proposed that every monastery should establish "Brotherhoods of Orthodox Pilgrims in Defense of the Faith." All lay brotherhoods would combine to form an "All People's Union of Orthodox Zealots of the Holy Faith." These lay brotherhoods would defend the monasteries from "enemies of the church" and act as mediators between the secular officials and the monasteries. The congress unanimously approved the bishop's request. These lay brotherhoods would play a very important role in the lives of the monasteries after the Bolshevik revolution.[67] Aside from organizing defense groups, the congress also stressed the need to strengthen Church propaganda. They decided to publish brochures and leaflets defending monasteries and detailing the government's repressive measures against them and distribute these to the people. The monasteries would collaborate in publishing a monastic newspaper, which would discuss news of Church life and reflections of modern life from the point of view of Orthodoxy.[68]

The 1917 Sobor

After months of planning and pre-sobor discussions, the All-Russian Sobor officially convened on August 15, 1917, in Moscow. All together 564 representatives met, divided almost equally between clergy and laity. Lay participation was a very important addition to the sobor. Previous church councils in Russian Orthodoxy had always been composed exclusively of bishops and archbishops. Much debate centered on whether to include the laity. It was finally decided that the inclusion of the laity was necessary to create a council that would represent the people as a whole. In this decision the Church demonstrated its commitment to the principle of sobornost. The delegates were divided into various committees to discuss important issues. The two topics that deserve attention here for their indirect impact on the status of monasteries are the relationship between Church and state and the election of a patriarch.

The committee on the relationship between Church and state met during September and November, 1917, and much discussion centered on the question of separating the two bodies. The basic issue was whether Russia should follow the model of the United States, France, and Belgium, where Church and state occupy separate spheres of influence, or the German model, where the government had authority over the Church. The representatives decided that Russia's circumstances did not correspond well with the policy of separation of Church and state, although they noted that the pre-sobor commission had advocated this course of action. That body, along with calling for separation of Church and state, insisted that in the Russian government, the Orthodox Church must occupy first position among all religious denominations. It also demanded that the Orthodox Church be favored by the government, as befitting the religion of the majority of the people. The commission also stressed that "in accordance with the new Russian government's recognition of freedom of conscience, the Russian Orthodox Church must possess this freedom in its entirety."[69] Other delegates, namely A. V. Vasiliev and E. N. Trubetskoi, voiced dissenting opinions. They stated that the Russian government could not speak of the separation of Church and state; rather, the Church should enjoy the right of self-determination. They decided that the Church should remain a free institution in the government, but that it should have a privileged position in Russia.[70]

The commission's final report reveals its decision regarding the future legal situation of the Orthodox Church in Russia. The first two articles emphasize the previously stated positions regarding the Church's privileged place in the Russian government and the government policy that religion must favor the Orthodox Church. They also demanded that the Church be exempt from taxes, that the state provide money for the Church, and that monastics, priests, and psalters be exempt from military service. At the same time, these articles stress the complete separation of Church and state and the restriction against the violation of each other's laws by the two entities. There is an inherent contradiction in these two phrases, demonstrating that the sobor delegates did not completely understand what the term "separation of Church and the state" actually meant.[71] In countries where the Church is separate from the state, all churches are financially independent of the government, and no church is favored over the others. If the Orthodox Church wanted to be a state church, as it historically had been, then that presupposed the Church giving up some control to the government.

One delegate, A. F. Odarchenko, seems to have been aware of this contradiction and wrote a dissenting opinion. He criticized the wording of the second article, comparing the situation that the representatives had placed the Orthodox church in to the situation of the Anglican Church in Great Britain.[72] He noted that the second article "does not recognize the church's independence from the government in areas central to church life, such as church law, church courts, church government, but only confers on the church the right of 'self-government' in these realms." He stated that the delegates do not fully understand the term "self-government" *(samoupravlenie)* and confuse it with independence *(nezavisimost')*. He claimed that the exact definition of "self-government" is "subordination of one (lower) power to another (higher) power. Such a definition leaves the Orthodox Church subordinate to the government in areas of the courts, government, and law. This is the situation of the Anglican church, but this is unacceptable to the Orthodox Church."[73]

If the issue of the relationship between Church and state was not fully and clearly resolved, the question of the patriarchate definitely was. After much theological debate over whether a patriarch was canonical, the delegates all agreed that the patriarchate was a historically Russian institution that should be reinstated. The current political situation contributed to a sense of urgency in resolving the issue, for the Bolsheviks had begun their seizure of power in October, while the discussions were continuing. This revolutionary situation added a new dimension to the question of what role the patriarch would play as the head of the Church. In a speech before the session, Bishop Mitrofan of Astrakhan stated the need for a patriarch who would provide spiritual leadership and who "would lift the hearts of the Russian people, would summon them to a better life and to great deeds and would himself lead the way." The patriarch was clearly regarded as a leader in troubled times and not merely as an administrative head. Other delegates spoke in apocalyptic terms, discussing the patriarchate as fulfilling the role of a "bastion against evil."[74]

In this atmosphere of crisis, the council worked surprisingly well. Quickly voting to restore the patriarchate, the council elected Tikhon Belin, metropolitan of Moscow, to serve as Russia's first patriarch in more than two hundred years. Tikhon was an excellent choice for this position. The son of a priest, he had spent all of his life in service to the Church. He had served eight years as bishop of the Aleutian Islands and North America and seven years as archbishop of Yaroslavl. He was appointed archbishop of Vilna in 1913, but the German invasion compelled him to leave his post in 1915. Two years later, Tikhon replaced Makarii as metropolitan of Moscow. A moderate, Tikhon was accepted by the delegates as a good choice for patriarch. Tikhon's humility and lack of formal education led many people in both the Church and the government to characterize him as weak; however, as later events demonstrated, Tikhon had a very strong sense of duty and could not easily be intimidated. He later demonstrated his courage in resistance to the Bolshevik authorities.[75]

The Church's position on the eve of the resolution remained precarious. Its efforts to reform itself produced mixed results. On one hand, its attempts may be seen as failures since it did not succeed in reaching the lower urban classes or the intelligentsia, a fact that hurt the Church deeply after the revolution. The lack of unity between the parish clergy and the monastics further hampered the cause of reform. World War I and the Church's support for the war effort in the face of widespread opposition also antagonized many segments of the population, who felt that the Church was out of touch with popular opinion.

The monasteries, as the backbone of Russian Orthodoxy, faced a tenuous future on the eve of the Bolshevik revolution. Continued propaganda, both from inside and outside the Church, contributed to the popular perception of monasteries as places of immorality. Tales of Rasputin's deeds heightened this belief and further discredited the monasteries. Lack of unity and disagreements about monastic administration also hampered attempts at reform. Despite these negative conditions, there were reasons to view the monasteries' situation in 1917 in a positive light. The organizational and moral reforms proposed at the pre-sobor commission on monasteries and monasticism in 1917 demonstrate that monks and nuns recognized that the key to surviving in a new and potentially hostile environment necessitated a close examination of current conditions and a willingness to address problems. The formation of lay brotherhoods to protect the monasteries also signaled a realization that the monasteries needed a core of active defenders. Had the Bolshevik revolution not interfered, monasticism may have experienced another revival. As it was, by engaging in reforms and taking preventative measures, the monasteries in many ways proved able to meet the challenges of the coming years.

CHAPTER 2

Revolution, Civil War, and Famine, 1917–1922

IN HIS ESSAY "The Role of Dual Models in the Dynamics of Russian Culture," Yuri Lotman observes that "for Russia at its various historical epochs it is not conservatism that is typical, but on the contrary both reactionary and progressive tendencies."[1] The dual model that Lotman discusses is the "old vs. the new." For a new idea or way of life to take root in Russian society, the old must be discredited and destroyed. Although Lotman examines the time periods of the introduction of Christianity to Russia and the Petrine reforms, the same phrase may also be applied to the Bolsheviks and the "old regime" of Russian society. In order to build their brave new world, Russia's new masters would have to destroy the old. Lotman also states that "a vital factor in the self-definition of any cultural phenomenon is a polemic with hostile ideologies since in the process of such a polemic its own position is formulated and the opponent's position is significantly transformed."[2] This statement is central to understanding church-state relations during the period of the Bolshevik revolution and the civil war. Communism needed the Church to serve as a contrast and a projection of much that was wrong with the old regime. Likewise, the Church needed Communism to bolster its position as defender of Russia and traditional lifestyles. Each contributed to the formation of the other's self-conception.

Even though the February revolution of 1917 and the new provisional government caused the Orthodox Church problems, the Bolshevik revolution on October 24, 1917, proved the greatest threat in its long history. The Bolsheviks' blatantly atheistic and violent rhetoric immediately set up an antagonistic relationship between the Church and the new regime. Yet, despite the Bolsheviks' determination to break the power of the Church and create an atheistic state, they also realized that they needed to remain practical and proceed with caution. The monasteries played an important role in this conflict, as their land and their treasures became Bolshevik targets for nationalization. To prevent seizure of church and monastery property, the monasteries used various methods ranging from violence to propaganda. The results of these tactics remained mixed. On the one hand, although the Bolsheviks converted many monasteries to secular use, most monks and nuns were able to continue to live on monastery land and to preserve their sense of community. On the other hand, the internal dissensions within the Church hindered it from launching an effective counterattack.

In his writings Karl Marx devoted much attention to the problem of religion. His critique of religion is very unified, as Delos B. McKown asserts. To demonstrate his thesis, McKown breaks Marx's critique of religion into twelve points, only a few of which need be mentioned here. First, Marx was relentlessly hostile toward religious beliefs. However, beyond using spoken and written words, he neither practiced nor advocated tactics designed to destroy religion. Second, Marx believed that objects of religious belief not only governed man but rendered him degraded and slavish in the process. Third, he maintained the existence of a close relation between the interests of religious institutions and those of secular property, whether movable or immovable. Finally, he believed in the eventual disappearance of religion.[3]

Lenin agreed with most of Marx's assertions, although he differed in the degree of hostility toward religion and metaphysics in general. Although Lenin repeatedly stated that religious questions should not be elevated to first rank, nonetheless his actions demonstrated that the issue of religion was very important to him. Like Marx, he believed that religion would disappear after the proletarian revolution. The differences between Marx and Lenin concerning religion are due mainly to the differing churches they had contact with in their respective countries. In Marx's Germany, the Lutheran church, which was allied with the bourgeoisie, was growing weaker by the year. Also, in the West there was a growing sense of agnosticism and atheism. Marx therefore felt more optimistic that the church would simply "whither away" on its own. Lenin on the other hand faced a church that was allied with the aristocracy, was very strong institutionally, and enjoyed broad support from the peasantry. Lenin felt that he could not afford to allow the church to fall on its own; he realized that to prevent religion from reasserting its place in the nation, the Bolsheviks needed to take proactive measures, such as propaganda and agitation.[4]

However, a division within the Communist Party concerning religion soon became apparent. The "soft-liners" were people such as the writer Maxim Gorky, Alexander Bogdanov (Lenin's chief rival within the Bolshevik Party), and the future minister of education, Anatoli Lunacharskii. This faction was influenced by Gorky's theory of "god building." In this conception, socialism "could become a surrogate religion of the masses." He took the Christian virtue of self-sacrifice and applied it to socialist ideology.[5] Lunacharskii was perhaps one of the most vocal of the god builders. He was a romantic who did not believe that his love of the arts was incompatible with his position as a revolutionary. He once stated that "[as a youth] art and religion . . . occupied the center of my attention, yet not as an aesthete, but as a Marxist." He saw art and religion as "means of emotional expression and, in particular, expression of the individual need for communion with others. Religion . . . carried the individual outside himself in search of fellowship: religion is a bond."[6] Although not a believer, Lunacharskii had respect for the cultural heritage of the churches and monasteries and did not agree with the view that they should be destroyed. He was emotional over this issue to the extent that when he heard false reports that St. Basil's Cathedral had been destroyed during the Moscow revolt, he burst into tears at a Sovnarkom meeting and ran crying from the room, saying: "I cannot stand it! I cannot bear the monstrous destruction of beauty and tradition." On November 2, 1917, he resigned from the Sovnarkom. In a published statement he declared that if atheism meant destroying beautiful architectural masterpieces, then he wanted no part of it.[7] He believed that there was a way to reconcile religion with Communism.[8] Lenin and his faction of hard-liners, which included Leon Trotsky and Nikolai Bukharin, regarded religion as nothing more than another way for the rich to exploit the poor. In a response to Lunacharskii, Lenin wrote: "Those who toil and live in want all their lives are taught by religion to be submissive and patient while here on earth, and to take comfort in the hope of a heavenly reward. But those who live by the labor of others are taught by religion to practice charity whilst on earth, thus offering them a very cheap way of justifying their existence as exploiters and selling them at a very modest price tickets to well-being in Heaven. Religion is opium for the people."[9]

The Clash between Church and State

Lenin believed that a communist state could be built only when religion was totally destroyed. Therefore, one of the first acts of the new regime was to nationalize all private land. On November 8, 1917, the "Decree on Land Nationalization" specified that "the landed estates, as also all appanages, the monasterial and church lands, with all of their livestock, implements, farm buildings, and everything pertaining thereto" henceforth belonged to the state. Until the constituent assembly met, the land would be placed under the control of the *volost* (village district) and the *uezd* (district)—the Soviets of Workers', Soldiers', and Peasants' Deputies (sovdeps). The Bolsheviks recognized these organizations as "the only mass organization of all the working and exploited classes capable of giving leadership to the struggle of these classes for their complete political and economic emancipation."[10] They were responsible for maintaining order while the lands were surveyed and inventoried prior to final redistribution (see Appendix A).[11] Therefore, it was left to the local authorities to administer the closing of the monasteries and churches and the land distribution, which accounts for much ambiguity and many inconsistencies in policy.[12]

This is most clearly illustrated in the villages, where the affairs of the church were still governed by the commune and the parish. The village soviets rarely prevented the priests from collecting fees for their services, and several village soviets even paid the priests out of their own funds. In the village of Kliuchi in Buguruslan uezd, the village soviet paid the priest a monthly salary of three hundred rubles to perform his services in church and also gave him an annual ration of two hundred *pud* of grain (one pud was roughly equivalent to thirty-five pounds). Another village priest in nearby Novo-Spasskoe reportedly made up to eight thousand rubles a month by charging for marriages, baptisms, and funerals, all with the soviet's blessing. However, other village soviets bitterly opposed such practices and remained avowedly atheistic.[13] One of the Bolshevik administrators in the volost of Zvenigorod (Moscow guberniia) wrote enthusiastically to Lenin describing their success in closing the monastery and transforming it into a factory. He wrote, "Your [Lenin's] portrait hangs in the monastery like an icon," and also spoke of placing Lenin's and other Bolshevik leaders' portraits in all of the workers' rooms "in the red corner" so that the workers could pray to them.[14] This last phrase was a deliberate play on words, since the icon corner is referred to in Russian as the *krasnii ugol*—"beautiful corner." *Krasnii* also means "red."

Despite Lenin's hostility to religion, he was above all a pragmatist. This accounts for some of his seemingly contradictory statements regarding religion as well as other matters. He had the foresight to realize that despite feelings of anticlericalism among the peasants and workers, many still expressed reluctance to engage in violent and destructive behavior against the churches. An intimate association of "Russianness" into Orthodoxy remained ingrained in the majority of the population, even among those who did not actively participate in Church life. Lenin therefore remained flexible in approaching religious matters; although he never lost sight of his original goal to eradicate religion, he recognized the usefulness of strategic and temporary retreat.

Although he shared Lenin's antireligious sentiments, Trotsky expressed impatience with Lenin's desire to approach the problem of religion slowly and carefully. In his book *Problems of Life,* Trotsky claimed that the struggle against religion was easier than might be expected. He based this claim on the assertion that the Russian peasant and worker had a "purely external relation" to the Church. In his view, the Church "never was successful in penetrating deeply into the consciousness of the masses, nor in blending its dogmas and canons with the inner emotions of the people." He considered that the Church provided more for social needs than spiritual ones, offering theatrical and ceremonial diversions from everyday life, and that religious practice was therefore "more of a habit than a living attachment to deeply held beliefs." In order to nullify the Church and make it obsolete to Russians, it was necessary to make other social diversions and entertainment available to the populace. He also believed it was necessary to educate the peasants and workers; once they could read, they would realize the falseness of religion and would no longer need the superstition that the Church provided. Therefore, education programs combined with entertainment would wipe away the already superficial attachment to religion.[15]

The Bolsheviks followed their nationalization decree of 1917 with several other laws designed to weaken the power of the Church. The "Revolutionary Divorce Law" and the "Marriage, Children, and Registration of Civil Status," both of December 31, 1917, secularized functions that the Church had previously claimed as its prerogative.[16] The biggest blow to the Church came with the publication of the "Decree of Separation of Church and State in Russia" on January 23, 1918 (see Appendix B). Even though both the Church and the Bolshevik state desired to be separate from one another, both sides held radically different interpretations of what this meant. As discussed earlier, the Church wanted to be separate from the state, while at the same time enjoying privileges and the protection of the state. The Bolsheviks interpreted separation of Church and state to mean that the Church was subordinate to the state.

Ostensibly, under this decree the freedom of religion was protected. Article three stipulated that "every citizen may profess any religious belief, or profess no belief at all." It also allowed religious rites to be performed, so long as they did not "interfere with the rights of the citizens of the Soviet Republic."[17] This ambiguous phrase allowed the authorities to prohibit religious activities at their discretion. The separation decree also contradicts the marriage decree by prohibiting religious rites from mixing with secular ones.[18]

The last two articles of the decree reiterate the land nationalization decree, which stripped the Church of its property, but the decree also gave the Church room to negotiate. After pronouncing all Church property "the property of the people," the last article allows "buildings and objects especially used for the purpose of worship shall be let, free of charge, to the respective religious associations, by resolution of the local or central state authorities."[19] This provision allowed lay brotherhoods to petition the government to turn buildings over to them.

Relic Exposures

Aside from passing laws weakening church power, the Soviet authorities sought to discredit the Church in the eyes of the people. The most dramatic and effective method was to expose "relic frauds" in the monasteries. Orthodoxy places great emphasis on preserving the bodies or parts of the bodies of saints. When a church is consecrated, the bones of one or more saints are placed in a hole in the altar as a reminder that the Christian church was built on the bones of its martyrs. As well, some monasteries have the entire bodies of saints lying in glass-covered caskets in their cathedrals. One manifestation of a person's saintliness is that the person's body is "incorrupt" after death—in other words, it does not decay. The most famous saints whose bodies lie in monasteries in Russia are St. Sergius of Radonezh in Holy Trinity-St. Sergius lavra in Sergeev Posad and St. Amvrosii in Optina Pustyn. Many pilgrims continue to come to these monasteries to pray to these saints and to seek miracles.[20]

The Bolsheviks viewed these practices as superstitious and barbaric. They believed that the "relics" that people came from all over the country to venerate were in reality made of wax or some other fraudulent material and that the monasteries used these "incorrupt" saints as a way to

Relics of Elder Ambrose, Optina Pustyn Monastery

trick ignorant peasants out of their money. They therefore engaged in a campaign to prove that monasteries were deceiving the people. They instructed officials to go to various monasteries, exhume relics, and perform tests to determine whether the relics were actually human bones. The Bolsheviks realized that the average Russian believer would protest this act; therefore, they gave careful instructions to local officials not to conduct these exposures on days when churches were crowded. Rather, they preferred to have a select group of people present. This group included representatives from the provincial Soviet committees, the Communist Party, and workers' and peasants' organizations. Doctors were also present to examine the relics and sign the necessary paperwork. Most important, the monastics themselves were forced to carry out the actual process of "exposing" the relics. They were also compelled to sign the affidavit to prevent believers from accusing the Soviets of sacrilege. The presence of monastics and clergy also added legitimacy to the entire proceedings.[21] These exposures were photographed, and atheist publications such as *Revoliutsiia i Tserkov* and later *Bezbozhnik* were filled with many lurid accounts of the discovery that so-called relics were actually made of wax and animal bone. An article in *Bezbozhnik* describes the relics of Rasnianski monastery in Kharkhov. The author asserts that the abbot would instruct the other monks to go out to meat shops and bring back bones of pigs, sheep, and cows to use as relics. These "relics" were to be taken to Moscow for laboratory tests to prove the monks' duplicity.[22]

There are many accounts of monks and nuns being tried in court for relic fraud, two of which are examined here. Both cases were tried in the Moscow People's Court, although the first incident actually took place in Smolensk guberniia. On June 22, 1920, the People's Court announced a verdict in the case against Abbess Serafima of the Vladimir-Ekaterina monastery and Hieromonk Dosifei Zhidkov of Donskoi monastery on charges of religious blackmail and counterrevolutionary activity. Although these two individuals stood trial, the minutes of the proceedings make it apparent that the real people on trial were Patriarch Tikhon and Bishop Nazari. Throughout the trial the judges consistently referred to the church's attempt to gain economic influence over the workers and peasants, the "dark, ignorant masses." According to one witness, Evdokia Volkova, after the government nationalized the land of the Vladimir-Ekaterina monastery, Abbess Serafima became desperate for money. She decided to bring in fake relics and a fake miracle-working icon in hopes of attracting more people. Volkova testified that Abbess Serafima said "after the appearance of the relics in the monastery, many pilgrims will come." She therefore ordered Volkova to go to Moscow and to receive this "miraculous" icon and relics from Patriarch Tikhon. Hieromonk Dosifei along with Bishop Nazari met her as representatives of the patriarch.

Although the judges found Dosifei and Serafima guilty and referred to them constantly as "sly" and "exploiters," they repeatedly stated that the two were committing these crimes under the direction and at the behest of Patriarch Tikhon and Bishop Nazari. In summing up, the court declared that "the real culprits are Tikhon and Nazari . . . they bear full blame for the actions of Serafima and Dosifei." Accordingly, the court handed down a sentence that reflected some leniency. Abbess Serafima was sentenced to ten years of hard labor, but in deference to her age, the court commuted the sentence to one year working at the Department of Social Security. The court sentenced Hieromonk Dosifei to five years of hard labor; however, because of his proletarian background, "he [was] not considered dangerous to the Republic." He was granted amnesty and was sent to work at the Bureau of Compulsory Labor "without depriving him of freedom." The court also stated that it would pursue a case against Tikhon and Nazari. The court further ruled that the "relics" would be transferred to a monastery and that brochures titled "The Suffering of the Vilenski Martyrs" would be confiscated and destroyed and that all pictures of the royal family would be removed from the nuns' cells. The fact that nuns then had pictures of the recently executed royal family was probably the real basis for counterrevolutionary charges.[23]

The second case occurred in October, 1920, also in the Moscow People's Court. Olga Mazinova, Vasilia Griaznova, and Abbess Aleftina of Paul Posad monastery in Moscow guberniia were accused of "constructing a cult factory and exploiting the working masses with religious superstition." Griaznova and Mazinova were laywomen who, according to the court, had organized a women's society in which they "spent large sums of money, received from the workers, to sustain their believers and other parasites." The two women were also accused of conspiring to spread propaganda concerning fake relics among the population. The punishment the court gave in this case was more severe than the previous one. Griaznova and Labzina were both deprived of their citizenship and sentenced to ten years of hard labor. Like Abbess Serafima, Abbess Aleftina was spared hard labor because of her age (she was eighty-six). However, she was still considered "a dangerous element to society" because she had "lived most of her life as a parasite on the body of the people." She was instead sent to a charity house where she would live out her days and do light work. The monastery would be confiscated and turned into a museum.[24]

These two cases illustrate the differing Bolshevik policy toward religion, particularly during the civil war years. Although both cases were tried in the same court five months apart, the verdicts differed greatly. In the first case, the court's leniency is explained by its desire to incriminate and eventually arrest Tikhon and Nazari. In the second case, the accused faced the same charges, but excepting the elderly abbess, the nuns were sentenced to hard labor. Several explanations may account for the difference in punishment in both of these cases. The lack of a direct mention of the patriarch or another bishop does not suggest another possible target for the court to focus on. The court doubtless had to prove to the people and to its superiors that it was firm in the fight against religion, and therefore, these nuns had to serve as examples. The social status of the accused also indicates a reason for the harsher sentence. Labzina and Griaznova were both described as "former merchants' wives." This would put them in a higher socioeconomic sphere than the workers and peasants whose interests the Bolsheviks professed to defend and who composed the people's court. Moreover, these women had started a factory within the monastery, indicating a taste for capitalism. Leaving aside Bolshevik anticapitalist rhetoric, Russians have traditionally exhibited mistrust of innovation and accumulation of wealth. The fact that the persons involved in these enterprises were women could also reflect a gender bias on the part of the judges. Another explanation could be simple arbitrariness on the part of the court.

The controversy over relics in Russia is not unique to the Bolsheviks. During the time of Peter the Great and his "spiritual regulation," many monks and nuns, as well as clergy, were accused of making fraudulent claims of miraculous icons and relics.[25] Those accused were placed on trial and, if found guilty, punished accordingly. However, some major differences are apparent when comparing these cases of relic exposure to the ones in the 1920s. The major difference is the motivation of the accusers and the nature of the trials. The earlier trials occurred in ecclesiastical courts, where the issue was never the legitimacy of relics in general. The concern of the clerics responsible was to prove that the relics in question were legitimate. The motivation was to preserve the integrity of relics in the Orthodox Church. Strict standards were used to determine whether a relic was genuine. In the cases of relic exposure during the 1920s, the atheistic government was trying to convince the population that the Church in general was fraudulent and that relics and miraculous icons did not exist. The motivation of these cases was to delegitimize the Orthodox Church in general.

Resistance to the Bolsheviks

There were many acts of resistance to the Bolsheviks' antireligious campaign, with various degrees of success. One explosive event occurred in 1919, when the Bolsheviks attempted to remove the body of St. Sergius of Radonezh from Holy Trinity lavra to an antireligious museum. When the authorities tried to "expose" the relics, they were met with great resistance from the local population. Sergei Volkov, then a seminary student, witnessed the scene. Despite attempts at secrecy, news spread that the Bolsheviks were coming to examine and possibly take away the relics of St. Sergius, one of Russia's most famous and beloved saints. At the beginning of Great Lent, the faithful gathered in the trapeza (refectory) chapel. One of the monks, Archimandrite Kronid, addressed the crowd, calling on them to defend "not monks, but a holy place, the place where St. Sergius walked." The Bolsheviks, afraid of possible violence, confiscated the keys to all of the churches and the bell tower, fearing that the monks would sound the alarm bell summoning the laity. They forbade people to enter the lavra by the main gate and surrounded the monastery with Red Army soldiers. The soldiers had instructions to shoot if they met with resistance. On the day of the relic exposure, the square near the monastery filled with people, mainly women. They strained at the gates, pushing the guards. Eventually they broke through the barriers and surged through the monastery gates. The guards fired into the air, but no one was killed.[26]

The Bolsheviks' determination to remove the body of St. Sergius provoked an angry letter from Patriarch Tikhon to the Council of People's Commissars. He quoted the Bolsheviks' laws against them, claiming that "the intention to remove the relics of St. Sergius affect our religious conscience and appears as an invasion of the civil power in internal life and the belief of the church. This action contradicts both the decree of separation of church and state, and the repeated statements from high central officials about freedom of religious expression and assurances that there will be no order to remove religious objects from churches."[27] The relics were not removed.

One of the most newsworthy and violent acts of protest occurred on January 19, 1918, when Alexandra Kollontai, the commissar of state welfare, ordered Kronstadt marines to enter the Alexander Nevsky lavra in St. Petersburg and confiscate the property for use as a shelter for the homeless and war invalids. This lavra occupies a very important place in Russian culture and history. Russia's most famous medieval hero, Prince Alexander Nevsky, is buried there. People came from thousands of miles to visit this monastery. It was therefore a symbol both to communists and to Orthodox believers. The communists viewed it as a symbol of the Old Russia they wished to destroy, and therefore the confiscation of it would send a powerful message that Communism had overcome the backwardness of Old Russia.

For the Orthodox, Alexander Nevsky lavra was a symbol of their faith and of all the old values and traditions that the Bolsheviks were attacking. Therefore, when the soldiers arrived, the monks were determined not to give up easily. The head of the lavra, Bishop Prokopii, refused to surrender the monastery's belongings. The Red Guards promptly arrested him. The monks rang the church bells in alarm, calling over two thousand people who lived nearby. Fighting broke out between the people defending the lavra, mostly women, and the Red Guards. During the riots, a priest, Fr. Skipetrov, was shot and killed. One interesting aspect of this incident was the behavior of the soldiers living in the vicinity of the lavra. The bells brought them to the lavra, where some of them sided with the Red Guards, but others defended the lavra against their fellow soldiers. The Red Guards were forced to leave the lavra without accomplishing their mission.[28]

The Bolsheviks did not expect the extreme violence that accompanied the attempts to nationalize church property, and many did not agree with Kollontai's order. V. D. Bonch-Bruevich, a scientist and a friend of Lenin's who was also an expert on sectarians, publicly stated that he was not an enemy of the Church and that he would "give his protection to the announced church demonstration which might arise out of this incident."[29] In a surprisingly candid newspaper account, the leaders at the Smolny in Petrograd (the Bolshevik headquarters) admitted that they had not foreseen that "Madame Alexandra Kollontai's decree would make such an impression on the population of Petrograd. Especially unexpected was the attitude of the soldiers toward the church that is being separated from the state."[30] They gave no other reference to the behavior of the soldiers, but this incident in the heart of Red Petrograd illustrated to the Bolsheviks that eradicating the influence of religion from people's lives would be more difficult than they had envisioned.[31]

The entire relics-exposing campaign lasted for two years, from October 23, 1918, to December 1, 1920. In all of Russia, a total of sixty-five inspections of relics occurred. At a Sovnarkom meeting in June, 1920, the council expressed satisfaction with the progress of the anti-relic-fraud campaign and vowed to "fully liquidate the cult of dead bodies." However, the committee acknowledged that the anti-relic campaign had been undertaken at a cost of great violence: Protests generally greeted the attempts of the authorities to carry out these exposures. In Perm guberniia alone, from June to December of 1918, ten protopriests, forty-one priests, five deacons, and thirty-six monastics were killed while defending their monasteries.[32]

A second occurrence further alarmed the Bolsheviks. On the same day of the attack on the lavra, Patriarch Tikhon issued a strongly worded message anathematizing the Bolshevik regime. He referred to the Soviets as "godless lords of darkness" and called on the faithful to "refrain from communicating with these monsters of the human race in any way whatever" and encouraged them to defend the church against the Soviets.[33] His statement essentially openly declared a state of war against the Bolshevik regime. The all-Russian church sobor, which was still in session, approved of the decree, but Count A. Olsufiev complained that it came too late to effect any benefit. The proper time for such an announcement would have been when the people had begun to attack the landlords' estates and factories.[34]

The sobor representatives realized the possible consequences of such an inflammatory statement. The murder of Metropolitan Vladimir of Kiev by armed bandits on January 25, 1918, and reports of arrests of bishops and priests further underscored the danger of antagonizing the new regime. However, the representatives agreed that the church provided the last hope to incite the faithful against Bolshevism and that they must take risks to achieve that goal. Thus, two days after the attack on the lavra, Metropolitan Veniamin of Petrograd led a religious procession through the city. The city party committee did not wish to have another outbreak of violence and ordered the soldiers not to interfere. Religious processions proved a very popular method of protest and occurred in other parts of Russia as well, most often accompanied by violence and arrests. In the wake of the Decree of Separation of Church and State and the Peace of Brest Litovsk, Patriarch Tikhon issued several other statements excommunicating the Bolsheviks, calling all Orthodox to wage war against them, and condemning them as traitors for signing the Brest-Litovsk Peace with Germany.

Many Orthodox laity and clergy responded to the patriarch's call. Religious agitation and protest spread throughout the provinces. In Iaroslavl, the parish councils refused to allow the local authorities to inventory the newly nationalized property. Violence ensued, which led the authorities to declare martial law. In Voronezh, a mob beat a commissar who was trying to inventory a monastery. In Tula, police fired on a religious procession held in protest of an official ban, killing thirteen. In other provinces, authorities recognized the strong religious feelings and rescinded bans against church processions. One Soviet antireligious journal estimated that from February to May, 1918, 687 people were killed in religious riots.[35]

Despite these demonstrations, the Church did not receive the popular response that it had hoped. The protests and violence that occurred were isolated and sporadic. No mass crusade against the Bolsheviks occurred, nor did a holy war to preserve the Orthodox Church in Russia happen. This was mainly due to restraint on the part of the Bolsheviks. Although they arrested and killed bishops and clergy, most of the violence against these latter occurred at the hands of returning soldiers and Red Guards, not by orders of the government. Many monastics seemed to realize this, as one petition to the commissariat of justice illustrates. The monks of the Alexander-Svirski monastery in Olonetski diocese (Petrograd guberniia) wrote a letter of complaint against the behavior of the Red Guards and soldiers in 1918. In October of that year, Red Army soldiers and officers had repeatedly broken into the monastery during services or meals, stolen sacred objects, and desecrated the shrine of a saint. They had drunk the communion wine and had stolen and ripped vestments, and when two of the monks protested, one of the commissars arrested them. The monks knew some of their attackers, remarking that many had been to the monastery before, either as pilgrims or as workers, and therefore knew where the valuables were kept. The monks sent the commissariat of justice a list of the stolen objects and demanded recompense. The commissariat responded that it would give the matter their attention.[36]

The restraint on the part of the government came from the desire not to make martyrs of clergy or monastics. For this reason also, the authorities did not arrest Patriarch Tikhon or disband the sobor. Also, despite announcing the new decrees, the government was slow to put them into effect. Many churches remained open, and their sacred objects remained untouched. The new government wisely recognized that it still needed to consolidate its power and that it would prove foolhardy to antagonize the majority of the population.

The Civil War, 1918–1921

The civil war further complicated church-state relations. The beginning of the civil war is sometimes dated from the day the Bolsheviks seized power in October, 1917. However, not until June, 1918, did serious fighting break out between pro- and anti-Communist forces. The civil war marked one of the most brutal periods in Russia's history. Having successfully staged their coup, the Bolsheviks were now engaged in a life-and-death battle with a variety of opponents, collectively known as the "Whites." The White forces were composed of diverse groups such as liberals, monarchists, socialist revolutionaries, Mensheviks, reactionary military circles, and other anti-Bolshevik factions. Both sides used terror to subdue parts of the country deemed sympathetic to the opposing side. No segment of society escaped this period unscathed, especially the Church.

The civil war had the effect of intensifying the Bolsheviks' antireligious campaign. They were especially harsh toward monasteries, which they regarded as "nests of counterrevolution." Because of their relative economic independence, they were difficult to control. At a time when the Bolshevik state faced attack and imminent defeat from its opponents, it was not inclined to tolerate acts of hostility from the Church. Speeches or activities that appeared even remotely threatening were immediately and brutally repressed. One instance from Poltava guberniia in August, 1919, describes a Bolshevik occupation of Spasso-Preobrashenski monastery. After robbing and desecrating the monastery, the Reds rounded up the monks and threatened to burn them. The approach of one of the White armies made this plan impossible, so the Reds took the monks to a railway station outside of the city and shot them. Out of twenty-five monks, seventeen were killed. The remainder managed to escape by feigning death.[37] In the town of Krolevetz in Tchernigov province, the clergy and monks of Rychlovsky monastery were put on trial. The abbot of the monastery and one of the priests received the death sentence. The judges voted to close the monastery and to "hand over the objects of service to other Church Communities."[38]

The Bolsheviks' suspicion of the church as an enemy proved justified. Although no concrete figures exist, the information available suggests that the majority of monks and clergy actively supported the White armies. Father Jonah, later bishop of Hankow, China, was one of these. Upon his ordination, he served as the senior chaplain of the Imperial Russian Army during the first World War. After the Bolshevik revolution he traveled to Perm, where the Bolsheviks arrested him and sent him to Tiumen province to stand trial. On his way, he was liberated by Kolchak's White army, which made him chief chaplain. After the Whites' defeat he fled to China.[39] Another monastic supporter of the Whites was Abbess Rufina of the Ioanno-Bogoslovski monastery near Ekaterina in Perm guberniia. When the Whites freed the area, Abbess Rufina ordered a religious procession, and the nuns presented each member of the military detachment with white fur hats and white garments. When the Whites retreated, they evacuated the inhabitants of the city, including the nuns.[40]

Documents from Siberia provide additional examples of the clergy and monastics offering material support to the Whites. While many clergy showed their support by offering services for the troops and some monasteries allowed the White forces to use their facilities to store weapons, some Siberian clergy and monks actually took up arms and formed "Regiments of Jesus." The reaction of peasant-soldiers in the Red Army to these regiments was sometimes mixed. Emelian Yaroslavsky, the future head of the League of the Militant Godless, tells an anecdote (possibly apocryphal) concerning this reaction. A detachment of peasants captured one Regiment of Jesus that contained many priests and monks. Most of these peasants were believers; accordingly, out of the group of prisoners they selected those deacons and monks who had the best singing voices and requested them to chant in the churches. The rest of the group they executed.[41]

Although the Whites are generally portrayed as sympathetic to the Church, there are some documented cases of White atrocities against monasteries. In the Caucasian town of Vladikavkaz was a women's monastery named Kizliar. The abbess there was Antonina. In the beginning of the 1917 revolution, the Bolsheviks burst into the monastery, stole articles, and murdered several of the protesting nuns. A year later Kizliar was seized by the Whites. The inhabitants of the monastery were grateful, thinking that the Whites had come to liberate them. However, one of the Whites independently ordered the destruction of the monastery and the murder of the nuns. Few escaped.[42]

Despite evidence of clerical support for the Whites, Patriarch Tikhon insisted throughout the civil war that the Church was not assisting the Whites. During the war, the patriarch changed his previous stance toward the Soviet government in official pronouncements. Whereas early declarations called for a holy war to preserve Old Russia, from mid-1919 on, a more conciliatory tone is evident. Tikhon ordered clerics and monastics to refrain from supporting political parties. Although he did not endorse the regime, he advocated neutrality. A year of house arrest in 1918 had convinced Tikhon of the futility of provoking the Soviet government. Later, on November 7, 1920, he took the precaution of issuing a circular that gave instructions on governing the Church should anything happen to him. This circular advised the diocesan bishops to establish a temporary church administration through joint action with neighboring dioceses in case they lost contact with the central church administration. It also gave the bishops permission to divide their areas into several dioceses and name new bishops if necessary. The important goal was to ensure that church life continued as smoothly as possible. This circular would later become the basis for the Karlovatskii synod. As John Curtiss notes, however, the significance of this statement is what was left unsaid; nowhere in the document is there anti-Soviet rhetoric, indicating that by this time the patriarch had either tacitly accepted the existence of the new regime or wished to avoid persecution or both.[43]

An example of the party's harsher attitude toward religion may be found in one of the resolutions adopted at the Eighth Party Congress in March, 1919. With the civil war in progress, the party decided that it needed to pursue its antireligious campaign more vigorously. The decree stated:

> With reference to religion, the All-Russian Communist Party does not content itself with the already decreed separation of church and state—ie with measures which are a part of the program of the bourgeois democracies, but never fulfilled in those democracies because of the many various ties binding capital with religious propaganda. The All-Russian Communist Party is guided by the conviction that only the realization of conscious and systematic social and economic activity of the masses will lead to the disappearance of religious prejudices. The aim of the Party is finally to destroy the ties between the exploiting classes and the organization of religious propaganda, at the same time helping the toiling masses actually to liberate their minds from religious superstitions, and organizing on a wide scale scientific educational and anti-religious propaganda. It is, however, necessary to avoid offending the religious susceptibilities of believers which leads only to the strengthening of religious fanaticism.[44]

The two departments that would oversee the Bolsheviks' religious policy during the civil war were the people's commissariat of justice (NARKOMIUST), particularly its eighth section, and the security apparatus, the Cheka. In March, 1919, NARKOMIUST wrote a circular objecting to the leniency of some courts in sentencing priests and monastics. Many were sentenced to monasteries or exiled outside the province. The NARKOMIUST argued that this practice was counterproductive and against Soviet principles, as it merely passed troublesome clerics along to a neighboring province. Those whom the courts convicted would have to serve more severe sentences.[45]

Nikolai Bukharin, the radical hard-liner, echoed this sentiment in his book *The ABC of Communism.* He wrote, "It is necessary at the present time to wage with the utmost vigor the war against religious prejudices, for the church has now definitely become a counter-revolutionary organization, and endeavors to use its religious influence over the masses in order to marshall them for the political struggle against the dictatorship of the proletariat. This is why the Soviet Power finds it necessary to engage at this juncture in widespread antireligious propaganda. Our aims can be secured by the delivery of special lectures, by the holding of debates, and by the publication of suitable literature."[46]

Like the party congress, Bukharin also counseled a cautious approach: He warned that the campaign against religion must be conducted with patience and considerateness, as well as with energy and perseverance. "The credulous crowd is extremely sensitive to anything which hurts its feelings. To thrust atheism upon the masses . . . and to make a mockery of the objects of popular reverence would not assist but would hinder the campaign against religion. If the church were to be persecuted, it would win sympathy among the masses, for persecution would remind them of the almost forgotten days when there was an association between religion and the defense of national freedom; . . . and in general, it would mobilize all of the vestiges of an ideology which is already beginning to die out."[47]

In addition to harsh rhetoric, the Bolsheviks frequently executed priests and monastics who were accused of supporting the Whites. This constant threat of danger forced the clergy to develop an underground communication system. This method is described by Elder Sampson of Pskov, who was living in the town of Tikhvin (east of St. Petersburg) as a novice at St. Sabbas of Krypetsk during the civil war. According to him, there were no young monks at the monastery, as they had all been conscripted from the monastery during the revolution. In 1919 Sampson was arrested because of his supposed resemblance to the Romanov family. He was shot by a firing squad, but when his fellow monks came to spirit his body away for burial, they found that he was still breathing. He recovered from his wounds and remained in Tikhvin as a lecturer of Russian history and literature in a military hospital.

In addition to these duties, he had a secret life—he served as subdeacon of the Bishop of Tikhvin, the future Patriarch Alexei I. Bishop Alexei "came there five times a year and gave me missions from Patriarch Tikhon. I would travel around to the different places where bishops were incarcerated and maintain the links between the hierarchs and the patriarch, with the Metropolitan of Novgorod and with the Metropolitan of Petrograd. They entrusted great secrets to me. I penetrated the prison where Archbishop Arsenius had been confined and became acquainted with him. . . . One time I came to give him a secret package. In front of me he read it, wrote a reply, gave it to me, but did not seal it. I brought it back through the prison checkpoint and returned the reply to (Bishop) Alexei, who governed the Novgorod diocese for him. This was the way Church affairs were handled at that time."[48]

One remarkable story illustrates the arbitrariness of Bolshevik policy toward the monasteries, particularly in rural areas. It concerns Abbess Antonina of Kizliar, in the Caucasus. As already mentioned, during the civil war the monastery was a victim of atrocities that both Reds and Whites committed. After the Whites retreated and the Bolsheviks took over, they tried to ascertain who had betrayed them to the Whites. They falsely charged Abbess Antonina with aiding the Whites and sentenced her to death. She fled to a monastery in Vladikavkaz, where the abbess hid her in an attic. The Bolsheviks offered a reward for her capture—three thousand gold rubles for whoever brought her in to the GPU (secret police), an incredibly large sum of money.[49] She stayed there for several months until she was betrayed by a GPU agent in the guise of a pilgrim to the monastery.

She then escaped and hid with a family in a nearby village. The nuns from the monastery came daily and brought food. After two weeks, Abbess Antonina decided to turn herself in to the GPU because she was worried about putting the family she was staying with at risk. The family pleaded for her to reconsider. She had already made up her mind, however, and, in full monastic garb with her gold abbess's cross, went to the local GPU. The mother of the family described their desolation as they sat in the house in silence, wondering what would be Abbess Antonina's fate. After several hours had passed, the eleven-year-old daughter exclaimed, "Here comes Matushka!"[50] They were amazed to see Abbess Antonina coming back to the house. She described to them what happened:

> "I went to the GPU. The guard asked me what my business was. I stated that I wanted to speak to the chief. They told me he was not available. I replied that only to him would I speak. After a short time, a door in the corridor opened, and the chief came out and invited me into his office. He asked what I wanted. I told him, "You have a price of 3000 rubles on my head, and I have come to turn myself in and claim the reward."
> "Who are you?" he said.
> "I am Abbess Antonina."
> "You? And you came to me yourself?"
> "Yes, and I bring you my head."

> He took out a photograph from a box, looked at it and looked at me. He told me, "You are free—go where you wish." As I was leaving, he said "In a year I will be obliged to give you some kind of legal punishment."[51]

After that meeting, Abbess Antonina returned to her original monastery in Kizliar. She lived there openly, and no one molested her. After a year had passed, she returned as promised to the GPU office, this time without her cross or monastic clothing. At the GPU she was imprisoned, but no officer abused or insulted her in any way, and she was made as comfortable as possible. After a year, she was again released and along with twelve nuns founded a skete in the mountainous village of Tuaps.[52]

The behavior of the GPU chief in this story opens up several lines of interpretation. In letting her go free for a year, he deliberately disobeyed the orders of his superiors. The abbess was a wanted felon, with rewards for her posted all over the Caucasus. He had no guarantee that she would voluntarily return to face her punishment. One possible reason is that he himself was a secret Christian. This seems unlikely, however. The most likely explanation for his action is that he admired her courage in turning herself in to the secret police and therefore did all that he could to help her and still obey his superiors. Whichever interpretation is correct, Abbess Antonina obviously had a profound effect on him, judging also from the treatment she received while in prison. The GPU was notorious for its brutality, yet Abbess Antonina was not even verbally insulted.

In 1920 the NARKOMIUST issued a statement claiming that "Painless but full dissolution of the monasteries is necessary, as they are the chief centers of influence of churchmen, nurseries of patriotism, and powerful screws in the exploiting machine of the old ruling classes."[53] The NARKOMIUST recommended first appropriating those monasteries that had been centers of counterrevolution. Whereas previous policy had desired to preserve monastery agriculture and economy, the new orders were to confiscate any businesses or manufacturing property. Local authorities could proceed with these instructions without obtaining permission from the central authorities.

Those monastery churches that had been transferred for the use of local parishes were temporarily exempt from harm. In 1921 the NARKOMIUST further clarified its position on the public use of monastery churches: It stated that, in general, the monastery church should be closed when the monastery was dissolved. Only in exceptional cases would the authorities allow the church to be turned over to a newly organized parish, on condition that the parish provide a separate entrance to the church and agree not to ring the bells.[54]

The monastics and neighboring laity did not meekly accept this announcement. Monks and clergy aroused the peasants to defend the monasteries, and in Zvenigorod and Nizhni Novgorod among other places, mobs reportedly beat those Communists who came to liquidate the monasteries. According to an article in *Revoliutsiia i Tserkov,* Patriarch Tikhon sent instructions to Archbishop Ionniki, abbot of the famous Novo-Ierusalimski monastery near Moscow, to seek the support of the pilgrims and other persons who revered the monastery and attempt to organize a brotherhood of defenders.[55]

Despite these instances of resistance, the authorities succeeded in closing many monasteries. Official statistics for all of Russia show that by 1920 the Communists had disbanded 673 monasteries and confiscated objects and capital totaling 4,247,667,540 rubles. They turned over approximately 827,540 desiatins of land to the peasantry and nationalized various monastic enterprises, for example, 84 factories, 436 dairies, 620 cattle barns, 1,112 rented dwellings, 708 hostels, 311 apiaries, and 277 hospitals and shelters. The Communists transformed these buildings for their own use. Out of these confiscated buildings, they created 48 sanitoria and health centers; 168 "institutions of social protection" (most likely homes for the aged); 197 schools and programs of the commissariat of education; 349 hospitals and sanitaria; 2 maternity homes and children's shelters; 287 Soviet institutions; 188 military establishments; and 14 labor camps.[56]

According to Alexander Solzhenitsyn, the first forced-labor camp was established in an empty convent in Nizhni Novgorod on September 6, 1918, with five thousand inmates. The Soviets preferred to use former monasteries as prisons because they were enclosed by strong walls; they had good solid buildings; and they were empty. Besides these practical considerations, what better way to show contempt for a religious building than to turn it into a place of torture and imprisonment. The prisoners even had a saying: "A holy place is never empty." Some of the most notorious of these latter establishments were Solovki monastery in the north; Andronnikov (where the famous icon painter Andrei Rublev once lived); Novospassky; and Ivanovsky in Moscow.[57]

Solovki had a special attraction for the Bolsheviks as it had served as a state prison from 1718 until 1903. The Tsarist government had imprisoned church and political dissidents there, including Alexander Pushkin's uncle P. Gannibal. In the beginning of the Soviet regime, after the Bolsheviks had confiscated the monastery, they allowed the monks to stay, forced them to work harder on the farm, and sent the herring that the monks caught to Moscow. However, because the Soviets resented the continued presence of religious objects, on May 25, 1923, they looted the monastery and set it on fire. They drove the monks out and converted the monastery into a prison. The Soviets allowed a few useful ones to remain, such as the fishing *artel* (cooperative marketing system), which continued until 1930. According to Solzhenitsyn, after the monk fishermen left, "no one could manage to find that particular herring in the sea any more, and it was as if it had completely disappeared."[58]

Other monks who remained included cattle specialists on Muksalma; Father Methodius, the cabbage salter; and Father Samson, the foundry specialist. They had a special plot of land separate from the camp with their own exit, called the Herring Gates. The Soviets referred to it as a workers' commune but also allowed them to use the Onufriyev Church at the cemetery "out of condescension for their total stupefaction."[59] The Soviets must have regarded these monks as "loyal" to allow them to stay on monastery land. Before the Stalinist purges, the main prerequisite for being considered loyal was not being an overt threat. That was enough of a guarantee for the Soviets.

Attempts at Accommodation

Aside from violent incidents, the church also pursued peaceful methods of negotiating with the Bolsheviks. One episode suggests that the government was willing to compromise with the Church. On March 15, 1918, the sobor heard a report from a delegation that had recently met with government representatives in the Kremlin. Although both sides registered complaints, the discussions proved remarkably amicable. The government officials declared that they were not hostile to religion but were favorable to it, particularly the Orthodox Church. They expressed regret over the violent events but stated that both nationalization of Church property and separation of Church and state must remain. However, they believed that some differences between Church and state could be resolved. One commissar stated, "We are attempting to construct socialism in Russia. Christ himself was a socialist, and the only difference in our attempts lies in the fact that we are promoting socialism by means of compulsion."[60]

The promulgation of the commissariat of justice's "Resolution concerning Execution of the Separation of Church and State and of School from Church" on August 24, 1918, illustrates the Bolsheviks' conception of compromise. This document reiterates the earlier separation decree depriving the Church of its rights as a juridical entity. In terms of property, it officially placed all church and monastery land under permanent control of the local sovdeps. Local members of the religious "cults" composed of at least twenty people could petition the sovdeps to use the buildings free of charge and for religious purposes only. If the petition was granted, the members agreed to assume full financial responsibility for the property's upkeep (see Appendix C). Property that was not specifically used for religious purposes, such as factories and fishing grounds, was not included under this clause and henceforth belonged to the state.[61]

Another provision of the resolution, which hurt the church more than land confiscation, involved the Church's monetary assets. All monies that the church and other religious organizations had in banks was to be confiscated and turned over to the sovdeps. Another law that was directed specifically against the monasteries forbade them to charge money for burials on monastery grounds. This eliminated a very important source of income for them. These laws made churches and monasteries financially dependent on their parishioners. The timetable for full confiscation of Church property was two months. The instruction also gave permission for the construction of new churches under the supervision of the sovdeps and with the understanding that this property would be nationalized as well. Despite all of these restrictions, the parishioners were able to attend church services fairly regularly as long as they had the funds to pay for them.[62]

In other negotiations between the sobor delegates and government officials, the latter refused to consider demands to annul the decree of separation of Church and state and the nationalization of Church property. However, they allowed some clergy and monastics to receive land for their own use. Within the people's commissariat of justice, the newly formed Eighth Department for Carrying out the Decree of Separation of Church and State issued the following circular: "It is clear that aged monks and nuns who are unable to work must be evicted from the monasteries so that social prosperity can be on a level with other citizens of the Russian Republic. However, among the monastic population it is necessary to differentiate between the working elements in the monasteries and those who exploit religion. It is necessary not to deprive those laboring elements of the possibility to use their rights, calling them to obey the laws of the Soviet republic according to the socialization of land, etc. It goes without saying, that the land department of the local soviets will give to these elements allotments of land, stock, and a quarterly allowance which must be received in the places for land allotments."[63]

These "model agricultural monasteries" would still be nationalized, however. The monks and nuns would cease to own the land they worked and instead would be employees of the state. These *sovkhozi*[64] would be under the direction of both monastics and the sovdeps. The products of the sovkhozi were not designated for the monks' and nuns' consumption, but rather to meet the economic needs of the government. The government strove to undermine the religious connection of these communes in part by forbidding any preaching on "purely religious themes."[65] Such restrictions were sometimes only a formality. In Kostroma province, for example, the local authorities built a sovkhoz on the grounds of the Bogoliubski women's monastery. Although officially the sovkhoz and the monastery belonged to the state, in practice not much changed. The abbess still occupied her former administrative position of authority, and the nuns still worshiped in their church. In Shamordino women's monastery in Kaluga oblast, later a sovkhoz, there were even two councils composed of nuns who administered the sovkhoz.[66]

A 1922 government report provided many details on the working of the Shamordino monastery sovkhoz. It had a total of 409 people. It is not clear how many of these were nuns, although the number was most likely very small; according to another report, before the Bolshevik revolution, there were 200 nuns in the whole diocese. By 1922 there were only 125.[67] On the sovkhoz were small farms composed of both "state and nonstate" monastics. The nuns working as state workers received pay, while the nonstate nuns received lodging. The report stressed that nearly all of the state nuns were from the proletariat or the peasantry. This suggests that social class determined the monastics' position within the sovkhoz. All nuns adhered to their monastic life, and three priests on the sovkhoz regularly conducted services. An addendum to this report noted that services were conducted at the monastery every day.[68]

Interestingly, there is also evidence that the Bolsheviks put pressure on many monasteries to join the Communist Party as a precondition to remaining open. Both Abbess Aleksia of St. Nikolas women's monastery in Medinski uezd (Kaluga oblast) and the nuns of Valdaisky Korotsky monastery in Novgorod complained to Moscow that they were threatened by the local authorities to either join the local Communist Party or face eviction. The central authorities in Moscow informed them that they did not have to join any party.[69]

This insistence that the monasteries join the local Communist Party raises many questions. Why would the local party want these "counter-revolutionaries" to belong to their organization? Did this not violate the separation between Church and state? One possible explanation is that the local party officials felt that the presence of monks and nuns would add legitimacy to the party in the eyes of the religious people who lived around the monastery. Another likely reason for this insistence is that the local party officials felt that the monks and nuns could do less political damage to the Bolsheviks if they were members of the party.

The Success of the Brotherhoods

Such situations as well as the clause in the separation decree giving land to the people enabled the monastics to take advantage of the government's inconsistent policies regarding Church land. Here, the newly formed brotherhoods played a very important role in preserving the monasteries. The establishment of such organizations was discussed in the pre-sobor committees of 1917 and were officially formed in April, 1918, upon the direction of the sobor. These brotherhoods, pledged to defend Church property, were united under an all-Russian council of parish brotherhood organizations. In addition to forming these brotherhoods, the Church vowed to accelerate the propaganda effort, and in the Petrograd diocese, a journal called for establishing a network of parish cooperatives, schools, and courts. The purpose was to form a tightly knit network that would counter Bolshevik propaganda and activity. According to P. N. Miliukov, the general opinion among sobor members was that the Bolsheviks "would break their necks on the church."[70] The Church would become increasingly dependent on these grassroots organizations after the sobor disbanded in August, 1918, due to lack of funds. Although there was a new administrative organ called the synod, which would assist the patriarch in his administrative duties, it had virtually no power. The patriarch was now left virtually defenseless and even more dependent on informal organizations for support.

These brotherhoods achieved notable success in preserving monastic property. On January 30, 1919, the brotherhood of St. Daniel sent a petition to the department of justice requesting permission to use the church at the St. Daniel monastery in Moscow for religious purposes. They also asked for "free and unlimited use of church buildings of our monastery." Five hundred fifty-six people signed this statement, including many monks. One month later the justice department granted their request. The justice department required that the brotherhood formally register with it and pay a deposit of fifty rubles.[71]

One of the most interesting appeals to the government came from the parish society of the Ivanovskii women's monastery. In a long statement the anonymous writer stressed that "the internal life of the monastery is based on strict communist beginnings; the directing statutes . . . do not allow the possession of private property." To further emphasize the monastery's "communism" the document explained in detail how the monastery operated. Rooms were divided equally among the nuns; they all participated in agricultural labor; and all ate the same kind of food in a common dining room. No one received preferential treatment. As an appeal to the Bolsheviks' commitment to the proletariat, the writer also emphasized that all of the girls in the monastery came from working-class families. She concluded by emphasizing the monastery's uniqueness: "Nuns from other monasteries have not succeeded in imitating our strict society. We all firmly repeat, that over the last hundred years, our monastery has been the image of laboring communism and for this reason we ask that our monastery be preserved."[72]

This petition illustrates that at least some of the monastics discovered a way to use the Communists' language to preserve their own communities. By appropriating the revolutionary verbiage, they tried to portray themselves as fulfilling communist ideals. Regardless of whether the parish society of Ivanovskii monastery actually believed in Christian socialism and that they embodied it is unknown and ultimately not relevant. The importance of the document lies in the fact that it recognized the value of language and rhetoric in appealing to the authorities. Because resistance ultimately proved ineffective, the parish societies realized that success lay in trying to convince the Soviets that they did not pose a threat to the new regime; they accepted the Communist government and were not seeking to undermine it.

Monastery Kolkhozi

During the first year after the revolution, more monasteries took the initiative and converted themselves into agricultural communes, or *kolkhozi.*

Kolkhozi offered a better alternative than the state-run sovkhozi. In the kolkhoz, people pooled their land and resources, worked the land together, and marketed the produce collectively. Unlike the sovkhoz system, the nuns had more control over their goods and could choose a manager from their own ranks.

The decision to become a labor commune was not without controversy. In every diocese the matter was thoroughly debated. Minutes from a diocese council meeting in Kaluga illustrate the concerns that monks and nuns expressed about the transition from monastery to commune. The council heard petitions from abbots and abbesses about turning their monasteries into communes. Father Nikon from Optina Pustyn advised that the only option for preserving the monasteries lay in forming communes according to Soviet guidelines. The most compelling testimony came from one of the abbesses. Abbess Aleksia of the St. Nikolas monastery in the village of Medinski was in the process of converting her monastery into a commune. She had already formed a council of nuns for this purpose. She took this step after being threatened with eviction by the local sovdep. They told her that the only way for the monastery to remain intact was to become a commune. After conducting a vote among the nuns, eighty-one of whom were in favor of forming a commune, Abbess Aleksia communicated with the war commissariat in Moscow. She was told that the monastery would be under the control of the local sovdep and that the nuns could remain and would not be harassed. This information convinced the diocese council to grant the right of the monasteries to become communes.[73]

Every diocese went through similar meetings and debates. Although many monastics initially expressed a reluctance to participate, they soon realized that labor communes were a better alternative than eviction, return to "the world," and loss of any semblance of community. The idea gained more support after seeing the success of the first officially Church-sanctioned monastery commune in 1919 in Novgorod. The nuns of Leushinski monastery had formed a labor artel that had proved so successful that the Petrograd episcopal council wrote that other monasteries should "take this monastery as an example." After hearing such praise, Patriarch Tikhon officially gave his blessing to continue setting up such establishments. By March, 1921, official statistics stated that out of a total of 400 monasteries in twenty-four provinces of the Russian Federation, 116 had become collectivized in some form.[74] In Moscow province alone, 18 monasteries were reorganized into agricultural communes and artels.[75]

Smolensk guberniia contained four such monastery sovkhozi, and Archangel, six.[76]

The transformation was not very difficult. Monastery life by nature is collective; monasteries are expected to be as self-sufficient as possible, and as discussed earlier, every monk or nun worked the land or did other chores to ensure the monastery's survival. They typically grew enough food for themselves to live on and when possible grew a surplus to sell in neighboring villages. More monasteries therefore petitioned the government to become agricultural collectives, and in most instances, their requests were granted. Both sides benefited from this arrangement; the monasteries were able to preserve their way of life, and the communists were able to benefit from the communes' economic output. The monastics turned over part of their harvest to the government and paid a fee to allow their operation.

In many cases the monastics did not have access to the entire monastery; the officials appropriated several buildings for their own use and gave the monks and nuns the remainder. For example, Nikolski monastery in Moscow remained under church control. However, the monks had control over only one building; the others were occupied by a school and the local forestry council. In Egorevskii uezd, Kalachevskii monastery was used for invalid housing and for the council of the volsoviet. Until 1919 the authorities permitted the monks of Holy Trinity lavra in Sergeev Posad to live on the premises of the former Theological Academy and even provided them firewood.[77] After the monks there were evicted in November 1919, they were offered the option of moving to Gefimanski skete (a small community of monks) three kilometers away. There, under the direction of Brother Porfiri, they transformed themselves into an agricultural commune under the control of the local authorities. Some of the monks, including Archimandrite Kronid, returned to the town of Sergeev Posad, where they lived in private apartments.[78]

Optina Pustyn was another monastery that made use of the opportunity of forming an agricultural artel. In the immediate aftermath of the Bolshevik revolution, many monks left. However, the few that stayed organized an agricultural artel. Some nuns from the nearby convent of Shamardino came to Optina and also worked in the artel. Interestingly, the concept of an agricultural artel attracted older monks more than younger ones. The young monks quickly became disenchanted with the heavy workload and resented the fact that they no longer were able to participate in the services or had time to pray in their cells. Only one young monk, Brother Ilya Zhirnov, stayed until the artel closed in 1923. The rest left and either went to other monasteries or returned to civilian life. Father Nikon, considered by many to be the last Optina elder, ran the artel and was the main person responsible for Optina's preservation until its final closure in 1928. Despite his dedication and experience, the artel provided barely enough food for the remaining monks. In addition to his administrative expertise, he also served as a spiritual father not only for the remaining monastics but also for the villagers.[79]

The Bolsheviks took credit for any success of the monastic communes and indicated that they would not exist if it were not for the support of local authorities. As an example, the Bolsheviks cited the Antoniev-Spiiskom monastery in Archangel. The local officials organized this artel in 1920, and according to official accounts, the monks "welcomed Soviet power as the true expression of the will of the working mass and supported struggling for their freedom." As proof of their revolutionary ideals, the monks also resolved "to reorganize (the monastery) as a laboring society of culture and belief composed of honest citizens of the Soviet republic."[80]

Such arrangements did not satisfy everyone. Many monastics deeply resented the presence of Soviet agencies, such as forestry commissions and schools, on their property. They regarded any kind of compromise with the Bolsheviks as admitting defeat, as a letter from the monks of the Nikolo-Babaevskii monastery to Lenin illustrates. The abbot and forty-seven monks protested the decision of the Kostroma revolutionary council to force all monastics in the province to work in artels.[81] As well, the government did not always uphold its promises to the monastery communes, as the case of Nikolo-Perevinski monastery illustrates. In March, 1918, the brothers wrote a desperate appeal to the patriarch, stating that the land committee was reneging on its promises to allow the monks to farm the land. The new laws stated that the monastery could not use any of the land for its own subsistence and left them only eight pud of rye and 120 meri (measures) of potatoes. Abbot John explained that the land committee also denied the monastery flour, and the monks had no money to buy necessities. The inhabitants of the monastery already lacked enough food to eat, and he feared that "if we do not get any rye or potatoes, we will be faced with starvation and will have to leave."[82]

A similar event occurred in Serpukhovski Devichy women's monastery in Serpukhovski volost (Moscow guberniia) in July, 1918. The local sovdep had allowed the monastery to use the kitchen garden as well as sixteen desiatins of meadow and to pasture sixteen cows. Now the sovdep declared that the previous arrangement was invalid since there were new people on the land committee. Nikolai Kuznetsov, a member of the sobor, wrote the Soviet of People's Commissariat to tell the volost committee that it did not have the right to arbitrarily overturn such decisions and that the fate of more than one hundred women living at the monastery depended on access to the land. However, the commissariat responded that it had looked into the matter and considered it satisfactory.[83]

Not all monasteries experienced misfortune in their new status as government sovkhozi. In Kostroma province, the situation of the Bogoliubski women's monastery actually improved after it was transferred to the authority of the Kostroma provincial land department. It received for its use 1,511 desiatins of land, 48 houses and other agricultural buildings, 77 head of cattle, 40 roosters, and 1.2 thousand puds of grain.[84] Such prosperity was rare, though, and was subject to confiscation at any time.

Such examples of arbitrariness reinforced the Church's distrust of the Bolsheviks and provoked a major debate within the Church over the issue of cooperating with them. The sobor issued a statement on April 6/19, 1918, condemning those clergy and laity who had disobeyed their superiors and in church matters had turned "to the civil authorities hostile to the church," thus bringing it harm. The decree also threatened recalcitrant clergy with defrocking and excommunication.[85] However, according to the liberal Dean Vvedevenskii, Patriarch Tikhon never dared to enforce this decree.[86] Nevertheless, he and other leading clergy continued to oppose the Soviet government. They called for processions and a national day of repentance and advocated measures to recover confiscated church property. In another defiant action against the Bolsheviks, the sobor issued a bold statement on April 5/18 declaring that only it and the patriarch had the authority to administer or dispose of church property.[87]

Many radical Communists likewise did not approve of allowing the monks and nuns to continue to live in their monasteries. They viewed these arrangements as betraying the antireligious struggle that was central to Communism. A letter from NARKOMIUST (people's committee of justice) in 1919 to all of the *zemotdels* (land departments) illustrates the conflict among members of the government regarding the monastery communes. It states that recent reports from NARKOMZEM (people's committee on land) referring to monastery communes, artels, and land seizure from monasteries "demonstrates the complete misunderstanding of the carrying out of the declaration of January 22, 1919, of the separation of church and state and that they [the zemotdels] are assisting in the evasion of this decree with their defense of these people."[88] NARKOMIUST then issued the following guidelines for interpreting the law. Among them, religious groups could not be registered as agricultural unions and therefore could not receive land or livestock from the government. However, monasteries and church did have the right to receive land and stock from the government as compensation for buildings confiscated for government use. Within "official" agricultural communes and artels, monastics and clerics could not be members because article 65 of the constitution deprived them of voting rights. The decree excepted novices, lay workers from the monastery, and peasants from areas surrounding a monastery from this rule. These people would be permitted to work in agricultural communes because they had been "exploited by the theological organizations belonging to the church or monastery." The "church agricultural communes" could not use government money to pay for the maintenance of religious buildings or objects.[89]

The desire to segregate church agriculture from "legitimate" communes illustrates a concern for the effect that the monastics and clergy would have on the peasants. It also demonstrated to the radicals in the government that the monasteries were not given preferential treatment. This delicate balance between the Communists and the Church sometimes produced paradoxical situations. For example, the Nikitskii monastery in Tula province transformed itself into a commune in 1919. Two years later the Tula government announced that the monastery commune would be liquidated. The monks complained to VTsIK (all-Russian central executive committee). After an examination the committee declared that "the artel has proved itself to be a fully functional and productive collective." The committee overturned the local government's decision and allowed the monastery artel to remain open.[90]

This case has several unique characteristics: first, it demonstrates the continuing disagreement in the Soviet government on the subject of religion. Despite the various decrees and guidelines emphasizing the status of monastics and clergy as nonpersons and the dispossession of land, the national government agreed to let the monks continue to keep their community. Second, it illustrates the lack of consistency in Soviet policy toward the Church. Local governments could sometimes be more severe than the federal.

However, the reverse could also be true. In a report to the all-Russian central executive committee, the Nizhnegorod guberniia committee explained why it rescinded its earlier decision to liquidate the agricultural monastic communes and distribute the land to smaller peasant villages. This report is especially revealing in that describes in detail how a local government changed its thinking about the monastery communes. After the initial order came from the federal government to confiscate all monastery lands, the Nizhnegorod guberniia committee decided that it would be more useful to use the existing monastery agriculture. This worked to everyone's satisfaction; the monastics wanted to preserve their communities, and the local authorities did not want to destroy prosperity based on the agriculture and small industry of the monasteries. Therefore, the guberniia committee judged it expedient to allow the working elements of the monasteries, such as experienced workers familiar with agricultural practices, to continue their farming.[91]

However, in September of 1919, the guberniia committee decided that the monastery communes were too ideologically problematic to continue to support. The committee complained that the monastery collectives "serve directly or indirectly to reinforce religious feelings in many workers, having more influence on the surrounding population and withholding the process of the development of Soviet consciousness." On soviet collectives the peasants would lose their connection to the monasteries and be more influenced by "soviet elements." The committee therefore decided either to place the monastery collectives under the direction of the local soviet workers and peasants deputies or to give the land directly to peasants and workers.[92]

The committee soon discovered that the monastery collectives and artels were "in excellent condition" and that breaking them up led to "drops in labor intensity and agricultural production." The land committee also discovered that the monastery kolkhozes that were transferred to peasants and workers led to a rise in theft and other social problems in addition to low agricultural productivity and a decline in the condition of both crops and livestock. As a result, the monastery communes and artels complained to the executive committee that they were not being treated fairly in the current policy and that the redistribution was harmful not just to them, but also to the status of agriculture as a whole. The executive committee gathered reports from party and government officials and concluded that the monastery artels and communes "honestly fulfilled their production and that their labor serves not only their basic needs, but also serves many soviet establishments." In the face of this evidence, the

Nizhnegorod executive committee concluded that its former policy of transferring the monastery communes to peasants "is ruinous and affects the condition of monastery agriculture, and for this reason, on August 28, the committee changes its decision in contradiction to the decree of separation of church and state, and offers the following:

1) Not to deprive the working elements of the monastery of the right that all citizens have to use land granted by the Soviet Republic.

2) To struggle with religious prejudices and dark superstitious masses, not through repression, but with good schools, propaganda, communism, and organized agriculture along communist lines.

3) To concern ourselves with the goals of creating model farms."[93]

As this frank report demonstrates, the Nizhnegorod committee decided that the monastery communes were a necessary evil that could not be destroyed yet. When the communist model was strengthened, then the monastery model of agriculture could be eradicated.

Another case of local pressure persuading authorities to keep open monastery communes occurred with the Elizabeth Society. Originally located in Tver guberniia, the society of sixteen nuns had moved to the Shakhovski monastery in Moscow guberniia in late 1919. After they moved there, they practiced agriculture and ran a school for orphans. In 1920 the authorities discussed liquidating the society and building their own school on the grounds that the society did not have the required number of twenty people to function according to the regulations. In response, the society wrote a protest letter to the Moscow guberniia, testifying to its socialist labor character. The citizens of the village of Nr'ev wrote a letter stating that the church of the Elizabeth Society served the needs of their parish and requested that the society's buildings not be confiscated.[94]

The special commission appointed to liquidate the Elizabeth Society concluded that despite the society's small membership, it demonstrated more advantages than liabilities. Despite its small numbers, its few members did strenuous work without hiring local labor. They also operated a sewing school in the village and encouraged the local population to participate. The fact that the local believers petitioned for the retention of the church also had an effect on the commission's decision, concluding that since article 13 of the decree of separation of church and state allowed religious buildings to be let free of charge to religious groups, to liquidate the monastery would be impossible. The committee decided that the school could continue in the main buildings of the monastery and that those nuns and priests who were qualified would teach there. The church would continue to serve the local parish. However, certain conditions were imposed. The society of nuns would have to disband, with those sisters serving as teachers staying in the school. The remaining sisters, "in view of their insistent wish to stay on the old property, "would be formed into an agricultural collective." The committee also prohibited the society from adding new members.

This compromise allowed the authorities to exercise their authority by formally abolishing the society and preventing it from spreading. At the same time, the authorities also managed to preserve those qualities of the society that they deemed most useful to them, such as its sewing school and its agriculture. They placated the villagers by allowing them their parish church and ensured that the school would be closely monitored so that the nuns and priests would not be bad influences on the local population. On the surface it might appear that the authorities received the greater advantage. However, the nuns also benefited. Despite the restrictions, the nuns were allowed to remain together and in this way maintained their community. They were also able to provide for themselves and worship in their church.[95]

While many monasteries became communes, a few, possessing great historical and architectural merit, were converted into museums. This process occurred at Novodevichy in Moscow, Troitse-Sergeev (Holy Trinity) lavra in Sergeev Posad (renamed Zagorsk), and Donskoi monastery in Moscow. Monks and nuns generally resisted such transformations, but as with the agricultural communes, some saw advantages in having the monasteries turned into museums. Not only would the architectural beauty be preserved, but there was also a possibility for monks and nuns to continue to live at the monastery in the capacity of caretakers.

One prominent proponent of turning Troitse-Sergeev lavra into a museum was Pavel Florensky. Although not a monastic, Florensky greatly admired the simplicity of monastic life, and he often made pilgrimages to Optina Pustyn, where he developed a close relationship to Elder Anatole. Later he became even more intimately familiar with monastic life as a professor of mathematics at the Moscow Theological Academy, located on the grounds of Troitse-Sergeev lavra. After the seminary was closed, he continued to work for the state. A gifted scientist as well as an ordained priest, Florensky used his respected position in the scientific community to lobby successfully for the preservation of Troitse-Sergeev lavra.[96] He later pressed for the restoration of Optina Pustyn as a museum. He was not as successful in this endeavor, however, as only part of the monastery was preserved.[97]

In the spring of 1919, the commissariat of justice sent out questionnaires to various monasteries and churches in Moscow province concerning the effect of the decree of separation of church and state on people's lives. The questionnaire contained thirty-six questions covering all concerns of the local liquidation committee, from the confiscation of church and monastic property to the reaction of the population to the decree. Various questions addressed the progress of the nationalization of the monasteries and monastic property and the number of remaining monasteries. They also discussed the status of the monastery communes and their use of labor, the fate of those monastics who had left the monasteries, and those monasteries that were under the direction of the department of museums and monuments.

Unfortunately, few of the questionnaires remain. The ones that are preserved illustrate the shrinking monastic population in the monasteries and also demonstrate the gradual switch to agricultural artels. For example, in Kalinovski uezd, the Uspenski monastery had 15 monks and 7 novices, down from the prerevolutionary figure of 19 monks and 23 novices. They organized themselves into the first officially recognized labor commune in Moscow in the spring of 1918. Alexeivski monastery, which had also become an agricultural commune, had a mixed population: forty men and sixty-four women, whose average age was thirty-four. Forty-eight were listed as agricultural workers. This survey does not state how many of them, if any, were monastics; however, it is likely that monastics made up a sizeable part of the commune. Likewise, the Nikolski monastery in Vologorski guberniia does not give any concrete numbers to show how many people lived there but states only that the monastery was used as living quarters for "working elements" and that they were honest people who were "preserving monastery agriculture."[98]

The Persistence of Religious Life

Despite the renewed antireligious campaign during the civil war, the peasants' faith generally did not weaken significantly. Young men conscripted into the army and exposed to the outside world were more susceptible to communist propaganda. However, the majority of the peasants remained isolated and largely illiterate. If anything, the civil war strengthened the

Church's position in the villages; in a period of uncertainty and fear of the future, the Church stood for tradition and reassurance. Much to the party's dismay, there were many reports of Communist Party members who still professed their faith, particularly in rural areas. The head of the guberniia department for village work in Smolensk openly admitted that the party had virtually no influence in the rural cooperatives and sovkhozes; rather, these organizations were dominated "by priests and kulaks (rich peasants)."[99]

The executive committee of the Makarievskogo uezd financial department wrote a letter to the Kostroma guberniia financial department requesting that a priest named Maltsev be allowed to continue to serve on the financial council. The committee cited as proof of his qualifications Maltsev's experience as an accountant and the fact that he had not had a parish since 1914. Most importantly, the committee considered that if Maltsev was kicked out, "the Ufimotdel would lose a man who is loyal to the principles and experiences of the workers, especially the hard experiences of the Ufimov workers."[100] According to A. Okninsky, a volost executive committee member of Tambov province, church attendance increased during the civil war years.[101] As well, returning Red Army soldiers soon forgot their atheist indoctrination. Village tradition, which largely revolved around the church, often proved stronger than short-term communist teachings.

The antireligious policies of the Bolsheviks not only did not discourage those people who were already monastics but also failed to deter young men and women who wanted to become monks and nuns. Mother Serafima was one such person. When the revolution broke out, she was seventeen years old and living in Moscow, the daughter of a pharmacist who also served as a deacon in the church. She wanted to enter medical school but was denied the opportunity when the administrators discovered that her father was an ordained deacon. Through her father's connections, she finally had an opportunity to study medicine at Moscow University. She passed the courses she took and worked as a nurse at the local clinic while continuing to study to become a doctor. While doing so, she continued to go to church and became acquainted with a bishop of Egor'evski province in Moscow who introduced her to monasticism. He was arrested shortly thereafter but was quickly released and returned to Moscow, where he had family. Mother Serafima led a double life in those days: She was nurse, a medical student, and at the same time a novice, tonsured into monasticism in 1922. Although she was very aware of the dangers of being a monastic during this period and saw many monks, nuns, and clergy close to her suffer arrest, exile, and execution, their experiences strengthened her belief and her desire to become a nun. She spoke of the spiritual part of her "double life" as being "deeper, more real."[102]

Religious feeling continued in urban areas as well. One citizen complained in 1919 that the streets of Moscow were plastered with posters of churchmen announcing religious concerts, prayer meetings, and lectures by former theological academy professors. At Easter, the Cheka (secret police) in Moscow released Bishop Nikandr and four other clerics from prison and allowed them to serve liturgy. NARKOMIUST also announced that these releases, as well as Patriarch Tikhon's freedom from house arrest, demonstrated that the government was not persecuting the Church.[103] According to one report from the United States Ambassador to Rome, religious feeling in urban areas not only continued but even overshadowed that in the rural areas. He wrote: "the Orthodox Church is strongest in the cities and along the railways; wherever, in fact, Bolshevik control is strongest, religious feeling, necessarily opposed to that control, has been growing."[104]

Although the persistence of religious feeling surprised many contemporary observers and also has the same effect on many historians, according to Yuri Lotman, the phenomenon is an age-old Russian response to dissatisfaction with current life. "Widespread dissatisfaction with the whole pattern of Russian life . . . was expressed in a series of popular movements and took the form of a demand for a return to the old ways. . . . Positive concepts such as piety and orthodoxy are given the epithet 'ancient'. The specific character of Russian culture . . . was that the connection with the past objectively made itself felt most sharply when subjectively there was a predominant orientation towards a total break with it."[105] In other words, when people felt that they were in danger of losing a cultural or national tradition, they held on to it even tighter. Even if they had expressed indifference or complained about it previously, the threat of losing it evoked nostalgia and encouraged their resistance.

Famine

A still greater threat to the monasteries occurred toward the end of the civil war, when Russia, already weakened from six years of fighting, faced a famine in the fall of 1920. Although the famine occurred mainly in the

Volga and Ukraine regions, it affected all of the former empire, as those areas provided most of the wheat for the entire country. As conditions worsened in the winter of 1921, people from the country flocked to the cities in search of relief, adding to the problem of overcrowding and spreading diseases such as typhus. Although the Soviet government tried to alleviate the crisis, it soon became apparent that large-scale relief was necessary, including that from foreign countries. The American Relief Administration, the Quakers, the Vatican, and the Nansen Committee were a few of the organizations that contributed to the cause. However, even this assistance proved insufficient in view of the magnitude of the problem.

Patriarch Tikhon realized that the famine provided an opportunity for the church to demonstrate that it was not the parasite that the Soviet government claimed and that it could provide much-needed services to the country. Therefore, he issued an appeal to the Eastern patriarchs, the Pope, the Archbishop of Canterbury, and the Protestant Episcopal Bishops of New York to help end the famine. He also asked the Russian Orthodox faithful to contribute. He established an all-Russian church committee to coordinate the collections, and the parish brotherhoods handled the local contributions of food and money. Despite this gesture of cooperation, the Soviet authorities distrusted Tikhon's motivation and refused to allow the church to have a separate organization. The government insisted that the church turn over any funds to the state so that the relief could be centralized. However, the church's contributions proved pitifully small—only nine million rubles in the last six months of 1921.[106] The government then reversed its earlier decision and on January 2, 1922, ruled that the church could actively solicit funds for the famine in conjunction with the Central Committee for Aid to the Starving (POMGOL). The churches and monasteries would collect money and food and turn them over to the local or central POMGOL agencies, which would give the church's account credit. The church would also participate in the distribution of the money and food.

Soon the government decided that the church was not contributing enough to the famine relief and should donate the gold and silver items used in the church services as well. Although this technically was state property, the government had not used it for famine relief, and many churches continued to possess their sacred items. The government claimed that the sale of these items could help feed millions of people. The church balked at this idea, but as the Soviet government stepped up its rhetoric and accused the church of insincerity in fighting the famine, the patriarch stated that the church could sell those valuables not sanctified for holy use in the church services. He encouraged the Orthodox faithful to donate gold and silver adornments on the icons, gold and jewels from old vestments, bracelets, medallions, and other such objects to the POMGOL. This compromise on the church treasures did not satisfy the government, and articles began to appear in the papers demanding that the church surrender *all* of its valuables. Newspapers printed accounts of nuns, priests, and congregations donating their institutions' valuables to the cause and insinuated that those who did not were not being patriotic.[107]

The government decided to take a more aggressive approach to the question of using church valuables for famine relief. However, some time elapsed before the authorities implemented these new policies. One article in *Pravda* on February 11 reported that the central executive committee had ordered the confiscation of valuables to begin immediately. The next day *Izvestiia* featured a statement denying that any concrete action had been decided. finally, on February 26 the central executive committee decreed that the local soviets would carry out the removal of all of the valuables in churches and monasteries within one month. In theory, only those items that "would not harm the interests of the cult" would be removed, and groups of believers would participate in the distribution.[108] In reality, no valuables were exempt from confiscation, and POMGOL rarely if ever consulted with laity or clergy about the use of the funds. It soon became clear that the state, by refusing to compromise, did not desire the treasures so much as it desired the destruction of the Church.

Clerical and popular reaction to the Soviets' announced policy toward the church valuables was mixed. Some more liberal churchmen and monastics favored the donation of valuables, even consecrated ones, for humanitarian purposes. They pointed out that nowhere in canon law is it forbidden to use church treasure for secular needs. What is forbidden is the use of church treasure to obtain personal wealth. In defense of this policy, they cited instances of churches and monasteries giving up their valuables for the good of the nation. One oft-quoted example was the abbot of Iur'ev monastery who, in 1916, donated church treasure to fight the war.[109]

Despite these arguments, Patriarch Tikhon and other clergy claimed that there was an enormous difference between those earlier examples of sacrifice of church vessels and the current situation. In the earlier cases the government in authority was not in opposition to the church and trying to destroy it. This attitude is summarized in Patriarch Tikhon's response to the peasants' observations that the tsars had taken church treasure in time of need: "The tsars took, but they also gave."[110] Such negative reaction to the announcement of the confiscation of church valuables proved more widespread than the positive reaction.

Nevertheless, the Church leaders' failure to take a united and clear stand hurt the Church. As in the beginning of the revolution, when Bolsheviks tried to inventory or confiscate church or monastery items, many outbreaks of violence occurred. After a particularly violent episode in the province of Shuia in 1922, the Politburo, in Lenin's absence, voted to delay further confiscations for an indefinite period. They did not want to provoke the peasants unnecessarily and feared that implementing an unpopular policy through violent means could plunge the country into civil war again, just as the Bolsheviks had finally gained the peasants' allegiance. When Lenin returned, he was displeased at the verdict and overruled it. The following letter to Molotov on March 19, 1922, demonstrates Lenin's understanding of the confrontational situation developing between Church and state and his deliberate use of the famine to destroy the Church. He wrote:

> I think here that our enemy is committing an enormous strategic mistake in trying to drag us into a decisive battle at a time when it is particularly hopeless and particularly disadvantageous for him. On the contrary, for us this moment is not only exceptionally favorable, but generally the only moment when we can, with 99 out of 100 chances of total success, smash the enemy and secure for ourselves an indispensable position for many decades to come. It is precisely now and only now, when in the starving regions people are eating human flesh and hundreds if not thousands of corpses are littering the streets, that we can (and therefore must) carry out the confiscation of church valuables with the most savage and merciless energy, not stopping short of crushing any resistance. It is precisely now and only now that the enormous majority of the peasant mass will be for us or at any rate will not be in a condition to support in any decisive way that handful of Black Hundred clergy and reactionary urban petty bourgeoisie who can and want to attempt a policy of violent resistance to the Soviet decree....
>
> We must, come what may, carry out the confiscation of the church valuables ... and this can be done successfully only now. All

> considerations indicate that later we will be unable to do this, because no other moment except that of desperate hunger will give us a mood among the broad peasant masses that will guarantee us the sympathy of these masses or at least their neutrality, in the sense that victory in the struggle for the confiscation of the valuables will be indisputable and entirely ours.
>
> ... [F]or us, after Genoa, Russia's international position in all likelihood will be such or may be such that harsh measures against reactionary clergy will be politically irrational and perhaps even highly dangerous. At present we are fully assured of victory over the reactionary clergy.
>
> ... Therefore, I come to the categorical conclusion that precisely at this moment we must give battle to the Black Hundred clergy in the most decisive and merciless manner and crush its resistance with such brutality that it will not forget it for decades to come.
>
> ... At the party congress arrange a secret meeting on this matter of nearly all of the delegates. ... [P]ass a secret resolution of the congress that the confiscation of valuables, in particular of the richest abbeys, monasteries, and churches, should be conducted with merciless determination, unconditionally stopping at nothing, and in the briefest possible time. The greater the number of the reactionary clergy and reactionary bourgeoisie we succeed in executing the better. We must teach these people a lesson right now, so that they will not dare even think of any resistance for several decades.[111]

Lenin's letter served to stop any thought the government had about possibly relaxing the policy of confiscating church valuables. In the aftermath of the letter, the government instituted even harsher measures against those clergy and laity who protested the seizure of church treasure. The clergy involved in the events at Shuia were tried, arrested, and sentenced to death. Frank Golder, a member of the American Relief Association, observed the trial of eleven clerics in Petrograd, including the metropolitan, bishops, priests, and theological professors. He commented that their attitude during the trial "deeply disappointed" those people who supported the Church. Instead of saying "Yes, I did it, and I have nothing to take back," they denied everything and behaved defensively, seeking to save themselves.[112] They were all sentenced to death, but six of them had their sentences commuted to prison terms, and the remaining five were shot. Golder reported that after the executions were carried out, stories of the slain clergy became part of Russian martyrology. Some of the legends surrounding them claimed that "on the day of the condemnation, Lenin got his first stroke, and the second on the day of execution; and at the very moment when the judge pronounced sentence his favorite son was run over by a streetcar. When the priests were lined up to be shot the soldiers refused to fire, and that in order to deceive the firing squad the priests were sent back to their cells to be shaved and dressed in convicts' clothes. On the way back the priests confessed to one another and read prayers from the appropriate services. When they were finally lined up with a lot of thieves, the soldiers shot them."[113] Most of these stories are probably apocryphal; however, they nonetheless illustrate the power and persistence of faith under persecution, much as stories of miraculous occurrences involving saints gave encouragement to the early Christians.

The entire episode of confiscating church valuables only aroused the population against the Soviets, and in the end the amount of money collected from the church did not serve to end the famine. Frank Golder cited a *Pravda* article of July 13, 1922, stating that "the total proceeds from the church treasures of the Petrograd Government will buy about 10,000 puds of flour. Assuming that the other administrative units of Russia will give an equal amount the total will be in the neighborhood of 500,000 puds, about 500,000 dollars. This is too low and it would probably be nearer right to multiply it by ten in view of the fact that statements have been made that the State Bank has advanced about 6,000,000 gold rubles on the church treasures. When one stops to consider the cost of collecting, the ill feeling it has created, he cannot help wondering what was behind it all."[114]

Ironically, the church itself provided the Soviets with the most effective weapon against it. This involved the creation of the Karlovatskii synod in 1921. As mentioned earlier, while under arrest Patriarch Tikhon had issued a statement authorizing the bishops to form a temporary diocesan government in the event that they lost contact with the central church administration. Using this decree as proof of legitimacy, a group of émigré bishops formed a sobor in the Serbian town of Sremski Karlovatskii. The reactionary Metropolitan Antonii Khrapovitsky of Kiev and Kharkov presided over the council consisting of fifteen bishops and many lower clergy. Many of these individuals were strong supporters of the White movement. The laity who were involved were typically the "old guard" of Russia—members of the nobility, army officers, and former court officials.

Ostensibly the Karlovatskii synod was to decide questions concerning the administration of the Russian Orthodox churches outside of Russia. However, it soon became evident that the synod had a definite political agenda. In a resolution to the Russian refugees abroad given on November 21 and December 3, 1921, the synod referred to the deceased Tsar Nicholas II as a martyr and called for the return of a monarchy. The synod also placed blame for the famine squarely on the shoulders of the Bolsheviks and appealed to the Russians abroad to make donations for famine relief to the Karlovatskii synod, who would forward them to the patriarch.[115] The blatantly anti-Soviet rhetoric of the synod fueled Soviet suspicions of the Church in Russia. The government accused Tikhon of authorizing and encouraging the Karlovatskii synod to undermine Soviet authority. The truth was that Tikhon did not support the Karlovatskii synod and maintained that the bishops took his earlier declaration out of context and used it to legitimate their statements. Despite Tikhon's protestations, he was arrested and indicted in May, 1922, on charges of counterrevolutionary activity. The most compelling evidence against him came from other bishops and more liberal priests who disagreed with Tikhon's denunciations of turning over consecrated objects. After his trial, Tikhon was sent to prison. From his cell he faced not only attack from the Soviets but also a revolt of the white clergy, a topic that I address later.

Since 1917 Russia had endured two revolutions, one civil war, and a famine. In their drive to create a "brave new world" the Bolsheviks had begun to destroy all vestiges of the Old Regime. The assassination of the royal family, the elimination of former nobles and tsarist officials, and especially the suppression of the Orthodox Church were deemed necessary in order to build socialism. Of all of these representatives of the Old Regime, none proved harder to abolish than the Orthodox Church, the main reason for whose resiliency may be found in monasticism. Unlike the official Church, monasteries proved more flexible. They had the advantage of occupying good agricultural land, and the monastics were capable farm workers. As shown earlier, the monastics adapted to the conditions of a collective farm relatively easily and were quick to use communist rhetoric to try to preserve their communities. The government soon realized that they needed the monastics' productivity, at least until they had built up society to the point where the peasants and workers could take over and run it efficiently.

In addition to their contributions to agriculture, those monasteries that had cultural significance were able to convince the authorities to turn them into museums. In this endeavor they were aided by the minister of education, Anatoli Lunacharskii, who admired the monasteries' cultural treasures. Although the monks and nuns doubtless did not enjoy having their consecrated vessels on display as artifacts, the museums allowed them to preserve objects that would otherwise have been destroyed. Some monks and nuns were also allowed to stay at such monasteries in the capacity of caretakers.

In summarizing the experience of the monastics during this period, one may conclude that they used the instability that the revolutions and the civil war caused to their advantage. The bulk of the Bolsheviks' attention during this time remained focused on attaining and keeping power. They persecuted the Church, but they also realized that they could not afford to alienate large segments of the population. They did as much to weaken the Church as they could without arousing the ire of the people; when they met resistance, the government in many cases prudently retreated. The Bolsheviks also left several loopholes in their new laws that the monasteries were able to exploit, such as allowing lay societies to assume control over the monastic buildings for religious use. Another aspect of early Bolshevik ideology which served monasteries well involved their concept of loyalty. In the early part of the Bolshevik revolution and the civil war, silence equaled complicity and acceptance. The Bolsheviks for the most part followed Lenin's dictum, "Those who are not against us are for us." The paranoia of the Stalin years, when it was not enough to keep silent, had not yet occurred.

In this period of revolution and civil war, monks and nuns saw their positions vary from initial violent persecution, to a reluctant acknowledgment that monasteries could have some productive value, and back to severe persecution during the famine of 1921. They learned to use the Bolsheviks' rules and ideologies to their advantage and often quoted the Bolsheviks' own laws against them. The monks and nuns who had been displaced after the monasteries' closures either went to other monasteries or found other ways of living that would still allow them to continue their monastic way of life. Thus far, monks and nuns had survived using their flexibility and ingenuity. However, their ability to persevere would be sorely tested during the rest of the decade as the antireligious campaign strengthened and as the nation faced the new challenge of forced collectivization.

CHAPTER 3

The New Economic Policy Years, 1921–1928

DURING THE CIVIL WAR, while the Bolsheviks were fighting for their survival, they implemented "war communism," a collection of social, economic, and political regulations that to many Russians appeared draconian. Such tactics included tight restrictions on private trade and production and the confiscation of food from peasants to feed the army. By the end of the civil war, the people had grown restless under these severe conditions and began demonstrating their discontent. Peasant revolts broke out in Tambov province and elsewhere in late 1920, and workers in Petrograd and other cities launched strikes protesting harsh working conditions. Additionally, the strain of the civil war also produced evidence of disunity within the Communist Party. The climax came in March, 1921, when sailors in Kronstadt revolted, seizing the fortress and demanding land, bread, and a Soviet government without the Bolsheviks. After that incident the Bolshevik leaders realized that they needed to abolish war communism, since they had defeated the Whites and had effectively consolidated their power. Any attempt to continue to implement war communism seemed certain to result in more bloodshed and threatened to undo any progress that the Bolsheviks had made. Thus began the period of the "New Economic Policy," or NEP.

Historians tend to view the events of the 1920s in Russia as a pendulum, swinging widely from the harshness of war communism through the relative liberalism of NEP back to strict authoritarianism under Stalin. They considered NEP to be a peaceful interlude between two bloody eras—the civil war and the brutal collectivization that began in the late 1920s. Historians have traditionally focused on the power struggle among Stalin, Trotsky, Zinoviev, and Kamenev to succeed Lenin as supreme leader. Although this aspect of the period is important, the neglect of other societal facets carries with it the danger of oversimplifying NEP. As

Sheila Fitzpatrick, Alexander Rabinowitch, and Richard Stites observe in the introduction to *Russia in the Era of NEP,* this was "a period in which those in power were forced somehow to come to terms with complex social and cultural residues of pre-revolutionary Russia, implicitly at odds with ongoing goals of building a socialist or communist order."[1] Lenin himself realized that society needed "breathing space" and that socialism was not something that could be forced on it. Rather, a slower approach combining tradition with change would more likely ensure the cooperation of the majority of Russians.

In its most basic form, NEP involved the relaxation of strictures on the economy. The countryside in particular received the most attention. A fixed tax replaced the previous policy of grain requisitioning, and private trade cautiously returned. The ultimate goal was to create a mixed economy composed of private and state institutions. By permitting bourgeois factory managers to resume their old positions of authority and welcoming back skilled émigrés, Lenin hoped to restore the economy devastated by seven years of war and revolution. With the stabilization of the economy would come party unity and an easing of social tension.

However, Bolshevik economic programs alone do not provide a complete understanding of NEP. New approaches to cultural and social policies also played major roles. Instead of slowly yielding to communist principles, strong traditional attitudes reappeared within both the general population and the party and refused to fade away. This set the stage for a renewed conflict between old and new behavior patterns. At best, these pre-revolutionary social and cultural forms could be incorporated into the new society, albeit with difficulty. At worst, they were impediments to the party's basic goals for Russia and its future. Somehow, whether through attrition, repression, or absorption, the legacies of the past had to be overcome.[2]

At the same time as there were economic and social relaxations, a tightening in the political sector occurred. The party purge of 1923, the expulsion of Russian intellectuals, and the trial of Socialist revolutionaries all indicated that the New Economic Policy did not represent a change in one-party rule.

As with the period following the October Revolution, one of the greatest obstacles facing the Bolsheviks in building their new society continued to be the Orthodox Church. As discussed earlier, despite persecution and laws designed to virtually outlaw religion, the Church had survived. Its perseverance was in large part due to monasticism as well as the courage of both white clergy and laity. Monks and nuns had lived through the revolutions and civil war because of their flexibility and ingenuity. NEP provided opportunities for them to use the prevailing political system to preserve their communities, but it also frequently presented challenges to their existence.

NEP and Religion

Although NEP was often characterized by a relaxation of harsh policies in the economic and political sectors, the Soviet government's policy toward religion during this period was contradictory. The central committee realized the challenge of continuing the struggle against religion while at the same time not antagonizing the peasants. It sent out a circular within the party stressing the importance of not overemphasizing antireligious propaganda while the party was still adjusting to NEP. In a special meeting for antireligious propagandists held on May 7, 1921, communist officials unveiled NEP's religious policy. The guidelines stated that the antireligious campaign should not offend believers and that the party should not expose itself to international criticism.[3] A secretary of the central committee, Emelyan Yaroslavsky, made this new religious course public in an article in *Pravda* on April 21, 1921.[4]

Despite this change in policy, persecution of the Church continued, although not as brutally as during the initial years of revolution and civil war. The Soviets staged trials of clergy and laity in an attempt to prove to the outside world that the new Soviet state was "just"—that no one was imprisoned or executed without a "fair" trial. The famine of 1921–1922 and the subsequent seizure of Church valuables provided an excuse for the government to arrest and execute many leading clergy. Dimitry Pospielovsky cites the total number of clergy killed from 1917 to 1922 at 8,100, of which 2,691 were married priests, 1,962 were monks and male novices, and 3,447 were nuns and female novices.[5] In addition to launching a full attack on the Church, the Soviets decided to try to weaken the Church internally. The Church had long suffered from internal divisions; the Soviets realized that the best way to destroy the Church would be to foster these divisions and cause it to collapse from within. Without unity, it could not launch an adequate defense.

The Living Church

As noted earlier, during the sobors of 1905 and 1917, divisions among the clergy arose over the question of restoring the patriarchate. The liberal white parish clergy opposed it on the grounds that their interests would not be represented. They resented the monopoly of power that the monastics enjoyed. However, they had been outvoted at the 1917 sobor, which restored the patriarchate and chose Tikhon as the first patriarch in more than two hundred years. Nevertheless, this did not end the attempts of reformist clergy to gain power and make reforms. After the 1917 revolution, priests led by Dean Alexander Vvedenskii tried to organize an underground movement of progressive clergy but were unsuccessful. By 1919 and 1920, partly due to the chaos of the civil war, the liberal clergy showed signs of revival. This prompted Patriarch Tikhon to issue a strongly worded decree forbidding any liturgical or doctrinal changes in the Church under threat of severe penalties. However, Metropolitan Veniamin of Petrograd protected liberal clerics, and they survived unmolested. They still resented the monks' monopoly of power, however, and felt that the black clergy did not adequately represent the parish priests' interests. The liberal clergy waited for a suitable moment to renew their attacks against the patriarchal Church.[6]

The opportunity came during the 1921 famine and the dispute over using Church valuables to aid the famine relief effort. The liberal clergy were aided in their endeavor by the party, which had relaxed its previous policy of harsh attacks against religion. The Bolsheviks had long been divided about the course that the antireligious campaign should take. As one observer has noted, NEP "brought the differences in the party over religion into sharper focus."[7] At the eighth party congress in 1919, the members expressed for the first time the party's intent to eradicate religion. The tenth party congress in 1921 called for an antireligious campaign among workers. In August of 1921, the plenary meeting of the central committee issued an eleven-point instruction on how to interpret article 13 of the eighth party congress.[8] As discussed earlier, this article recognized the difficulty that the Bolsheviks faced in destroying religion without offending believers and fostering religious fanaticism. The instruction regarding this article made a distinction between educated and uneducated believers. The former might be admitted to the party if they could prove their devotion to communism despite being Christians. This deviation from earlier practice regarding religion was in line with overall NEP policy. Emelian Yaroslavsky, the secretary of the central committee and the future head of the League of the Militant Godless, and Commissar of Enlightenment Anatoli Lunacharskii agreed with this approach. Hard-liners such as Leon Trotsky, the architect of the plan to create a

Church schism, disagreed. In many ways, the disagreement over Church policy was symptomatic of disagreements in other areas, such as the economy.[9]

This new policy to support the pro-Soviet faction in the Church was expressed in an editorial in *Izvestia* in March, 1922, which stated that the government should aid "that more democratic part of the clergy that finds within themselves some sort of common feeling with the suffering masses, and protect it against the violence of those Church hierarchs who are definitely hostile to the laboring masses and dream only of bringing back the old order."[10] These sentiments quickly translated into official policy. On May 9, 1922, Patriarch Tikhon testified at the "trial of the fifty-four," a sensational trial in which fifty-four defendants (mostly priests) as well as the patriarch himself faced accusations that they had incited anti-Bolshevik riots by encouraging the people to resist the government campaign to confiscate Church valuables. Tikhon was indicted and placed under house arrest. Of the other defendants, ten men and one woman were sentenced to death; ten were acquitted or released, and the rest received prison sentences of five to ten years each. Five of the death sentences were later commuted to prison terms.[11]

After the patriarch's arrest, events moved quickly. In early May, the head of the sixth section of the GPU, Evgenyi Aleksandrovich Tuchkov, met with some of the rebellious clergy in Moscow, and on May 12 a delegation of liberal priests visited Tikhon during his imprisonment and accused him of being responsible for the Church's current weakened condition. They claimed that because of his counterrevolutionary activity during the civil war, which included supporting people who were opposed to the Soviet regime, many clergy had been arrested and/or killed, and consequently the Church was in a state of disarray. They demanded that Tikhon temporarily surrender his power to another hierarch and allow the Church to call another sobor. Powerless, the patriarch had no choice but to agree. However, he insisted on turning over authority to the more conservative Metropolitan Agafangel of Iaroslavl.[12]

Ten days after this meeting, the same clergy wrote an appeal to the faithful, titled "To the Believing Sons of the Orthodox Church." It stated that the workers' and peasants' government, which operated by the will of God, desired to combat famine, epidemics, and other disasters which befell Russia, but "the leaders of the Church took the side of the enemies of the people, as shown by the outbreaks when the Church valuables were requisitioned. . . . [T]he people, however, did not support this program of the hierarchs, but condemned those who wished to use the national calamity for their own political ends." The clergy also called for an end to the civil war against the state.[13] This appeal ignored the fact that the majority of the people who rioted against the confiscation of Church valuables were ordinary believers who were responding to government provocation. These were not cases of a few select leaders organizing anti-government demonstrations; most of these protests were spontaneous reactions to official policy.

The liberal clergy were not satisfied with the arrangement that they had fashioned with Patriarch Tikhon. They viewed Metropolitan Agafangel as too conservative and plotted an administrative coup. Father Kalinovskii fabricated a story to a reporter alleging that the patriarch had agreed that the Church should be governed by the "Temporary Higher Church Administration." This body consisted of Father Kalinovskii himself, Father Krasnitskii, Bishops Antonin and Leonid, and others, all liberal clergy. They assumed control over all diocesan affairs and took immediate steps to call a sobor.[14] Thus, the Church coup occurred swiftly and bloodlessly; with Patriarch Tikhon under house arrest, Metropolitan Veniamin in prison, and Metropolitan Agafangel arrested and exiled, the liberal clergy faced no opposition. Other more conservative reformists, such as Nikolai Berdyaev, were living in exile, and although they continued to take an active interest in the affairs of the homeland, their participation necessarily was limited.

The new group called itself "The Living Church," thereby implying that the Patriarchal Church was a moribund institution. Although they staged the coup themselves, strong evidence suggests that the party supported them, clandestinely at first, and then openly. The Soviet government initially claimed that it was impartial in religious matters, but its actions in response to the split in the Orthodox Church demonstrate the opposite. Clearly they realized that the reformers offered the Soviets the possibility of destroying the Church for them. They would support the Living Church for only a short time, as Lunacharskii suggested to Lenin in 1921:

> A significant part of the clergy, undoubtedly sensing the stability of the Soviet regime, wants to be reconciled with it. Of course, this renovated Orthodoxy with a Christian socialist lining is not at all desired and finally . . . will be eliminated and disappear. But, as an active opposition to the reactionary patriarch and his supporters . . . it can

> play its role because it is based mainly on the peasant masses, the backward merchant class, and the more backward part of the proletariat. For these groups, such a temporary center of clerical unity is a great shift to the left of the one that they still find in the reactionary Orthodox church.... We cannot, of course, support the activity of Soviet Orthodoxy. It might, however, be advantageous to render aid secretly and to create in the religious arena several transitional stages (on the way to atheism) for the peasant masses.[15]

Bolshevik support for the Living Church also suggests an underlying fear of monasticism. As Edward Roslof points out in his work on the Living Church (also referred to as the "renovationist movement"), the Bolsheviks "hoped to confine Orthodoxy to parish churches, outside which all religious activity was forbidden and inside which only purely cultic functions were allowed."[16] By fostering the parish clergy's antimonastic feeling, the Bolsheviks hoped to neutralize the popularity and influence of the monastics.

Following Lunacharskii's suggestions, the Soviets allowed the Living Church to operate in relative freedom, whereas those clerics adhering to the Patriarchal Church were arrested on grounds of "counterrevolutionary activity." The Living Church openly advocated cooperating with the Soviet government, as the inaugural article in its journal, *The Living Church (Zhivaia Tserkov')*, attests. It states that the recent violence and conflict over the Church valuables demonstrated that "under certain conditions the government could not remain aloof from the Orthodox Church, but had to take positive action concerning it." Because the Soviet constitution did not provide any legal organs for negotiating with the Church, the Living Church encouraged the establishment of a special committee of laymen and clergy to organize those "who recognize the righteousness of the Russian Social Revolution and are loyal in respect to the Soviet power, to protect them against the patriarchal administration, and unite them on a nationwide scale for development of a general program on church matters and relations with the state."[17]

Having achieved their coup, the renovationists tried to force their radical reforms on Orthodox parishes and dioceses across Russia. Their changes included allowing priests to remarry in the event of divorce or death, ordaining nonmonastic clergy as bishops, adopting the Gregorian calendar in place of the Julian, using the vernacular in church services in place of Old Church Slavonic, and abolishing the patriarchate. They also promised parish priests financial independence from both parishioners and bishops. These ideas earned the Living Church the loyalty of many of the parish clergy.

The Living Church organized itself along much the same lines as the Bolshevik Party. The parish priests were seen as the vanguard of the Church revolution. They were formed into "cells," and hierarchs in every diocese directed the renovation of the churches at the local level. During the first year of its existence, the Living Church received the full support of the Soviet authorities. Any bishops or clergy who resisted the attempts of the renovationists to impose their authority faced removal from office and often arrest and exile by the local police.

The apex of the renovationists' power came at the All-Russian Church Council (sobor) in 1923 in Moscow. Despite its name, the sobor proved less than inclusive. All of the delegates were handpicked by the renovationists and reflected their views. At the sobor, the delegates confirmed the reforms that the renovationist clergy were already promulgating, namely the ordination of married clergy to the episcopate, the adoption of the Gregorian calendar, and the use of Russian in the service. The delegates also decided to reform monasticism. In one session specifically devoted to monasteries and monasticism, they stated that the report on monasticism by protopriest N. Popov was "dangerous" in that it tried to hide negative aspects of monasticism and praised Professor Belolikov for exposing the truth about monastic life. The delegates agreed that, although monasticism had played a role in the cultural development of early Rus, it was irrelevant to modern life. The alleged financial excesses and immoral sexual behavior that occurred in monasteries were not acceptable. Furthermore, the committee accused monks in the Kievo-Pecherskaia lavra of participating in the murder of Metropolitan Vladimir on January 25, 1918, although they give no motive for the alleged accomplices. The committee therefore recommended that all monasteries be closed and traditional monastic life abolished. They succeeded in getting several monasteries turned over to their control, including the famous Kievo-Pecherskaia lavra. The monks who remained on the property resisted the influence of the Living Church by forming prayer groups that met in one of the monastery churches.[18]

The Living Church delegates also proposed transforming the existing monastery buildings into places where "laboring Christian brotherhoods" could gather away from the noise and crowds of the city. The focus of these societies would be to bring people together through the gospels and to attain freedom through work, equality, and brotherhood. Another idea came from the renovationist Bishop Antonin. He advocated using the monastic model as a method of spiritually regenerating the Russian people. Rather than eliminating monasteries entirely, he proposed limiting the number of monks and nuns. He also suggested that monasteries would better serve society by dispensing Christian charity to the poor.[19]

Although the reformers decided to preserve some aspects of monasticism, such as a life based on work and prayer, they aimed to change its character by co-opting and "sovietizing" it. The traditional goal of monastic life was to attain salvation through humility and a strict regimen of work, prayer, and obedience to one's elders. This last concept was abhorrent to the renovationists. They envisioned their "new" monasteries as retreat centers where people could come to escape the trials of city life and achieve unity through work and brotherhood. The renovationists would use the monasteries as opportunities to evangelize the word of God.

One anonymous letter to the "Journal of the Holy Russian Synod of the Orthodox Church" *(Vestnik Rossiiskai sviashchennogo sinoda pravoslavnoi tserkvi)* supported the 1923 sobor's concept for transforming the monasteries. What sets this letter apart from other supporters is that it was allegedly written by a monk. If this letter is genuine, it would be one of the few instances of monastic support for renovationism. The writer states that he is a monk but "has not had the opportunity" to belong to any monastery. However, he has visited many monasteries, including Mount Athos in Greece, which in his eyes adds legitimacy to his views. His lack of participation in a monastic community alone raises questions about the writer's position. Had he been tonsured to monasticism and become a "secret monastic"? Or was he a self-proclaimed "monk" who practiced the monastic life without the benefit of tonsure? Why had he not joined a monastery? Was it out of necessity or choice? Some monasteries were still in existence during this time, so it would have been possible to be a part of a monastic community.

Although his personal circumstances are unknown, the author discusses the 1923 sobor's reactions to the monasteries and concurs with its view that monasteries are anachronistic and need to be "reformed." He claims that monastics appear "unable and indisposed to labor under the direction of the modern laws of work."[20] On the occasions that monastics do work, they soon turn away from it, as they are not used to physical labor. He makes this statement completely ignoring the evidence of the many monastery collectives functioning not only with the approval, but also with the endorsement, of the Soviet government.

The writer posits what he views as the two most important questions regarding the future of monasticism. The first is where to place the "tens of thousands" of men and women of all ages who have been displaced from the monasteries, including children who have been living and studying at monastic-run schools. The second question is how to utilize this "black army" that "remains without work." He endorses the sobor's idea of allowing monks and nuns to stay in their monasteries, on the condition that they allow laypeople to visit and use the monasteries as centers of spiritual retreat.[21] These conditions were designed to undermine the monastery's function as a place where monastics could withdraw from the secular world. Although the monasteries had always allowed laypeople to visit and stay overnight, they were always separated from the monastics. Guests stayed in separate residences away from the main monastery. The sobor's new policies would have laity involved in every aspect of monastic life, opening the monasteries to an influx of secular society. With laypeople constantly coming and going, a strict monastic lifestyle would be impossible to maintain.

Regarding the question of how the Church should use the black clergy, the writer takes a utilitarian view of monasticism. He claims that the monastics have never allowed themselves to serve the Church or society. They have shut themselves off from the world and, because of their egoism, focus only on their own salvation. He criticizes them for their isolation and claims that they are disregarding Scripture's call to save others. He contrasts this with the Catholic monks, who emphasize serving the community. However, this criticism is flawed, as the Catholic Church has two types of monastic orders: those who serve and those who are cloistered. He believes that Russian monks and nuns should be more involved in society by serving in village churches, hospitals, and orphanages. He ignores the fact that monasteries have been doing precisely that for centuries.[22]

What would prompt a self-proclaimed monk to espouse such antimonastic rhetoric and support the renovationist cause? One possible explanation is that the writer was not a monk but a renovationist supporter who used the "monastic touch" to add legitimacy to his views. If the writer were in fact a monk, other interpretations could account for his attitude. One is that he grew disillusioned with the monastic life and sincerely believed that monasticism would have to change to survive. Two strong outside influences are evident in his writing: the Protestant conception of the Church as servant of society, and Christian socialism. The writer could have had contact with the various Protestant sects in Russia, which had a powerful presence in some areas of the country. Both Protestantism and Christian socialism view the Church in a utilitarian model as a tool to serve society.

In general, there was a strong Christian socialist strain to the renovationist movement, leading to charges that adherents were engaging in pro-Soviet propaganda. Statements by some renovationist hierarchs, such as Bishop Aleksei of Smolensk, lend credence to this accusation. In an attempt to accept the Communist Revolution, Aleksei allegedly proclaimed, "The atheists do divine work and the commune is the ideal of Christianity."[23] One of the more moderate renovationists, Boris Titlinov, claimed that monks from the Antonievo-Siiski monastery in Archangel desired to form a commune and composed a resolution stating that they "understood the situation between the RSFSR and religion, and resolved to give a great welcome to the Soviet power as expressing the true will of the working masses."[24] Such a statement seems questionable and almost certainly was designed to garner support for the renovationist cause. By claiming that conservative monastics endorsed the Soviet government, the reformers added a sense of legitimacy to their program. However, Valaam monastery in the Russian Far North was unusual in that it was a center of renovationism. Several accounts of monks at Valaam discuss the persecution of monks who refused to adhere to the new reforms, especially changing from the Julian calendar to the Gregorian one. Father Boris of Valaam wrote that on September 25, 1925, the abbot of Valaam expelled those monks who refused to accept the new calendar.[25] Another monk, Elder Michael, described how, in 1925, Hieromonk Polycarp was exiled to Russia for writing critical articles about the Church administration. In November of 1925, the Church leadership sent a committee to Valaam to investigate each brother and to establish his loyalties. By the end of 1926, forty-four brothers had been expelled from Valaam, and another forty-eight had left voluntarily.[26]

With the 1923 sobor, the renovationists reached the peak of their power. After that event, their influence declined precipitously. Three explanations appear to account for this decline and ultimate failure of renovationism: internal divisions within the Living Church, popular opposition to the renovationists, aided by Tikhon, and the government's abandonment of its tool. Shortly after the Living Church's formation in 1922, other splinter renovationist groups began to appear. The first was Bishop Antonin's group, "The League of Regeneration in the Church." Others, such as Dean Alexander Vvedenskii's "League of Congregations of the Ancient Apostolic Church," the "Russian People's Church," and the "Free Laboring Church" followed.[27] These divisions were accentuated by the fact that the Living Church represented a very narrow constituency, mainly urban parish priests. It did not include other groups in its program and succeeded in attracting only a very small number of laymen. Additionally, renovationist support was strongest in the urban areas and appealed particularly to the more intellectual priests and believers.

Rural laity and priests tended to resent any attempts at radical change, although in some areas the clergy and laity remained divided between renovationism and "Tikhonism." This was the case in Smolensk province, where according to a government report, out of 736 priests in the region, 301 were Tikhonites, 344 declared themselves renovationists, and 91 did not profess any following. The uezds of Vyazma, Sychevsk, Yartsevo, and Smolensk were renovationism's strongholds. The laity, however, remained loyal to Patriarch Tikhon, as evidenced by the number of petitions for his liberation.[28] Since the laity had played an increasingly important role in parish politics since the revolution, their support was crucial to the reformers. The laity had signed contracts for use of the church buildings and were responsible for maintenance and paying the priests' salaries. Without the laity's cooperation, the Living Church could not succeed.

Unfortunately for the Living Church, the laity generally proved to be of a more conservative frame of mind. Many remained loyal to Patriarch Tikhon and resented the slanderous remarks about him. They regarded the attacks on the monasteries as assaults on the bastion of Orthodoxy. They also resisted the reforms that the renovationists proposed, especially involving the change in the calendar. Additionally, many parish council members were rich peasants who opposed the Soviets and resented the renovationists' support of them.[29] They regarded the Living Church as a Bolshevik creation and believed that the ideas it preached were heretical. They responded to the proposed changes with petitions to the commissariat of justice requesting that state officials stop supporting the renovationists, arresting and removing noncooperative hierarchs, and interfering in parish affairs. This attitude was expressed in a GPU report from Leningrad province in July, 1925. The parish council of a church in

Benitskaia volost protested that the renovationists were "commissars in cassocks. They support Soviet power because it pays them. They betray the people. They don't believe in God; they burn icons and rob churches. God has sent Soviet power to punish us for our sins."[30] Parishioners also used violence against renovationists. In one instance, a mob stoned Dean Alexander Vvedenski, while various other provinces (such as Saratov) reported violent responses to renovationist clergy who attempted to perform religious services.[31]

Patriarch Tikhon, although under house arrest, continued to fight against the renovationists. He and his supporters, dubbed "Tikhonites," set up autocephalous dioceses in Petrograd, Kaluga, Minsk, and about half a dozen other places.[32] They also actively participated in propaganda. In this last endeavor monastics played a large role. One instance involved a religious procession from Ustiuga to Kotovalo led by a renovationist bishop. The Tikhonites sent monks ahead of the procession to warn people not to receive the bishop because "he was a communist imposter."[33] Tikhon also continued the practice of using monks and nuns as couriers to imprisoned and exiled hierarchs. As clerics who did not serve in parishes, they had more freedom of movement and greater anonymity than those in Church administration. One of these "messenger nuns" was Mother Alipii Bol'shakovoi, a nun from Theodorovski Pereslavski women's monastery. In 1924, after Tikhon's release and reinstatement, he rewarded her with a gold cross for her work in "sustaining and serving confined and exiled hierarchs."[34]

In June, 1923, the Soviets released Patriarch Tikhon from his home confinement in exchange for a statement of loyalty.[35] His freedom allowed him to launch an effective but subtle counterattack. In a gesture that showed his commitment to monasticism, he made his first public statement at Donskoi monastery in Moscow. He declared that he was not an enemy of the people and stated that the Church's role was to do the work of Christ and not engage in politics. He politely refused to meet with the leaders of the Living Church and reiterated the position that the Church must adhere to canonical law. This last phrase was a subtle indication that he had no intention of giving in to the demands of the Living Church to allow married bishops.[36]

Tikhon's strategy of not overtly attacking either the government or the Living Church while still maintaining his traditional position ultimately paid off. Beginning in late 1923, many churches formerly associated with the Living Church petitioned the Church hierarchy to return to the fold.

Some, like the letter from the Vladimir province, professed "profound dissatisfaction and hatred of the popular masses in the parish toward the church authorities headed by the so-called Living Church."[37] Although Tikhon appeared to have recovered his former position of authority, he and his supporters were not completely out of danger. A 1924 letter from the renovationist synod to Soviet President Mikhail Kalinin expressed outrage at Tikhon's freedom and warned of his conspiring to lead a group of monastics in counterrevolutionary activities.[38] In November, 1924, a lay brother, Y. A. Polozov, was murdered by bandits at the Donskoi monastery, where the patriarch resided. Tikhon was there at the time, and it is not clear whether the murder was a result of a robbery or an attempted assassination.[39] The very next month, fifteen monks were arrested at Kievo-Pecherskaia lavra after police found a large quantity of precious stones and metals hidden in the cellars, along with counterrevolutionary correspondence with Patriarch Tikhon and other "counterrevolutionary" figures. The patriarch hastily wrote a letter published in *Izvestiia* denying any involvement and claiming that he knew of no counterrevolutionary activity among the monks of the lavra.[40]

In 1924 the Soviet government began to rescind support for the renovationists. There were two main reasons for this. One was the international protests that accompanied the arrest of Patriarch Tikhon; the other was the fear that the renovationists would actually succeed in building a Soviet Church. That was the last thing the Soviets wanted. They also realized that the popular response to the Living Church was decidedly negative. Accordingly, the authorities followed a policy throughout the remainder of NEP that would play different factions of the renovationists against each other. In this they were effective. Both the official Church and the renovationists were administratively weak; many people rejected both the Patriarchal Church and the Living Church and joined sects such as the Baptists and other Protestant groups.[41]

By the end of 1924 renovationism had effectively come to an end, although remnants of the movement existed well into the 1940s. Evidence of this impotence may be seen in a report by E. M. Yaroslavsky: "As for the renovationist movement, it must be noted that it has practically ceased to exist. It has an organization but for the most part it is of no consequence. The renovationists play virtually no role in the villages; they have absolutely no organization there. In the larger cities the Tikhonites have a rather significant influence; they are succeeding in re-establishing their former power there."[42]

Further evidence of the weakness of the renovationists appeared in 1924, when many high-ranking renovationist clergy publicly repented and asked Patriarch Tikhon for their readmittance to the Church. Among those penitents were Archbishop Konstantin of Kostroma, Bishop Artemii of Petrograd, and Archbishop Serafim of Irkutsk. One of the most important of those who repented was Metropolitan Sergei of Iaroslavl, who had been an ardent supporter of the Living Church in 1923. After serving a period in prison, he went to Moscow in March, 1924, where he made a public confession clad in the simple robes of a monk. Tikhon forgave him and restored him to the rank of metropolitan.[43]

In addition to fomenting factionalism within the Church, the Soviets' NEP policy also promoted competition between the Russian Orthodox Church and other Christian sects. The Church had long fought the influence of sects such as the Tolstoyans, the Dukhobors, and the Molokans. Most of these groups had roots in the Orthodox Church but had broken off relations and maintained their own beliefs and practices. The patriarchate rejected these sects as un-Christian and did not consider them legitimate. At the eighth party congress, the party established a commission called "the Organizational Commission on the resettlement of Sectarians" (Orgkomsekt) to foster close cooperation between the government and sectarians. The duties of the Orgkomsekt were to encourage sectarian agricultural communes and obtain land for them.[44] These sectarian communes would naturally be in direct competition with the monastery communes.[45] The institutional support that the Communist Party provided for the sectarians signaled the beginning of a renewed attack on the monasteries. The party had decided that although the monastery communes had proven productive during the civil war, sectarian communes would be more loyal. Sectarianism was stronger in some areas than others. Smolensk guberniia in particular attracted as many as 2,300 in 1925, with the numbers growing by 200 a year.[46] Like its treatment of the renovationists, after 1924, the party reevaluated this support and began to persecute the sectarians as well.

Renewing the Antireligious Campaign

The Soviets pursued two simultaneous policies toward the Orthodox Church during NEP. In addition to manipulating Church politics, they also renewed the antireligious propaganda campaign. As previously discussed, there was a faction of the Communist Party that disagreed with the hard-line approach and instead favored using the educational system to fight religion. Commissar of Education Lunacharskii was the major proponent of this "middle course" that avoided both headlong attacks against the Church and meddling in Church affairs. Instead, he believed that educating the peasants in natural history and science along with exposing the shortcomings of the clergy would make the people realize how backward and exploitative religion was and cause them to abandon it of their own accord.

The Bolsheviks did not use this propaganda tactic much during the civil war, as they were too concerned with winning that conflict to devote attention and money to the antireligious struggle. Although the commissariat of justice had published the antireligious journal *Revoliutsiia i Tserkov* since 1919 and communism was now officially taught in place of religion in the schools, little was done otherwise to educate the masses. Lunacharskii experimented with staging debates between clergy and atheists. However, these backfired when the clergy frequently emerged the victors. After the civil war ended, Lenin wrote a letter to the central committee in 1921 calling for the establishment of a society of "militant atheists" to lead the fight against religion. However, throughout 1921 and 1922, work on that project proceeded slowly. Publishers produced antireligious books and pamphlets, mostly translations from Western authors, but the shortage of both paper and competent antireligious workers delayed the pace.

One group that embraced the antireligious movement aggressively and wholeheartedly was the Komsomol (Young Communist League). This organization was composed of young people who had fought in the war and frequently participated in the confiscation of Church valuables in the early period of separation of Church and state. At first the party endorsed the activities of the Komsomol, which included holding antireligious carnivals and demonstrations and arbitrarily closing churches; however, these aroused the wrath of the peasants and engendered anti-Soviet feeling among the population, something the government did not want.

By 1923 the subject of antireligious propaganda had reached such importance that the party made it a subject for debate at both the twelfth and thirteenth party congresses, held in 1923 and 1924, respectively. The results of a secret 1923 census underlined the necessity for making religious policy a priority. The census indicated that 3,126,541 people were involved in religious organizations compared with 1,737,053 in 1910.[47] Those figures showed that religion had increased rather than declined during the first five years of the Bolshevik regime. These numbers necessitated some kind of government response.

At the twelfth party congress in 1923, the triumvirate of Zinoviev, Kamenev, and Stalin favored a more conciliatory policy toward religion. They condemned the arbitrary closing of churches and called for propaganda focusing on a materialistic interpretation of social life, addressing mainly the rural areas. Such a reversal of policy paralleled the political decline of Trotsky, who favored a more aggressive approach, and revealed the political maneuvering within the party to determine who would succeed Lenin.

The general secretary of the Communist Party, Iosif Stalin, in particular decried the excesses of the antireligious campaigns. This reaction did not come as a result of genuine concern for the people. Rather, Stalin realized that the people were not happy with the current antireligious policies and the party was in danger of losing their support. In characteristic fashion, he blamed local party officials for the offenses. In a letter to all party bodies, Stalin used language foreshadowing his famous "Dizzy with Success" speech in 1930: "[Several recent events] indicate how carelessly, unseriously, and lightheartedly some local organs of the party and state considered so important a question as freedom of religious conscience. It seems that these organizations and organs of power do not understand the fact that their brutal, indiscreet acts against believers, who constitute a huge majority of the population, cause incalculable damage to Soviet power and are threatening to destroy the achievements of the party."[48]

As general secretary, Stalin forbade the arbitrary closing of churches and other houses of worship, superfluous taxation, and arrests of a "religious character." However, he stressed that these prohibitions did not mean that the party was relaxing its vigilance against religion. On the contrary, the party would be alert to those groups who would use religion as a counterrevolutionary tool and at the same time take a slow, tactful approach toward debunking religion.[49]

The thirteenth party congress met in May, 1924, and confirmed the "religious NEP" that the twelfth party congress had initiated. However, this congress did not merely reiterate the conclusions of its predecessor. The party leaders did not officially acknowledge the change to a more conciliatory course until after the thirteenth congress. The year in between the two congresses was filled with much debate, particularly with regard to the question of the sectarians. The thirteenth party congress voted to continue the policy of supporting them. However, as Arto

Luukaanen points out, the real importance of the thirteenth congress was that "it constituted a short breathing space in the political struggle over the future of the Soviet Union." Both hard-liners and moderates were satisfied with the resolutions adopted; the hard-liners viewed the new policy merely as a temporary setback, whereas the moderates believed that a "long and steady transition period" was on the horizon.[50] The congress also recognized the need to expand antireligious propaganda. A group devoted solely to educating the people about the folly of religion was sorely needed.

The League of the Godless

The "League of the Godless" (in Russian, *Bezbozhniki*) first arose as a means to support the newspaper *Bezbozhnik* (the Godless), established in 1922. Membership grew slowly; by 1929 the group claimed a total of 8,928 cells with 465,498 members. Out of that number, 30 percent were Komsomols, another 30 percent were Communists, and the remaining 40 percent were non-party members. In terms of social class, 40 percent of members were workers, 30 percent peasants, 20 percent were white-collar workers, and 10 percent were not reported. Only 20 percent of all members were women.[51]

Surprisingly, some of the key officials in the Bezbozhnik movement were former priests. They were visible in all levels of the organization, particularly during the early NEP period. Daniel Peris places this phenomenon in the broader context of the Bolsheviks' recognition after the civil war that efficient administration of the country necessitated the skills of "bourgeois specialists," those "skilled individuals occupying a wide variety of technical and administrative positions during the prerevolutionary period."[52] Although technically not bourgeois, the clergy were classified as enemies of the people, and the Bezbozhniki realized that to effectively mobilize their fellows, they needed people with an inside view of the enemy. Recruitment proved easier than originally supposed. The clergy occupied a castelike system and were thought of as people more fated than "called" to that vocation. Therefore, in seminaries and among the lower clergy there was much discontent that the Soviet was able to capitalize on. Indeed, it was in a seminary that Iosif Stalin was first exposed to Marxist ideology.[53]

One aspect of Yaroslavsky's league upon which many contemporary observers and historians commented was its conscious transference of religious forms and the structure of Orthodoxy to the new Soviet state. The use of former clergy may have contributed to this but cannot be viewed as the main cause. Nonetheless, Yaroslavsky admitted that part of the league's goals was cultural substitution, that is, borrowing the forms and practices of Orthodoxy to create a new Soviet religion.[54]

One of the league's most frequent targets was monasticism. *Bezbozhnik* and other antireligious journals actively participated in the "relic fraud" exposures in the civil war period. During NEP, articles lamented the continued existence of monasteries and the lack of effective propaganda against them. Many of these articles explicitly criticize the government for allowing the monasteries to exist. The journal *Antireligioznik* published an article in 1926 about the Troitse-Sergeev lavra in Sergeev Posad, near Moscow. The author complained that although the monastery was closed by a decision of the authorities, the fact remained that "many monks continue to live there under the guise of labor artels, collectives, and such, in full view of the authorities." The monks continued to wear their monastic clothes and conduct services, consciously breaking the law. *Antireligioznik* also accused the monks of engaging in counterpropaganda against the Soviets. It claimed that the monks wrote anonymous "letters from heaven" and used fake bleeding crosses while preaching about the second coming of Christ in order to scare the peasants and drive them away from communism.[55]

To combat the influence of the monks on the surrounding population, *Antireligioznik* proposed organizing an antireligious excursion to the lavra. Such a trip, the journal argued, would be sure to attract believers, and the guide could use the opportunity to expose the monastery for the exploitative and corrupt institution that it was. The tour would emphasize the political role of the monasteries, the separation of Church and state, the antiworker bias of the monasteries, and particularly the corrupt and immoral lives of the monks. The guides would have to conduct much research on the monastery in advance in order to be prepared to answer any questions. The article criticized the current tours of the monastery (converted into a museum since 1922), complaining that they focused on the architectural and artistic merit of the monastery and often did not contain any reference to antireligious propaganda. The article concluded that after an effective antireligious tour, people would become so disillusioned with the monasteries that the latter would lose their influence.[56]

The Bezbozhniki's greatest opposition and competition came from within the villages. As the monasteries used the Soviet institution of the collective farm to preserve themselves, so the rural parish clergy and laity used both traditional village institutions such as the *skhod* (village assembly) and the new institution of the *soviet* (village council) to protect religious life in the countryside during NEP. Clergy and laity gained valuable political experience in both institutions. They pressed the skhod to enact measures, especially financial, that benefited the village church. The village councils also defended the church by blocking the secularization of church property. In an ironic twist, the villagers were able to use a Soviet institution to forestall cultural and political encroachment on religious activity and reintegrated religion and politics.[57]

Failure of the Antireligious Campaign

The antireligious movement by and large proved to be a failure during the NEP period. In a ground-breaking study of the Bezbozhniki and rural religion, Glennys Young cites four main reasons that the antireligious campaign suffered in general, some of which have already been mentioned. One involved the militaristic and violent methods of the Bezbozhniki, most of which were a legacy of the civil war. Another was the indifference of many Komsomol, party, and Red Army members to antireligious activities. A third reason was chronic material shortages, and the last reason was the counterattack of the religious villagers.

As to why the antireligious activities failed in the countryside, Young cites isolation from fellow comrades and institutions, the degree to which external factors (such as the presence of military personnel) determined the League's validity, and the religious strength of both Orthodox and sectarian movements in a given area.[58] The experience of Smolensk appears to confirm this explanation. At the end of 1925, the League of the Godless claimed only 2,500 members.[59] The agrarian nature and isolation of Smolensk and the alarming (both to the Soviets and to the Orthodox Church) spread of sectarianism account for the low figures. Official numbers listed 2,300 sectarian members in Smolensk province. They included members in twenty-seven evangelical communes and two larger organizations. Actual figures of sectarians may have been higher, with a growth rate of 200 new members per year.[60] The main reason for the weakness of the antireligious movement in Smolensk was again the power of the villagers and the parish clergy. It was not uncommon for the parish priest to serve on the village soviet and skhod and for these institutions to display icons in their meeting halls.

Much recent research has focused on peasant response to the antireligious propaganda. Although the Bezbozhniki targeted primarily rural areas, they did not neglect urban centers. Factory workers were required to attend talks and films and to read antireligious literature. The degree to which workers responded to the propaganda is unclear. Workers who were religious necessarily kept their opinions to themselves. They did not have the same opportunities to participate in local politics that the peasants did. They had no village soviets or assemblies that would enable them to defend their churches. Despite this, there is an indication that many workers remained religious. In 1922 the workers of the Moscow factory "Serp i Molot" petitioned the justice department to transfer the miracle-working icon of the Holy Trinity (Troitse-Sergeev) lavra to the chapel of St. Sergius in Rodozhoi Iamskoi settlement. Trotsky observed in 1923 that "a worker will not trouble to buy new icons, but has not sufficient will to discard the old ones. He does not go to church and reads *Bezbozhnik* but sends for a priest to christen his child—just in case." Trotsky dismissed these examples of religious ties among workers as vestiges, claiming that "religiousness among the Russian working classes practically does not exist."

A more realistic assessment of religiosity among the proletariat came from trade union official Mikhail Tomskii, who as late as 1928 asked a trade union congress, "If we dismissed all believers from our ranks, who would be left in the unions? The core of our unions would not be much larger than that of the party."[61] The following figures illustrate the numbers of urban religious societies in the Russian part of the Soviet Union in 1927 and 1928. Overall there were 4,345 registered religious societies in the cities in 1927. Of those, 59 percent were Orthodox. One year later the percentage of Orthodox in the cities increased by 1 percent from 59 percent to 60 percent out of a total of 4,266 registered societies. In comparison, the countryside had 31,678 total religious organizations in 1927, of which 71.5 percent were Orthodox and 32,539 in 1928, of which 72 percent were Orthodox. Even though it is not surprising that the countryside had more religious groups than the cities, these figures show that urban religious life, particularly in the Orthodox Church, was far from dead.[62]

Monasticism during NEP

Whereas the parishes retained some of their strength during NEP due to the parish councils, the monasteries' fate generally worsened. Beginning in 1923 the Soviets began closing some of the monastery communes, although many remained open until 1930. The authorities found various reasons for closing down these kolkhozes and artels. Among the explanations they gave were the low level of production by the monastery communes and the need to use those properties and resources for hospitals and schools. Many letters from the authorities discuss their fear of the monastics' influence over the population, particularly the peasants.[63] Sometimes, particularly if the artel was composed of nuns, they used the old charges of immoral behavior and a "parasitic" lifestyle. Such was the case with the Alexander Nevsky society, located on the grounds of the Akatevski women's monastery in Moscow guberniia. In 1924 a commission was established to investigate the monastery artel. The commission declared that the society was not a true artel, but rather a monastery disguised as an artel. The 162 members of the society, all nuns, were divided along class lines. It was charged that only forty-nine of these nuns were actually engaged in agricultural work. The rest were "parasites." The nuns who did the work and lived in the worst quarters were from the peasant class, while the bourgeois parasitic nuns had the best living arrangements and were permitted to remain idle. There were also reports that nuns engaged in immoral behavior with men and went out in the evenings in secular clothes. Because such behavior was inappropriate for nuns, the commission argued that the monastery was not legitimate and should be closed.[64]

The story of the Alexander Nevsky artel and its closure is not unusual. However, in reading the commission's report, several noticeable details emerge that merit further comment. That all of the members of the artel were nuns is in itself remarkable. The guidelines for agricultural communes in 1919 stipulated that they must be open to all who applied. Many of the local sovdeps ensured that the monastery sovkhozes and kolkhozes contained nonbelievers as well as monastics. This would weaken the power of the monastic communities and provide the sovdeps with spies within the monastery walls. That the nuns of Alexander Nevsky avoided these restrictions and preserved the monastic character of their artel illustrates that these government constraints were not always enforced. Furthermore, the commission's report describes the growing number of nuns tonsured into the monastery, all of whom were peasants from the local population. In 1921 alone, twenty-one women were tonsured as nuns.[65] Judging from the description of the service, these tonsures were done quite openly. Obviously the abbess felt comfortable enough to conduct these services in plain view of the authorities, some of whom were in attendance. This suggests that the local authorities tacitly condoned these activities. These tonsures attest not only to the survival of monasticism, but also to its growth. For a person to decide to become a monastic during a time when monasteries were being closed and monastics arrested demonstrates deep faith. The abbess and the nuns of the Alevander Nevsky artel allegedly attempted to bribe the commission sent to close the monastery by offering warm food and new shoes. The report condemns these bribery attempts and claims that the members of the commission refused them.

Many monasteries wrote formal complaints to the Moscow soviet (Mossovet) requesting that their artels remain open. These were very similar to earlier petitions from the civil war. Every request used socialist language designed to reassure the authorities that the monastery communes had the same goals as the Communists. These pleas all stressed the equal living conditions among the monastics and stressed the number of members who were from the peasant class. Some bolder petitions even accused the Soviets of being hypocritical, as a letter from Gefimanski skete in Sergeev Posad illustrates. The monks of this skete claimed that the Mossovet's decision to close the monastery artel in 1924 "is fully contradictory to the action of the organs of the Mossovet itself when it officially pronounced our artel the best in Sergeev uezd. Our artel was founded on March 3, 1919, with the permission of the Sergeev Volost Land Department. In 1923, the Moscow Guberniia Land Department agreed to extend the artel for nine years." Less than one year after this agreement , the Mossovet went back on its word when it decided to close the artel. The monks of Gefinamnski skete further stressed its record of productivity and used communist ideology and language to defend its existence. They claimed that none of the members of the artel had any personal property and that therefore the artel could be said to approximate a commune. They also emphasized the peasant background of most of the monks. The skete successfully defended itself and remained open as an artel until 1928.[66]

Two of the largest and best-known monasteries affected by the new wave of closings were Optina Pustyn in Kozelsk and Kievo-Pecherskaia lavra in Ukraine. The end of Optina Pustyn's "golden age" came in 1923, when the artel was closed and the rest of the monastery converted into a museum.[67] The real tragedy for monastics and laypeople, however, came that same year with the arrest of Elder Nektary. He was the last of the revered Optina elders, and his arrest and deportation symbolized the end of a revered tradition of eldership. After his arrest, he was transferred to a village near Kozelsk, which was easily accessible to his many followers. Despite his illness and the fact that he was officially under arrest, people continued to come to his lodgings in great numbers, including many nuns from closed convents. The elder's continued popularity so threatened the authorities that they moved him to a remote village thirty miles from Kozelsk, where he died in 1928.[68]

On the grounds of Optina Pustyn, twenty monks were allowed to remain to serve as museum workers; the rest were evicted. Some left the area and went back to their families; others settled in the nearby village of Kozelsk. By request of the nearby village of Stenino, the Kazanskii cathedral of the monastery was allowed to remain open and serve as a place of worship. Monks living in surrounding villages as well as the ones who still lived at Optina participated in the services. This situation lasted for only one year, after which the church was closed, in 1924. The museum and library continued to function, and several monks still lived in the skete.[69]

In addition to the exiled monks, nuns from the nearby convent of Shamordino, including the abbess, moved to Kozelsk to be closer to the monks. Soon many women arrived in Kozelsk, desiring to experience a spiritual life. In time a small monastic society developed in the village. Fr. Nikon, a spiritual son of Elder Nektary and considered by some to be the last Optina elder, took care of the spiritual needs of the monastics and served as a focus of religious life. The nuns and monks worked in the gardens (and in the commune when it existed) and the hospital. When the Kazanskii cathedral closed in 1924, they gathered to worship in the hospital kitchen, where two of the nuns worked. The closure of the church marked the end of monastery life at Optina, but not of monastic life in general. Most of the monks relocated to Kozelsk, the closest village to the monastery. Some lived with sympathetic villagers; other monks who had the means bought houses and lived together. One monk, Fr. Lavrentii Levchenko, was one of these latter. His situation was somewhat unique; his entire family were all monastics. They and some other monks all lived together and enjoyed greater comfort than they had had at the monastery. The place of worship shifted to St. George's church in Kozelsk.[70]

Fr. Nikon described the village of Kozelsk during this time as a "little monastery." The villagers got used to seeing the monks and nuns, and the church was filled for every service. Monastics and lay religious people from other places came to Kozelsk to be near the Optina monks and par-

Library of St. John's skete, Optina Pustyn Monastery

ticipate in an active religious community. This soon came to the attention of the local authorities, who published an article in the local newspaper that stated, "before we had only one monastery; now we have two," and "in the evening around every corner and in every alley you can see these 'black crows.'"[71]

Perceiving the presence of monks to be a threat to the building of socialism, the authorities arrested Fr. Nikon in 1927 and sent him to the nearby town of Kaluga. Several of his spiritual children followed him there and delivered things to him in prison. The authorities then transferred him first to Solovkii concentration camp and in 1929 to Karelia. In 1927 the government closed the Optina museum and transferred it to the authority of the Glavnauka (department of science). The remaining monks were told to leave. The last effort to preserve Optina had failed. After Fr. Nikon's arrest and the closure of the museum, few monks remained. The once thriving Optina Pustyn became a ghost of its former self.

The story of Kievo-Pecherskaia lavra in Ukraine followed mostly the same pattern as Optina Pustyn. From the letters of Archbishop Leonty of Chile, who at the time was a young novice, a graphic account of the last days of the monastery emerges. Kiev was one of the monastic centers in

Entrance to St. John's skete, Optina Pustyn Monastery

the Russian empire; more than 400 monks lived at the lavra. There were several other monasteries in proximity to Kiev lavra. The nearby Mikhailovsky monastery housed 30 monks; Troitse, 250; and Vydubctski, close to 40. Women's monasteries were numerous as well: Trolovski had 600 nuns; Pokrovski, 300; Vvedenski, 150; Lebedinski, 250; and Mezhigorski, 30. In the immediate aftermath of the 1918 laws, the authorities applied the same tactics of gradual encroachment that they had used on other monasteries. They conducted exposures of the relics and generally looted the monasteries. They took the vegetable gardens (which were their main source of existence) away from the monks. They left them barely enough to survive. This was done to make life more difficult in hopes that their resistance would gradually wither. The monks loved their monastery, however, and they endured hunger and cold and found work in the nearby villages to try to support it.[72]

Despite the monks' dedication, the authorities announced the closing of Kievo-Pecherskaia in 1924. This began an unequal struggle between the authorities and the religious people who wanted the lavra kept open. The latter wrote petitions that were occasionally granted; however, the extensions on the church and monastery did not last long. The closure of the monastery and the arrest of the monks became known on Easter of 1924; the monks responded by ringing the bells and summoning the faithful. Leonty describes the courtyard as overflowing with people by daybreak, among them Red Army guards. The authorities, fearful of riots, backed down.[73]

After Easter the Soviets arrested many of the monks on charges of hiding Church valuables. Leonty wryly comments that these charges persisted despite the fact that the Soviets had already stolen most of the Church valuables years before. After the arrests, only six monks out of the previous four hundred remained in the monastery. The rest had scattered. Some monks who escaped arrest left the monastery and moved to a small monastery named Kitaevski Pustyn. There they hoped to continue their community. Some of the elders moved to a home near the river, while younger monks settled on farms with believers and worked as laborers. Those older monks who were ill and could not live by themselves resided with villagers. Fr. Leonty and other able-bodied monks were taken prisoner by the Soviets and forced to work in the Goloseevski monastery forest in the winter without food or water. Many died from hunger.[74]

Those monasteries that escaped closure during this time became refuges for displaced monks and nuns. One such sanctuary was Vysoko-Petrovskii monastery in Moscow. Located in the center of the city, this fourteenth-century monastery served as an unusually strong center of spirituality and monastic life from 1923 until its closure in 1929. One nun, Mother Ignatia, referred to Vysoko-Petrovskii as the "desert in the capital."[75] During this period of persecution Vysoko-Petrovskii experienced the greatest spiritual revival in its history.

This revival started in 1923, when Bishop Bartholomew, the former director of the Moscow Theological Academy, arrived in the monastery. He was sent there by the authorities after they closed the academy. His emphasis on obedience and monastic rule made him a popular father confessor, and the monks soon elected him abbot. He also conducted an illegal seminary on the grounds of the monastery, composed of former professors from the theological academy. This underground seminary continued until 1928.

At the same time, monks from the Zosima Pustyn monastery arrived, having been dispossessed of their monastery. Some of these monks were known throughout Moscow and even throughout Russia for their wisdom and piety. Among them was Father Agafon, who was the greatest pastor among both monastics and laity. He alone had over four hundred people under his spiritual guidance. Bishop Bartholomew made him co-abbot, and together they played key roles in the spiritual growth of the monastery.[76]

Aside from serving as a haven for uprooted monks, Vysoko-Petrovskii also attracted many young women and men who desired to follow the monastic way of life. They received secret tonsure, and some of them, such as Metropolitan Filaret of Moscow, later became high-ranking Church officials. Others continued to live in the secular world and lived essentially a double life. They went to school or work and at the same time adhered to the monastic routine of work, prayer, and obedience to an elder.

One of these secret nuns was Mother Ignatia, a Muscovite by birth. Although she first came to the monastery in 1924, she did not receive tonsure until 1938. Having earned a degree in anthropology from Moscow University, she went on to become a specialist in the pathomorphology of tuberculosis. By the time she retired in the early 1980s, she had reached the pinnacle of her profession and was a noted specialist. But she considered her secular work secondary to her "real" profession as a monastic. Her memoirs provide a detailed description of monastic life in Moscow in the 1920s and early 1930s.[77]

Mother Ignatia believed that Vysoko-Petrovskii was responsible for preserving monasticism during the 1920s and 1930s. "The Fathers considered that monasticism must not die out. For this reason, all of their strength was devoted to maintaining the traditions of spiritual life."[78] Vysoko-Petrovskii was almost unique in that it was one of the few monasteries that had not been turned into an artel or museum but was actually allowed to function solely as a monastery until its closure in 1929. The monastery did not remain unmolested, however. Several of its churches were closed and monks arrested. Nevertheless, Vysoko-Petrovskii continued to attract not only monastics but also laity, as the monastery functioned as a parish church. Many Muscovites, including intellectuals and artists as well as "simple people," came to the daily church services.[79]

The story of Vysoko-Petrovskii and its growth illustrate how the persecutions and closures neither dampened people's hunger for monasticism nor weakened monasticism's ability to adapt to changing circumstances. The presence of an illegal seminary on the property and Vysoko-Petrovskii's growth as a center of spiritual development demonstrate people's desire for the wisdom and guidance of the monastics. It is doubtful that Vysoko would have become the center of spirituality had it not been for the closures of other monasteries and the atmosphere of persecution that prevailed.

A Second Schism and the Declaration of 1927

Two events that seriously affected the Church during the NEP period were the death of Lenin on January 21, 1924, and the death of Patriarch Tikhon on April 7, 1925. These two occurrences meant that the continued existence of the patriarchate was open to speculation. Whoever succeeded Lenin would determine future religious policy and also decide whether to approve the election of a new patriarch. Lenin's death inaugurated a power struggle within the Communist Party. Religious people knew that their fate depended on which faction of the party seized power. Trotsky and the other Leftists took a hard-line approach to religion, whereas the Right appeared to have a more pragmatic policy to religion.

Aside from their shock and grief at Patriarch Tikhon's death, the faithful were appalled and dismayed at the publication of a document in *Izvestiia,* allegedly written by Tikhon on his deathbed and published posthumously. This "testament" essentially supported the Soviet regime and called for the Church to support the workers' and peasants' government. He urged the Church to fight not the Soviets but the "true enemies" of Orthodoxy—sectarians, renovationists, the Godless, Roman Catholics, and Protestants. He repeatedly condemned those who opposed the Soviet government and urged the Church to cooperate with the government. Finally, he condemned the émigré clergy, especially the Karlovatskii synod.[80]

This message caused much consternation among the faithful, particularly the émigré clergy and their supporters. They immediately branded it a forgery. However, the document was delivered by two of the patriarch's closest confidants, Metropolitan Peter and Metropolitan Tikhon of the Urals. Other contemporaries declared that the handwriting was definitely Tikhon's. Many of the faithful continued to believe that even if the testament was written by him, it was composed under duress and therefore was not legitimate. However, other evidence indicates the testament's authenticity, as it remained consistent with Tikhon's public statements and willingness to cooperate with the government after his release from prison.

Patriarch Tikhon had designated Metropolitans Peter, Agafangel, and Kirill as possible successors until a sobor could be called to elect a new patriarch. The Soviets did not want a sobor to be called, nor did they want a new patriarch. Therefore, they did everything in their power to prevent a sobor from meeting. They arrested and exiled all three possible successors before any one of them could assume the position. One of the people instrumental in prohibiting the sobor from ever meeting was Iosif Stalin. Under duress, Metropolitan Peter appointed Metropolitan Sergei of Nizhni Novgorod to serve as deputy locum tenens (temporary head of the Church) until his release. Peter later tried to rescind Sergei's position, but Sergei defied him. Sergei had the support of other Tikhonite bishops, and in the end he remained in the position of locum tenens.[81]

The Soviet government did not approve of this choice, considering Sergei to be a leader of the right wing of the patriarchal Church. They arrested him several times, the last occurring in 1926 shortly after his appointment. The patriarchal Church's position was very precarious in 1926; of eleven possible candidates for locum tenens, ten were in prison or exile. While in prison, Metropolitan Sergei came to realize the futility of resisting the Soviets. Ultimately, when he was approached by the government for the purpose of securing a compromise between Church and state, he decided to cooperate. He appealed to the OGPU to legalize the Church with him as its head.[82] He further requested the formation of dioceses, the right to call a synod of bishops, and permission to print a journal and to have theological schools. In return, the government would have, if not outright Church support, then at least neutrality. These talks broke down, and Sergei was arrested again and imprisoned until 1927. However, by that time, the government had become convinced of Sergei's loyalty and granted most of his requests. Metropolitan Sergei, now the official head of the Church until a sobor could be called, made his agreement known to the people in the famous "Declaration of 1927."

This declaration announced that the Orthodox Church was now restored to the legal position that it had lost after the Bolshevik Revolution and called on the faithful to be loyal to the Soviet government. This, however, proved not to be the case. Although the government promised legality, a series of laws passed in 1929 ensured that the Church would remain without juridical rights. Not until 1943 did the Church have its legal rights restored. In the statement, Sergei stated that it was possible to be both a true Orthodox Christian and at the same time a loyal Soviet citizen. He claimed that Orthodox Christians recognized the Soviet Union as "our secular native land, whose joys are our joys and whose failures are our failures. Every blow aimed at the Union . . . is regarded by us as a blow directed against us."[83]

The 1927 Declaration has been the subject of much analysis by historians and religious writers and therefore is not exhaustively discussed here.[84] The main result was that it split the Church into two factions: the Patriarchal Church (sometimes called the "Sergianists") and the Karlovatskii synod (also known as the Catacomb Church). After publicizing this speech, Sergei communicated with the Karlovatskii synod and declared that, if it did not give a written statement of loyalty to the Soviets, then it would be excluded from the jurisdiction of the Moscow patriarchate. The Karlovatskii synod refused and formally broke off relations with the Patriarchal Church. Members of the synod accused Sergei of collaborating with the enemy of the Orthodox Church and branded him a traitor and a heretic. The right-wing clergy within Russia likewise opposed Sergei's position, referring to him as the "Red Patriarch," and formally ended relations with him.

The Declaration of 1927 formed the basis for the most serious and long-lasting schism within Russian Orthodoxy.[85] Parishes had to decide whether to remain with the Patriarchal Church or to break away and establish another church. Those clergy and laity who decided to split off from the official church faced a very difficult decision, for, whatever repugnance they felt regarding the declaration, the fact remained that Sergei had acted well within the canons of the Church. Therefore, those who left the Church were viewed by the state as counterrevolutionary and by the Church as ecclesiastically guilty of uncanonical behavior. The émigré clergy constituted most of the schismatics. Within Russia, most Orthodox at least passively accepted Sergei's declaration, including the Optina Elder Nektary, whom both sides regard as a saint.[86] Statistics from 1928 show 28,000 active churches belonging to the Patriarchal Church, compared to 3,364 renovationists.[87]

Nevertheless, the promulgation of the declaration resulted in two separate Orthodox Churches existing in Russia, one legal and the other illegal. The schismatic group called themselves the "Catacomb Church" or the "True Orthodox Church." They established their own secret parishes and monasteries and ordained their own priests and bishops. Officially they had no legitimacy either within or outside Russia, as they had broken with the Patriarchal Church. However, like the latter, the Catacomb Church based its authority on the late Patriarch Tikhon. This validity came from a story related by Dr. Michael A. Shishilenko (later Bishop Maxim of Serpukhov), a physician at the Tagantkoff state prison and the chief physician of Patriarch Tikhon. According to the doctor, the late patriarch had spoken freely with him about the state of the Church and not long before his death had expressed the opinion that "the only way for the Russian Orthodox Church would be the way into the catacombs." He advised Dr. Shishilenko to secretly become a monk and even a bishop in case the higher church hierarchy "should become untrue to Christ and turn over its inner freedom to the Soviet State."[88]

After the declaration, Shishilenko secretly became a monk and then a bishop, taking the name Maxim. He continued to practice as a prison physician while fulfilling his clerical obligations. In 1929 he was arrested by the political police and sent to Solovki Island prison on charges of being a secret monk. While at Solovki, he continued to serve as a physician and as a priest.[89] Although it is not known how many people received secret tonsure within the Catacomb church, evidence suggest that Catacomb "monasteries" thrived in the labor camps, particularly in Solovki.[90] Many critics of the Patriarchal Church further accuse Sergei of having the secret police arrest and imprison clergy from the Catacomb church. Moreover, even though many monks and nuns were expelled from monasteries for not agreeing with the Patriarchal Church, there is no hard evidence available to substantiate these accusations.

Another cleric who vociferously campaigned against Sergei's declaration was a married priest named Valentin Sventitsky. He served as the parish priest of St. Nicholas on Elias Street in Moscow. Although not a monastic himself, he traveled many times to Optina Pustyn, where he became a disciple of Elder Anatole. He admired the discipline of monastics and delivered a series of lectures in Moscow from 1921 to 1926 on the application of monastic discipline to daily life in a secular world that was hostile toward Christianity.[91] In these lectures he particularly emphasized the necessity to strive for ceaseless prayer, also known as "prayer of the heart." Father Valentin's preaching came at a crucial moment for Orthodoxy and monasticism. Because the government was closing more and more monasteries, Father Valentin's instructions stressed that one did not need to live in a monastery to become a monastic. He spoke of the real walls of monasticism as being "the walls between the heart and the world. . . . Very few people at this time can live behind monastery walls. But all people have the possibility to live in a state of spiritual monasticism."[92] These lectures became the cornerstone for a secret monastic movement after 1930, when all of the monasteries were officially closed. These "monasteries in the world" became a regular feature of Orthodox life in the Soviet period. A contemporary of Fr. Valentin's, S. I. Fudel, remarked, "It is a remarkable fact that even in 1925 in the city of Moscow, this man managed to arouse people in his parish to a life of intense prayer. He did much for the general defense of faith." Father Valentin was one of the most vociferous opponents of Metropolitan Sergei's declaration and in 1928 was arrested on charges of counterrevolutionary activity. He died in exile in Siberia.[93]

In summarizing the Soviet response to religion during the NEP period, at first glance it appears chaotic and contradictory—organizing attacks on religion while at the same time making concessions to it. However, upon closer examination, the Soviet government seemed to have both a short-term and a long-term plan for religion. For the present, the Soviets recognized that they needed to establish some kind of working relationship with the Church. They would be willing to grant the Church some allowances and rights in exchange for its loyalty. However, the Soviets did not lose sight of the long-term goal of eradicating religion—hence the intensification of the antireligious propaganda. The fifteenth party congress in 1927 signaled the beginning of the change in party policy toward the Church, when Stalin remarked that the weakening of the antireligious struggle needed to be overcome.[94] The end of NEP and the period of collectivization would indeed witness an intensification of antireligious policies and a return to the harsher methods prevalent during the civil war.

Like the Soviet government, the monasteries also had both a short- and a long-term plan for dealing with the antireligious policies of the Soviets. The short-term plan was to continue to seek legitimate means to keep their monastery communes open, even if that meant appearing to cooperate with the regime. They rightly perceived that the Soviet government would soon begin to react more harshly toward religion in general and monasticism in particular. They therefore began preparing for a time when they would have to go underground. This meant establishing a network of elders and eldresses and trusted laypeople to build "monasteries in the world." These men and women would form the bulwark of monasticism during the ruthless years of collectivization and the intensified antireligious campaign.

CHAPTER 4

The Good Friday of Russian Monasticism, 1928–1934

BY 1928 THE SOVIET UNION had reached another turning point. The previous decade had witnessed two revolutions, a change from a monarchy to an experimental form of governance based upon communist ideals, but strongly influenced by the experience of civil war and famine. The New Economic Policy (NEP) had been designed to rebuild the country and to restore faith in the ruling government. By 1928, however, many party officials believed that NEP had outlived its usefulness. The end of NEP signaled a turn toward a more authoritarian form of government that would have lasting consequences politically, socially, and economically.

The end of the New Economic Policy also signaled the end of the party's relatively temperate attitude toward religion. As discussed earlier, the twelfth and thirteenth party congresses displayed a more tolerant policy toward religion in general and the Orthodox Church in particular. In 1928 there were still differences within the party between the hard-and soft-liners about how to approach the question of religion. Stalin had previously allied himself with the moderates, deploring the excesses of the antireligious propaganda. However, by the beginning of 1929 he had consolidated power and was poised to pursue a more aggressive policy toward the Church. He foreshadowed this firmer policy earlier in 1927, when he stated publicly that "the Party cannot be neutral in its relations toward religion, and it will conduct antireligious propaganda against it." More ominously, he went on to say that the party could not oversee antireligious work until the "counterrevolutionary clergy" were all liquidated.[1]

The New Economic Policy, despite having achieved some notable successes, was proving problematic in many ways. Within the party there were objections over the future path of NEP. Should it be a short-term solution, or should it be the basis for the nation's long-term economic plan? If the latter, then the party leaders would have to sacrifice the ideal of building a socialist society, since in many ways NEP was contradictory to the ideology of socialism.

Aside from dogmatic disagreements over NEP, serious concerns about the economy remained. Although the agricultural sector recovered rapidly from the effects of the civil war and the famine, the industrial sphere lagged behind. The party needed to do something to bridge the disparity between these two areas. There was also the problem of uneven grain distribution between urban and rural areas. The problem was not that the harvest had been bad, but rather that the peasants were reluctant to turn over their produce to the state.[2] The party could have redressed this imbalance by using intelligent fiscal and market policies, but its dogmatic commitment to Marxist theory precluded taking that path. The result was the dual policy of collectivization and industrialization. These two methods would dominate the next decade and have a lasting effect on the nation. Perhaps the most important change involved the government's role in implementing these policies. Government planning became the third part of the Soviet trinity that was to totally change the relationship between state and society. In the words of Moshe Levin, the state "did more than just 'guiding': it substituted itself for society, to become the sole initiator of action and controller of all important spheres of life."[3]

The Great Turn, 1929–1930

The chief purposes of collectivization were to bring the peasants under state control, ensure a steady supply of grain to the cities and the army, and put an end to petit-bourgeois attitudes in the countryside. A secondary aim was to provide a market for industrialization.[4] The Russian countryside was still unmechanized and largely inefficient. More modern machinery would guarantee better harvests and cheaper produce. These goals would be achieved by consolidating the small, private peasant farms into large collective entities. Nobody would have any private property; homes, livestock, and equipment would all be held in common. Although collective farms had existed during the civil war, participation was strictly voluntary. As examined earlier, many monasteries made use of this trend and became very successful communes. The state-run farms, however, suffered from inefficiency and lack of skilled farmers. The Soviets felt that the solution to this imbalance lay in totally collectivizing all of the farms.

Peasants would be either persuaded or forced to join these new enterprises.

Collectivization had a social side as well. By bringing the peasant class under state control, it would be easier for the government to ensure that peasants would remain docile. For collectivization to succeed, a cultural revolution was needed to educate the "dark masses" in the countryside. The party needed to reeducate the peasants to think along communist lines. Despite the party's disdain for the peasants, they still made up almost ninety percent of the Russian population and remained a volatile social class. Of particular concern was the group of wealthier peasants referred to as the *kulaks*.[5] Stalin blamed them for the uneven food distribution between the cities and the countryside, and concluded that the only way to solve the problem was to dispossess this "parasitic group." Many kulaks also happened to be patrons of the Church. Because of their relative wealth, they contributed money to the parish church, were members of the parish councils, and in general were very important to rural religious life. The destruction of the kulak class therefore would also be a blow to the Church, as it would eliminate its chief financial support.

Along with collectivization, the Soviets also renewed their attacks against the Church. Aside from needing a scapegoat to blame when things did not go well, the Soviets also realized that if the kulaks were important to the Church, then the reverse was also true. The Church had a vested interest in encouraging the peasants to resist collectivization, since the new system would hurt it financially and politically by depriving the Church of its main source of income and local political support. Thus, a dual policy of anti-church measures and anti-kulak measures would eliminate all opposition and speed up the collectivization process.

Collectivization began slowly in 1928, and without any specific plan. The Komsomol[6] and other activists went to the countryside in great numbers. Their ostensible mission was to encourage the peasants to form collective farms and while doing so compel them to give up grain and livestock. They had another purpose as well, and that involved bringing "enlightenment" to the rural areas. The primary target of the Komsomol in this endeavor was the Church. Komsomol members viewed the Church as the source of backwardness in the countryside and used both coercion and brute force in order to stamp it out.

However, the attempt by the Soviets to place the blame on the Church and the kulaks backfired. Stalin's tactics were predicated on the fact that class struggle existed in the countryside and that the so-called *bedniaks* (poor peasants) and *sredniaks* (middle peasants) would approve of the authorities' actions against their "class enemy" and cooperate with them. The truth was that the "class warfare" among the peasants was largely mythical. The whole concept of dividing the peasantry into three separate subclasses was a Stalinist idea and did not reflect at all the actual situation in the countryside. The peasants themselves realized this, as an editorial to the newspaper *Krestianskaia gazeta* illustrates.[7] Although it is true that many poorer peasants envied and resented their richer counterparts, there was no spontaneous revolt against the kulaks. In fact, when the Komsomol manipulated the *skhod* (village assemblies) to banish kulaks from their midst, many poor and middle peasants defended them.[8]

Thus, the main result of attacking the kulaks was the further alienation of the majority of the peasantry, who were already opposed to losing their land and livestock. They viewed the collectivization policy as a second enserfment. The peasants well remembered the brutality of the civil war period and war communism, when the Bolsheviks forcibly took grain from them. Some Smolensk officials reported several peasants prophetically stating that "now they are confiscating bread from the kulak; tomorrow they will turn against the poor and middle peasant."[9] This cynicism is also explained by the fact that many of these kulaks had been poor peasants who had worked hard and taken advantage of NEP to better their positions. Peasants also deeply resented the government's simultaneous attack on the Church. Many of them tied collectivization to the antireligious campaign and refused to participate in a "Godless" enterprise.

Despite agitation in the countryside during 1928, the process of dekulakization did not begin until early 1929 and at first was conducted only sporadically. Not until May 1929 did the council of people's commissars announce a formal definition of a kulak. Only one of the following criteria was sufficient to designate one as a kulak: "1) hiring of permanent workers for agricultural work or artisan industry, 2) ownership of an industrial enterprise such as a flour mill, dairy, establishment or equipment for husking, for wool carding or combing, for making starch or potato flour, for drying fruit or vegetables, and so forth—but only if provided with an engine or water wheel, 3) the hiring out, permanently or seasonally, of complex agricultural machines driven by an engine, 4) the hiring out, permanently or seasonally, of equipped premises for dwelling or business purposes, 5) the presence of members in the family who are engaged in commerce or usury or who have other sources of income not derived from labor. *This last provision specifically includes ministers of cults*" (emphasis added).[10]

The problem was that almost any peasant could fit that definition of a kulak; at one point or another, almost any peasant would have hired out a machine or employed a person for seasonal labor or rented out part of his property to another person for money. This definition also affected the monastery communes that had until now been tolerated and in many cases even protected by the central authorities since most of the monastery communes relied on hired workers to perform some of the labor. Moreover, a central administrative order gave provincial authorities the power to determine which peasants were kulaks and what measures would be taken against them. Local antikulak acts frequently included increasing kulaks' taxes by three times the amount that other peasants paid. Failure to pay the required amount meant that local officials could impose heavy fines and take away the kulaks' property.

Aside from dispossessing the kulaks of their property, further measures included denying suffrage. Although this deprivation might appear unimportant since most peasants never voted, the fact was that being labeled a *lishenets* (deprived person) was noted in personal records. If a peasant wanted to move to a different part of the country, his record followed him and would hinder him from finding employment. Additionally, being deprived of voting rights frequently meant that other penalties were to follow, such as loss of lodging, food rations, and medical service and exile.

Although dekulakization had been taking place for a year on a local level, not until December, 1929, did Stalin announce that the total liquidation of the kulaks as a class was an official aim of the government, and not until February, 1930, did the party produce formal legislation specifying how the elimination of the kulaks was to occur. Ironically, by this time, the kulaks were already economically destroyed, as they had nothing else left to confiscate. Nevertheless, the ideology of class struggle that the Soviets propagated demanded that the kulaks be eradicated. To justify this policy, the Soviets broadened the definition of a kulak and the whole dekulakization process took on a life of its own.

New Position of Monasteries

In the battle for the countryside, the monasteries necessarily became targets of the Soviet collectivization campaign. By 1930 the authorities had closed all of the monasteries in the Soviet Union but one—Pskov-Pecherskaia, located in free Estonia. In examining the status of the monasteries during this period, one question stands out. Why were they unable to use collectivization to their advantage as they had in the past? As discussed earlier, during the civil war and through NEP, many times local and central authorities allowed and sometimes encouraged monastery collectives to remain open. They recognized that the monastery collectives were far too prosperous to close down and that local collectives were not advanced enough to replace monastery agriculture. They decided to allow the monastery communes to function until the communal farms grew stronger.

However, by 1928, compromise was not as much of an option as it had been in the past. This was mainly due to the stronger position of the government. During the revolution and civil war, the Bolsheviks were fighting for their very existence and needed to come to a modus vivendi with vestiges of the past, such as the Church. By 1928, however, the Bolsheviks were more secure in their power. In a report to the directors of the house of culture, Emelian Yaroslavsky stressed that the monasteries needed to be liquidated because of their influence and criticized the regime for allowing them to function as communes during the civil war. He also warned of the influence of former monks and nuns if something was not done to ensure their isolation.[11] Perhaps the best explanation for the change in the monasteries' position lies in the character of Iosif Stalin. In the case of the monasteries, Stalin was shrewd enough to recognize that if he allowed the monastery collectives to exist, they would be in direct competition with the kolkhozes. Because the monastery communes were obviously more efficient, they would highlight the Soviet farms' inferiority and attract more peasants. More important than economic rivalry, which was admittedly not as worrying, was the ideological competition that the monastery communes offered. Stalin did not and could not permit any struggle for authority in the countryside. Therefore, monastery communes must not continue to be allowed to exist.

Early signs of the monasteries' fate occurred during a politburo meeting in June, 1928. A new protocol stated that "the further liquidation of monasteries [is] vital for the aim of anti-religious propaganda." Therefore, members voted to establish a commission that would draw up measures for closing the monasteries. They stressed the need "to ensure that after the liquidation of the monasteries the monastery lands and buildings do not lie empty." The politburo also expressed concern over the fate of the displaced monastics, although not out of altruism. It claimed that monks and nuns were more dangerous when they were dispossessed than when they were in their monasteries. Itinerant monks and nuns were more likely to seek refuge with villagers and stir up sympathy and antisoviet feeling. The politburo therefore recommended that the government establish "settlements" where these monastics could live permanently and where the government could keep watch over them.[12]

One obstacle that the government faced in closing the monasteries was public feeling. Monasteries were a source of spirituality, especially in rural areas where the monasteries often served as the parish churches. Monks and nuns were not abstract ideas to the villagers, but rather were real people with whom they had close personal relationships. In addition, the monks often took their grievances to sympathetic foreign governments, particularly Britain. In 1931 a group of monks anonymously forwarded a copy of the new regulations regarding taxation of churches and detailed arrests and exile of priests and monks.[13] The Soviet government recognized that turning the monastics out of their residences would create ill will with the villagers. It attempted to counteract that with a propaganda campaign. In 1929 the antireligious journal *Bezbozhnik* published editorials allegedly written by peasants complaining of these "false" monastery kolkhozi. These letters may or may not have been genuine. *Bezbozhnik* frequently fabricated letters to the editor in order to further its antireligious point of view. All of these letters had several consistent themes. They accused the government of favoring the monasteries at the expense of the local peasants; they emphasized that the monastics had all been deprived of the right to vote and therefore should not have the right to own land; and finally, they demanded that these false communes be closed.

One letter discusses the status of a monastery in the village of Maino, Umianovskii okrug, that existed "under the pretext of a kolkhoz." The writer then criticized the Zemotdel (land department) for increasingly supporting the monks and neglecting the youth commune "Molodaia Gvardiia." The accusation was obvious; any government organization that allowed the monastery communes to function was doing so at the expense of "real" kolkhozi. The letter concluded by announcing that this travesty of justice had been remedied. A "special commission" had inspected the monastery kolkhoz and established that the monastery "had illegally appropriated the term 'working' and that its members had been deprived of voting rights long ago and that the main source of income was not farming, but rather was from religious services." The monastery commune was closed down on December 28, 1928. The property was then turned over to the Molodaia Gvardiia commune.[14]

Another letter echoes the preceding themes but is interesting for the detail of monastery communes that it provides. It is from the province of Saransk and describes a women's monastery that at the time of the revolution had three hundred desiatins of land.[15] Although the Bolsheviks officially nationalized it in 1919, they allowed the fifty-nine nuns to remain and the monastery to function as a "land society." By 1926 land tenure had been introduced that increased the nuns' holdings. The letter alleged that the local Zemotdel gave the nuns additional land at the expense of the peasants. However, this letter admits that some of the nuns in fact worked the land and were not "parasites." By 1927 someone—either the nuns or the Zemotdel—had sold the buildings of the monastery. But the purchasers immediately restored the buildings to the nuns for their own use. There was also a school in the monastery in which the nuns instructed the village schoolchildren.[16] Such statements illustrate the continuing ties between the villagers and the monasteries and suggest that wherever and however possible, peasants would help the monastics survive.

The 1929 Religious Laws

Not only did the Church lose its support base in the villages, but the Soviets enacted certain laws specifically designed to hurt it. The so-called April laws of 1929 proclaimed by the all-Russian central executive committee of Soviets (VTsIK) forbade religious organizations to organize mutual assistance funds, to materially aid church members, to organize meetings for women or children, to organize Bible or religious study, to organize handicraft groups, and to open libraries or medical societies. All clergy including monastics were also forbidden to participate in agricultural or business activities.[17] The purpose of these new laws was to undermine the Church's traditional role as a social institution. The Soviets wanted the people to depend only on the government for social services. Henceforth, the Church would concern itself only with conducting religious services. However, in a central standing commission of religious questions meeting, Tuchkov proposed that those priests and monastics who renounced their positions should be allowed to work in any position, except the military or the people's commissariat of enlightenment.[18] This proposal was accepted in a later meeting, and the laws were changed.[19]

At the same time, the authorities amended article 18 of the 1918 constitution. The original wording provided for "freedom of religious and antireligious propaganda." In May 1929 the new article read "freedom of religious worship and antireligious propaganda." The difference in wording may appear merely semantic, but upon closer examination, this slight change drastically alters the Church's position. In the original wording the Church had essentially equal footing with any other institution in terms of propaganda. The Church had been recognized as a distinct institution and had been allowed the freedom to spread its ideas. The amendment relegated the Church to the status of a subordinate body. It had permission to perform only religious services. The government was now the only institution that had the right to promote propaganda, whereas the Church could no longer retaliate and defend itself against ideological attacks. The commissariat of education also changed its policy regarding religion. Initially schools were required to conduct only nonreligious teaching. In 1929 a new statute specified that teachers conduct antireligious instruction. These two modifications of the law signaled that the government was about to go on the offensive in the war against religion.

Perhaps the most controversial antireligious decision that the Soviets made in 1929 involved removing church bells and melting them down for scrap metal. In order to further distance religion from the lives of people, Stalin prohibited churches in Moscow from ringing their bells. Since these bells no longer served a purpose, the government decided to put the metal to better use. In Moscow, for instance, the metal from bells was used to finish building an addition to the Lenin library. In other parts of Russia and Ukraine, the bells were ostensibly used to help the industrialization effort. The popular response to the bell removal campaign caught the Soviets off guard. They had calculated that it would not arouse much opposition. However, many villagers and some townspeople viewed the attempt to remove the bells as one more assault on their identity as Christian believers. There were many reports of people, particularly women, violently responding to party members taking the bells down. Stalin ordered that the removal be stopped but later renewed the project.[20]

"Storming the Heavens": The Renewal of the Antireligious Campaign

The League of the Godless assumed a large role in this renewed attack on religion. As mentioned earlier, the league originated during the NEP pe-

Bells, Optina Pustyn Monastery

riod and advocated eradicating religion through education. Emelian Yaroslavsky, the league's leader, did not approve of the violent methods used during the civil war. The league's second congress in 1929 officially adopted a moderate, culturalist policy. Specifically the league would focus on educational work, antireligious propaganda, and better training for antireligious workers. The league especially targeted women, who were widely perceived as more religious than men. The league devoted much time and effort to persuade women that the Church was exploiting them.[21] However, the league's relatively temperate approach would be tested with the promulgation of the 1929 laws and the harshness of dekulakization. One sign of this more aggressive approach appeared at the same 1929 conference when the league voted to add the word "militant" to its official name.

The league grew rapidly during this period. According to its own figures, membership rose from 100,000 in 1925 to 700,000 in 1929 and to 5 million in 1932.[22] However, despite these numbers, the league remained largely ineffective as an agent of atheism. Membership was usually nominal, and it was active only around major religious holidays. The general population displayed little interest in the league's secularization campaign, and it alienated those who believed that communism and religion were not mutually exclusive. Many rank-and-file party members still remained believers, albeit not always openly. However, one letter to Kalinin came from a Tambov party official who described himself as a "33 year old Christian-peasant" who had demonstrated his loyalty by fighting on the side of the Bolsheviks during the civil war. He defended his religious beliefs and effectively challenged anyone to prove that these beliefs made him a counterrevolutionary.[23] One anonymous letter to Kalinin expressed this frustration with the government's religious policy. Signed "one of many believing Russian people," the letter writer (most likely a woman) defended religion and religious believers. She claimed that there were millions of believers in Russia, and contrary to propaganda, many were from the working class. She also stated that "communism will never succeed if it does not get rid of atheism and a materialistic world view" and "without a higher power, it is impossible to build a new life."[24] Another letter from a member of the workers' union in Briansk guberniia pointed out that the party's antireligious measures were hurting the bedniaks and sredniaks, the two peasant groups whose interests the party claimed to represent.[25]

There are many explanations for the league's weakness, including factionalism within the league itself and overburdened antireligious workers. Perhaps the biggest reason, however, involved lack of support from the central party leadership. According to both regional league members and regional party officials, the central party bodies did not sufficiently promote their antireligious work. One example comes from the Iaroslavl guberniia in 1929. The local Godless group, attempting to close the Talgskii monastery, complained that "appropriate help is not rendered to local League organizations, which work extremely poorly without the party's assistance."[26]

This lack of patronage was further exacerbated by the inconsistent and contradictory orders to the league regarding how to conduct antireligious work. On the one hand, league members were told to intensify the campaign against churches. On the other hand, the party warned against actions that would alienate the peasants. A memo in May, 1929, from Tuchkov criticized local party organizations (which in effect included the league) for "underestimating the number of believers [which according to Tuchkov was eighty percent] . . . exaggerating the actual growth of religious sentiment among the peasantry, and they often rely excessively on antireligious and Komsomol organizations in the campaign against religious organizations. [The result is that] the closing of houses of worship is taking place in an erratic, chaotic way, ignoring directives of the party and Soviets and sometimes with total disrespect for objects of worship."[27] These mixed messages might be interpreted several ways. They could indicate that the party itself did not have a consistent plan for the execution of the antireligious campaign and that communication between local and central organs was often weak. They could also indicate that the central party officials were deliberately vague about their instructions so that they would have a scapegoat when people complained about the unrestraint of the antireligious campaign.

Evidence from the archives indicates that people complained, often vociferously. These complaints took the form of letters to powerful officials protesting the actions of the antireligious campaign. Kalinin was the most popular official to write to, not only because of his (mostly nominal) position as president of the Soviet Union, but also because he was widely regarded as a sympathetic and moderate figure. One group of villagers from the village of Mangusha in the Ukraine wrote to Kalinin complaining of the behavior of a group of Komsomols who had destroyed the local church and mercilessly beaten many of the villagers, including the elderly and children. This letter asked for protection and punishment for the offenders.[28]

The desire for a scapegoat was certainly evident in Stalin's "dizzy with success" speech in March, 1930. In this famous speech Stalin blamed local party officials for the "excesses" of the collectivization campaign. Hard on the heels of "dizzy with success," the central committee passed a new resolution, "on the struggle against distortions of the party line in the collective farm movement." This statement claimed that there were "inadmissible distortions of the Party line in the battle against religious prejudices. . . . There can be no doubt that such practices carried out under the flag of the 'leftists' provide grist for the mill of counter revolutionaries and have nothing in common with the Policy of our Party."[29] The resolution also prohibited any church closings unless "an overwhelming number of the population" agreed to it. Even then the oblast executive committee would have to confirm the decision. League workers in the provinces also complained that the central authorities often reversed church closings in response to peasant petitions.[30] Instances like these illustrate the continuing ambiguity of the Soviet government. Despite its resolve to totally obliterate religion, the regime realized that it could not completely disregard the attitudes of the people, particularly the peasants.

Resistance to Collectivization and the Antireligious Campaign

During the initial period of collectivization, peasants used both active and passive resistance to the government's policy. Reports of armed peasant attacks against Komsomol and party members frequently appeared in the press, although at that stage these disturbances could not be described as mass rebellion. Instances of large-scale passive resistance were more common than violence. The situation was severe; by 1930 the kulaks had lost thirty to forty percent of their means of production.[31] By 1931 the government had exiled (or "relocated," in Soviet parlance) 356,544 kulak families, totaling 1,679,528 people. Common places of exile included Kazakhstan, the Urals, and Siberia.[32]

Kulaks devised ways to circumvent the government by putting land in their poorer relatives' names, selling their crops to poor peasants at low prices, or selling to illegal private traders. The most common method of avoiding turning grain over to the state was burying it, either on private property or in the forests. Church property was also a favorite hiding place, which provided the Communists with another reason to raid churches and monasteries. Kulaks were not the only people to engage in this antigovernment behavior. Middle and poor peasants, including those living on collective farms, used the same tactics to evade official grain collection. When these methods did not work, they would turn their crop into hay, burn it, or throw it into the river.[33] These extreme measures illustrate the extent to which the peasants were alienated from the state.

When discussing resistance to collectivization, many history textbooks emphasize the peasants' desire to retain control over their land and its produce. This was true, but in their petitions to the government, the peasants made clear that they were not only protesting the economic policies of the government but were also against the state's attempts to destroy religion. A government report described the nature of the peasant responses as varying according to region. In those areas that were heavily targeted for grain procurement, peasant demonstrations focused mainly on the difficulty of obtaining food. In areas where church closings were common, the peasants "support faith, religion, the old way of life; and almost everywhere, they are against collectivization, against new forms of land distribution, [and] against the social restructuring of the countryside."[34]

Until recently, when discussing peasant resistance to the Soviet regime, Western historiography has focused mainly on the more extreme methods that clergy and laity used to combat Soviet policy, such as riots and sabotage. However, new research indicates that the clergy and the peasants increasingly used more politically sophisticated techniques. As they did during NEP, rural clergy relied on the village assemblies and the village soviets, both of which were hostile toward collectivization, to stave off church closings. One government report from May, 1929, complained that the kulaks "are beginning to adopt more sophisticated, openly counter-revolutionary tactics in the form of mass demonstrations, frequently connecting these demonstrations against the ongoing campaign to close churches. As a result, this network of underground kulak groups, which has already made its presence felt in the Soviet election campaign, today has resurfaced with impudent mass demonstrations with corresponding slogans and demands."[35]

In one example peasants from the village of Mikhailovskii staged an anticollectivization rebellion. This "mob of kulaks" ruled the village for the next two days, during which they called a meeting of the villagers, attended by nine hundred people, seven hundred of whom were women. They adopted a platform that included abolishing all existing collectives and restoring property rights and voting rights to all (including priests).[36] Elsewhere many peasants wrote letters to members of the government. One letter from Riazan' guberniia addressed to Stalin himself was particularly outspoken. The writer specifically blamed Stalin and other leaders "for all those comrades, i.e. members of society, who languish in jails, poverty, and back-breaking labor. You impede the march of life toward communism. You don't allow discussions of the concerns of the working masses with you by their representatives, who come to the capital to see the leaders."[37]

Government Response

The government faced an awkward situation in terms of how to respond to this popular resistance. On the one hand it had to suppress any opposition in order to reassert authority and deter others from rebelling. On the other hand, if the authorities acted too brutally, they risked provoking the peasants so severely that the country might degenerate into another civil war. In areas where unrest was particularly acute, local authorities expressly forbade using military force against the kulaks.[38] However, special brigades of soldiers designed to force peasants to collectivize already existed. Membership in these brigades was voluntary, and they were composed mainly of party or Komsomol members. Under control of the OGPU, not the military, their identities were kept secret for fear of retaliation from their fellow soldiers.

This fear reveals a fact that Soviet military historians have previously been reluctant to admit. Recent archival evidence shows, however, that Red Army soldiers were not as reliable in either the collectivization or the antireligious campaigns as had been thought. Soldiers who joined collective farms under duress were usually disillusioned with the lack of organization and the corruption that accompanied them. Many left the kolkhozi, and many more simply refused to join. In his recent work on the Red Army, Roger Reese discusses the boldness of many soldiers in their criticism of collectivization.[39] Soldiers often physically threatened their comrades who displayed procollectivization feelings. In one case soldiers attempted to murder their party cell leader in a dispute over dekulakization.[40]

Soldiers often displayed similar hostility toward the antireligious campaign. Most recruits came from villages, where the church was the center of everyday life. When these peasant-soldiers returned home on leave, they frequently participated in church activities. The League of the Militant Godless knew this and therefore placed considerable importance on work within the army. Yaroslavksy wrote an article discussing a particular incident involving a young Red Army soldier from the peasant class. Yaroslavsky claimed that the monasteries in particular exerted an influence over the peasants, as they had this boy. However, when the youth attended a relic exposure, he expressed anger at the Church for having deceived him and declared himself an atheist.[41] The message was clear; religious sentiment still lingered in the Red Army, and only the league's propaganda could eradicate it. The truth of the matter was that, like peasants, some soldiers actively resisted the league's attempts to make them atheists and continued to practice Christianity secretly. According to official army estimates, the average army division composed of 6,000 to 8,500 men contained from 4,500 to 6,500 believers.[42] Many peasants also protested the government's ending exemptions from the army for religious reasons. Kalinin received many letters protesting this policy and in general defending the place of religion in the countryside.[43]

Urban Monasticism

Even though the regime was closing many of the monasteries during this time, there were still opportunities for monastics to continue their way of life. As seen in the earlier examples, rural monastics often had the support of the village assemblies as well as individual peasants to help them preserve the communities. The closeness and the supposed religiosity of the peasants would appear to give rural monastics an advantage over their urban counterparts. However, according to some personal accounts, the life

Danilov Monastery, Moscow

of urban monastics could be easier. City life offered more opportunities for anonymity, even in a society that required an internal passport. It was also easier for former monastics to find work in a factory or a school. Moscow in particular offered a haven for clandestine monastic life because the Soviets often exiled bishops there so they could better keep watch over them. These bishops obtained their own apartments, which served as meeting places for local religious people. As well, many monastics who had been turned out of their monasteries came to these bishops for spiritual guidance.[44]

The last monastery in Moscow to close was Danilov monastery. The

Don Monastery, Moscow

official residence of the patriarch, Danilov had long occupied a prestigious position in Moscow. This monastery was also a favorite haven for both lay people and former monastics. Many laypeople who went there for services stayed and became monastics. When Danilov closed in 1930 and became a prison for children of "enemies of the people," the remaining monks either found their own apartments or lived in the homes of nearby parishioners. Nun Anna tells of one particular tradesman named Alexei Mikhailovich, in whose home many monks found refuge.[45] People who allowed monks and nuns to live in their homes did so at great risk to their professions and even their lives. If caught, they could become lishentsy or face exile or imprisonment.

Novodevichy Monastery, Moscow

Despite the hardship that monks and nuns faced during these years, there was also "a spiritual blooming of monasticism," according to A. E. Levitin-Krasnov, who was a "monk in the world." That is, he lived as a monk but was never formally tonsured. His account of religious life in Leningrad gives valuable insight into how urban monastics preserved their communities. Levitin-Krasnov was born in Moscow but spent much of his youth in Leningrad. One of his favorite monastic worship sites was the Novodevichy women's monastery.[46] As late as 1930, nuns were still living there, although the monastery was officially closed. The chapels remained open, and the remaining nuns (ninety, as opposed to the prerevolutionary number of six hundred) conducted their lives as usual. Levitin-Krasnov claims that monasticism was at its finest during this period, despite or maybe because of the persecution that the monks and nuns endured. "Semi-legal, constrained on all sides, expecting to be arrested at any minute, monasticism at this time differed because of the purity of its life. All mercenary, unscrupulous people had left monasticism."[47] Others also spoke of a deepening spirituality in the midst of persecution. Mother Serafima describes the pilgrims coming to Diveevo women's monastery in central Russia as especially devout and strongly connected to monasticism. The physical hardships and the danger involved discouraged any casual visitors.[48]

All Saints Church and Monastery, Moscow

Secret Monasticism

As mentioned earlier, the closure of monasteries led to the phenomenon of "monasteries without walls" and "monasticism in the world." There were two types of secret monastics. Those like Levitin-Krasnov, who desired the monastic life and would often obtain the blessing of a bishop or elder to lead a monastic life while outwardly living a secular lifestyle. They tried to follow the monastic vows and prayer life. They never actually took monastic vows, and many times they returned to the secular world and sometimes even married. Some went on to have successful careers. This was the case with Nina Frolovna, a well-known and respected Moscow surgeon who along with her sister was a secret nun. They sheltered three eldresses in their apartment during this period.[49] Another such monastic was the aforementioned Mother Ignatii. Such women and men were often able to use their professional success and social prestige to their advantage and thus escape detection.

The other type of secret monastics received secret tonsure and immediately severed all contacts with the outside world. They left their families and lived as virtual hermits. This latter group was composed mainly of young women.[50] Some of these young secret monastics made their decision with the blessing and knowledge of their parents. Others, such as Nun Anna and Levitin-Krasnov, came from nonbelieving households and either ran away to join a monastery or lived a secret life away from their families. Many secret monastics did not tell their families in order to protect them. As the Soviets closed more monasteries and as it became increasingly dangerous to go to churches and meet with priests and bishops, many young men and women who aspired to the monastic life formed their own societies and met secretly. There they would pray, read religious literature, and gain courage from each other. Mother Serafima, however, was ordered by her spiritual father, a bishop, never to speak of her monastic life with anyone. She never involved herself in any religious circles and remained alone except for her conversations with her spiritual father. Occasionally she would go to Sergeev Posad and visit some of the remaining monks who lived there. She was ordained a deaconess and had contact with other deaconesses when she went to church but never spoke with them or cultivated any relationships with them outside of church.[51] When asked whether the need for secrecy ever made her feel isolated or lonely, she replied that this secret was "her deepest happiness."[52]

Although being a monastic in the world was the most common form of secret monasticism, other monks and nuns established secret monasteries in caves or forests. After serving a prison sentence for "counterrevolutionary activities," abbess Antonina of Kizliar took twelve nuns and went to the town of Tuapse, where she founded a secret monastery in the mountains. News of this haven spread through the underground monastic network, and soon many nuns who were escaping persecution joined Abbess Antonina's group. In the same area were also fourteen monks who lived and worshiped in nearby caves and helped the nuns survive. When they were discovered by the secret police in 1927, most of the nuns and monks were immediately shot. As the leader, abbess Antonina was arrested and taken away. Her exact fate remains unknown.[53]

Abbess Rufina from Perm guberniia also kept alive the tradition of monasticism after she and the other nuns were evicted from their monastery during the civil war. The nuns from the former Ioanno-Bogoslovskii monastery formed the Bogoroditsa Smolenskii travelers' society. They became itinerants, moving from place to place and living with sympathetic laypeople. They finally emigrated to China in the late 1920s.[54] Evgenia Cheliabinskaia, also a nun from Perm, managed to avoid arrest until 1931, when she was captured and sent to Kazakhstan. She had been secretly meeting with other nuns in an apartment, which the authorities surveyed after being informed by a neighbor.[55]

Monks and nuns who had been dispossessed from their monasteries often gathered at people's homes to meet and conduct services. However, this could be risky, so they also began meeting in cemeteries. One group of nuns bought a house near a cemetery in Sergeev Posad so they could be close to their new "place of worship."[56] There was less chance of getting caught, and if the militia did come, they could scatter easily or pretend that they were visiting graves of friends or relatives. In Leningrad there were several spiritual "circles" that met in graveyards. Typically, members designated one grave to serve as a meeting place. In Leningrad it was either the grave of hieromonk Alexios or the grave of Alexander I before he was transferred to Peter and Paul fortress. A lamp was always kept burning before these graves, and pilgrims would often come there to light lamps and pray.[57] This practice of using graves as informal churches harkened back to the days of early Christianity, when persecuted Christians met in the catacombs to pray and gain strength. In many ways Christianity had come full circle—from tombs to elaborate cathedrals and back to tombs.

The "Good Friday" of Russian Monasticism: February 18, 1932

The relative calm that existed in the cities ended abruptly on the night of February 18, 1932. On that night, "all of Russian monasticism" was arrested and put into labor camps, signaling the beginning of a two-year repression. Although the monasteries had all been closed two years previously, dispossessed monks and nuns had not been subject to arrest on a massive scale. Arrests had occurred throughout the first five-year plan, but they were mainly sporadic. This was the first time that a systematic sweep of monastics occurred.

The question as to why the authorities chose 1932 to engage in mass arrests may be explained by the famine. This year was particularly brutal, and the monastics, as "parasites," served as convenient targets. In Leningrad alone, 316 monks and nuns were arrested and exiled to various labor camps throughout the Soviet Union.[58] Mass executions of clergy also occurred with regularity. In Rostov 120 monks and clergy were executed in 1932. In July of 1933, a scientific expedition near Irkutsk reported seeing a column of sixty men, all priests and monks, being marched to a forest. The soldiers asked each one, "Is there a God?" The scientists reported hearing the prisoners reply, "Yes, there is a God," followed by the sound of a gunshot.[59] At the height of this repression, Leningrad began a rampage of church closings—355 in one year.[60] This was partly due to the League of the Godless's declaration of a "five-year antireligious plan" that it claimed would "remove God from the territory of the Soviet Union" by May 1, 1937.[61]

The most common crime with which the Soviets charged monastics was "counterrevolutionary activity." This accusation encompassed a wide range of activity and usually meant that clergy were arrested merely on the basis of their occupation. Some, such as Mother Sofia of Raiskii monastery in Kazan, were arrested for operating secret monasteries.[62] In Perm, Archimandrite Tavrion was arrested for operating a secret school for children and blaming the Soviet government for poor agricultural conditions.[63] In Kozelsk in 1933, authorities arrested an unspecified number of monks and sent them to Marinskii labor camp in Novosibirsk.[64]

Exile and Prison

In keeping with the Soviets' desire to control the whereabouts of the newly dispossessed monks and nuns, they often incarcerated them in prisons and forced-labor camps. Two common destinations were Kazakhstan and Siberia. Despite their exile, monks and nuns were still able to keep a sense of community and even maintain contact with their fellow monastics who remained free. Nun Anna, living in Moscow, described how she and her friends, all secret nuns, would gather in the evenings at various train stations. They recognized the different trains that carried people into exile. For example, if a train had lattice on it, it was a "black crow" train; that is, it was carrying mainly monks and nuns. They would meet these trains and find out from the exiled monks and nuns what was occurring in other areas of Russia and then report back to the bishops in

Moscow.[65] This informal network made it possible to better gauge the government's methods and to prepare for coming situations.

Monks and nuns described the sense of community that often developed in exile. Young women and men who either aspired to be monastics or had already taken secret vows sometimes voluntarily went into exile with their spiritual elders to provide comfort and assistance. This was the case with two young women, Nina, aged 20, and Nastya, aged 24. They were part of a Moscow community of religious young women who attended services at church and the remaining monasteries whenever possible. When their mentor, Bishop Augustine, was arrested and sent into exile, they decided to go with him. He later said that he would have perished had they not been with him. Despite the hardship of exile, the three reported that it was not all bad because they had the companionship of other priests and monastics.[66] Some monastics found relief from the horrors of exile with sympathetic villagers. Such was the case with Mother Fomara, who lived with a peasant man and his son in their cottage during her three-year Siberian exile. Without their assistance, Mother Fomara, who was quite elderly, would not have survived her sentence.[67] Imprisoned clergy in Moscow described workers giving them a basket of eggs one year on Easter.[68]

The labor camps also provided opportunities for the monastics to preserve their communities despite harsh conditions. Camp officials typically singled out the religious prisoners in the camps for especially brutal treatment. Aleksandr Solzhenitsyn described how the religious prisoners were favorite candidates for the penalty compound, where they received the harshest labor. They kept whole barracks of "nuns" there who "had refused to do the devil's work" and for punishment held them in a penalty block up to their knees in water.[69] Religious women prisoners, especially nuns, were also frequently sexually assaulted by male and female guards. Solzhenitsyn commented, "we overlooked the fact that the sinful Orthodox Church had nonetheless nurtured daughters worthy of the first centuries of Christianity."[70]

However, even in this atmosphere of suffering and despair, monastics were able to meet and in some cases conduct services clandestinely. One account describes how a group of nuns at Butyrki prison in Moscow managed to celebrate Easter service while in prison. They dressed in white, set up a makeshift altar on an old decaying table, and sang the Easter hymns at midnight.[71] The continuation of these church rituals in prison helped to preserve a sense of normality despite the surroundings. It also proved inspirational to many regular prisoners in the camps. Sometimes nonbelievers who were in the camps sought out the monks and nuns for comfort and wisdom. Some, such as the wife of one of the camp bosses, converted to Christianity.[72] There were also many cases of secret tonsure.

Solovki

One of the first labor camps was located in Solovki monastery, near the White Sea. As mentioned earlier, a few of the resident monks were allowed to stay there even after it was turned into a prison camp. They were totally evicted in 1937. Many monks and nuns as well as priests and hierarchs were sentenced there as well, especially after the new round of monastery closings in 1928. Figures provided by the émigré church estimate that about 425 Orthodox clergy (including nuns) were in Solovki camp alone.[73] Despite the harsh conditions, Church life in the camps did not escape the influence of Church politics. The schism between supporters of Metropolitan Sergei and the Catacomb Church existed in the camps as well. Although hierarchs and clergy from both sides were sent to the camps, the émigré church still accused Metropolitan Sergei of ordering the arrest of opposition clergy despite the lack of any evidence.

The policy of holding religious services at Solovki changed throughout the years. Accounts from the years 1924 and 1925 state that religious services on Sundays and other holy days were forbidden. On major holidays such as Christmas and Easter, the workload was doubled to try to break the believers' spirit. However, beginning in 1925, camp authorities allowed clergy to conduct services in the cemetery near the fortress. These services were well attended, especially on holidays.

Of all of the religious holidays, Easter was the most celebrated in the camps. Easter is the holiest day in the Orthodox calendar. With its message of resurrection after death, it had an especially poignant meaning for those Orthodox clergy who were incarcerated. They had already experienced the death on "Good Friday" and were currently enduring the "descent into hell" through living in the camps. They believed that the resurrection of religion and monasticism would naturally follow. Personal accounts of Easter at Solovki emphasize this feeling of hope. Several describe their Easters on Solovki as the most spiritual experiences of their lives.[74]

This feeling extended even to nonbelievers. G. Andreev, a political prisoner on Solovki from 1927 to 1929 described Easter as a day when "it was impossible to have an empty and cold soul." In 1929 the authorities strictly forbade anyone except the monks and the higher clergy from conducting church services. Even so, Andreev managed to go to the Easter service that year and said that he had never before experienced a more meaningful Easter service.[75] I. M. Andreev, a prisoner in Solovki and also a doctor, described a secret Easter service that he went to in 1930. There were only ten people, including two nuns, and they whispered the entire service. Andreev and three other doctors were present at the service. When the guard came by at 4:00 A.M., after the service had just ended, the doctors pretended that they were treating the bishop.[76] Every account of Easter services on Solovki mentions that the priests and monks were even able to somehow procure the traditional Easter foods—eggs, lamb, wine for communion, and kulich, the traditional Easter bread.[77]

Some of the monks and priests received permission to conduct "reeducation" work among the prisoners. This included bringing them literature (doubtless after being approved by the camp authorities) and trying to instill a sense of morality in them. On the whole, priests and monks reported success in their endeavors.[78] One starets, Father Tavrion Batozsky, spent almost thirty years in camps, prisons, and internal exile, beginning in 1925. Before his death in 1978, he spoke of his time in prison as an opportunity to minister to people: "If you only knew how grateful I am to God for my wonderful life! Imagine, the good Lord had entrusted such a responsible pastoral work among prison inmates to me when I was still so young [27 at the time of his first arrest in 1925]. If I had not landed in the camps, how many people would never have heard the word of God!"[79]

Such instances reveal the paradoxes of the Soviet approach to religion. The Soviets sent these priests and monks to the labor camps for preaching and conducting religious services. Then they allowed and sometimes even encouraged these clergy to do the same things in the camps that they arrested them for in the first place. The Soviets later apparently became aware of this contradiction, as they stopped allowing clergy to work among the prisoners. However, this seemingly contradictory action on the part of the camp authorities in fact benefited them somewhat. By using the clergy to keep the criminals calm, the guards' jobs were made easier.

At the end of 1933, the defeat of monasticism and Orthodoxy seemed imminent. The monastery communes that had allowed monastics to preserve their communities ceased to exist, and the mass arrests and imprisonment of monastics in 1932 appeared to signal the destruction of monasticism. Despite the devastation, however, monasticism persevered. All of these stories illustrate the ingenuity that monks and nuns developed to preserve their sense of community during this period and underscore the true spirit of monasticism. Monasticism is a lifestyle based upon deep religious commitment and is independent of an institution. The Soviets could close all of the monasteries, but they could never eradicate their essence so long as monastics continued to exist. Despite the arrests and executions, the ranks of monasticism continued to be filled. This spirit of adaptation and courage would enable monasticism to survive the purges of 1937 to 1939.

CHAPTER 5

The Descent into Hell, 1934–1939

WITH THE END of the famine in 1933, another apparent thaw in the relationship between state and society occurred. Some contemporary observers such as Nicholas Timasheff refer to this period as "the Great Retreat," or the "Second NEP." According to this interpretation, Stalin realized that the population was not ready for drastic changes and therefore pursued a more moderate course.[1] The degree to which this assertion is valid is debatable. Certainly there was a noticeable ideological shift in the Soviet Union after the period of collectivization. The second five-year plan set more realistic goals, and the party abandoned its earlier rhetoric favoring class warfare. Agriculture was slowly starting to recover, and more traditional social values reappeared. Old bourgeois features of Soviet life reemerged, and Soviet high art and cinema adopted many qualities of old Russian culture.

The "Great Retreat," 1933–1935

The most conspicuous change in the government's new "detente" came with the change in the internal security organs. The party disbanded the old OGPU and in its place established the NKVD (people's commissariat of internal affairs) and imposed limitations on it in order to protect individual liberties. In 1934 officials disbanded the *troiki*, three-person field courts, and a resolution of people's commissars and the party's central committee detailed proper arrest procedures. Included in these guidelines was a prohibition on arresting anyone without the permission of the "appropriate procurator" and without sufficient evidence.[2] It appeared that Soviet society was moving more towards regular judicial procedures.

The government displayed a more tolerant approach even toward religion. Although the authorities did not reopen any churches or monasteries or release many clergy, neither did they embark upon new massive antireligious campaigns or engage in more mass arrests. On the contrary, the central standing commission on religious questions (CSCRQ, henceforth referred to as the "cult commission") often played the role of mediator between state and society. It tried to follow the will of the Communist Party, while abandoning the harsher antireligious policies of the collectivization period.[3] There was also a marked decrease in the number of antireligious articles in the press during this time.

This more relaxed approach encouraged many believers to take a more assertive role in church-state relations. This new outspokenness may be seen in one anonymous quote from Leningrad: "[I]n this year (1934) we must not only stick to our position, but also restore some of the rights illegally taken away from the church." Believers often wrote letters to the local and central authorities condemning the closure of churches and asking them to restore the churches to the believers. They used a tactic that had benefited them in the past: quoting the communists' rhetoric and laws to their advantage and appealing to the idea of justice. One letter argued that "churches are being closed and nothing is being given in return." Another letter claimed that persecution of religion went against foreign policy: "Litvinov told [U.S. President Franklin D.] Roosevelt that there is no persecution of the clergy in the USSR, while the GPU arrests the best priests simply because they have conscientiously fulfilled their pastoral duty and worked on the spiritual development of believers."[4]

The central authorities sensed the mood of the people and sometimes ruled in favor of believers. One example may be found in a letter from a member of the cult commission to the all-Russian central executive committee (VTsIK). In this letter the atheist member of the cult commission requests the VTsIK to reverse an earlier decision prohibiting a group of believers from using a local monastery church to meet. The letter protested that the Kolotskoi monastery church served several villages and using another location would deprive the people of their right to gather and worship. The VTsIK granted this petition and allowed the believers to worship at the former monastery.[5] It appeared that the Soviet Union was poised to experience a second NEP. This change of policy encouraged other countries, including the United States, to establish formal relations with the world's first Communist country.

Despite all of these examples of a "great retreat," there are also signs that this retreat was partly an illusion. Historians such as Arto Luukkanen, Sarah Davies, and Stephen Kotkin argue against Timasheff's conception of a Great Retreat, although they acknowledge that there was a temporary return to more traditional values. Kotkin asserts that Stalinism as a whole "far from being a partial retreat let alone a throwback to the Russian past, remained forward looking and progressive throughout."[6]

Luukkanen, although referring to the period 1933–1935 as "the good years of the 1930s," points out that the signs that the government was relaxing its antireligious stance need to be viewed with caution. As an example, he cites the fact that the number of complaints from believers to the cult commission declined significantly during the period 1933–1935. This could be interpreted as proving that the government's religious policies were in line with the will of the people. However, Luukkanen also states that one may interpret this reduction in petitions as evidence of frustration among the believers. If the government was intent on destroying religion, then there was no sense in complaining.[7]

It is also important to remember that during this period of detente, the Communist Party experienced another *chistka,* or purge. Beginning in 1932 many party members were stripped of their membership. This early "cleansing" was relatively lenient and not accompanied by arrest and imprisonment, as took place during the later purges of 1936–1938. However, it was an indication of things to come. Also, Luukkanen underscores the dilemma of the party in its religious policy during the "good years." On the one hand, the Stalinist leadership "wanted to consolidate its political mandate among ordinary people and favored a more moderate policy in relation to old traditional values." On the other hand, the government "was gradually tightening its political grip on newly established collective farms, factories and plants."[8]

In addition, as early as 1933 the internal security organs were already active, announcing discoveries of "nests of sabotage" in collective farms and factories. There were also complaints that religion continued to exist on the kolkhozi and that churches were camouflaging themselves behind "communist forms of slogans and languages."[9] Yaroslavsky warned against the party's being too complacent in the fight against religion, stating that "religion and religious organizations are up to this moment a risk for the working class and peasantry."[10] Peasants and women were still considered "weak" and more subject to the influence of religion and needed to be closely monitored.

Most important, during these "good years," an event occurred that would totally change the course of Soviet history. In 1934 Leningrad party leader Sergei Kirov was assassinated under questionable circumstances. Stalin blamed "counterrevolutionaries" for the murder; however, some historians believe that it was Stalin who ordered the murder of the popular party leader, who was widely believed to be a threat to Stalin's position as general secretary. This murder would provide the pretext for Stalin to carry out purges, first against the party and then against the general population.

The 1936 Constitution

The apparent "thaw" of the relationship between the Soviet state and society appeared to reach its climax in 1936 with the promulgation of the new constitution, also referred to as the "Stalin Constitution." This document was hailed as proof that the Soviet Union was the most democratic and just nation in the world. Much attention has been devoted to this constitution, leading the unwary reader to suspect that it was a radical departure from previous constitutions. In reality, the 1936 constitution did not significantly change any of the fundamental governmental principles of the regime already established by the earlier constitutions of 1918 and 1924. The Communist Party was still the only legal political party permitted, while the "fundamental freedoms" of speech, press, and assembly were again guaranteed. Subsequent events demonstrated just how meaningless these liberties really were.

Why then did the Congress of Soviets decide to write a new constitution? In a speech to the Extraordinary Eighth Congress of Soviets of the USSR on November 25, 1936, Stalin stated that the necessity for a new constitution arose from changes in the Soviet Union that had transpired since the previous constitution of 1924. He defined that document as a "program" outlining the goals of the Soviet Union in completing the socialist revolution. Stalin affirmed that by 1936 the nation had changed and the "experiment of forming a multinational state based on socialism has been completely successful. Therefore, a new constitution would speak of what already exists, of what has already been achieved and won now, at the present time."[11]

Another explanation for Stalin's desire for a new constitution is that it camouflaged the purges, which had begun in 1935 and would reach their bloody climax in 1937. The generous language of the constitution and its guarantees of the right to work, freedom of religion, and broadening of the electoral public was designed to show Stalin and the Soviet government in a benevolent light. The constitution was also intended to illustrate the superiority of communism over fascism, which was rapidly gaining strength in Germany, Spain, and Italy.

Despite the fact that the Stalin constitution in many ways affirmed the power and prominence of the Soviet state, certain elements represented a radical departure from previous political practices. One was its very public nature. After the committee was appointed to draw it up, the central executive committee announced that the constitution would be submitted for nationwide discussion. This was an unprecedented occurrence; usually Soviet laws were drafted and promulgated, often in secret, with no possibility for debate. The Soviet public responded with enthusiasm to these public deliberations. An estimated 36.5 million Soviet citizens attended these meetings. They submitted a total of 154,000 proposed amendments to the constitution, only 43 of which were adopted.[12]

A further notable feature of the 1936 constitution was the inclusion of several amendments that heralded significant changes from previous Soviet policy. The amendments that are discussed here concern religion. In reviewing the draft constitution, Stalin remarked on several amendments and additions that he felt needed to be added. He stated that the amendment to article 124, prohibiting religious rites, should be rejected because it "ran counter to the spirit of our Constitution." He also rejected the proposed amendment to article 135, which disenfranchised all ministers of religion, former White Guards, and all former rich people and persons "not engaged in socially useful occupations." As an explanation, Stalin stated that Soviet law disenfranchised the "non-working elements" only temporarily, when they "waged open war" against the Soviet state. Now, however, the Soviet government had crushed the opposition and become "an invincible force." In response to concerns that the former White Guards and priests would "worm their way into the supreme bodies of the country," Stalin replied, "What is there to be afraid of? In the first place, not all of the former kulaks, priests, White Guards are hostile to the Soviet government. In the second place, if the people in some places do elect hostile persons, it shows that our propaganda work was very badly organized and we shall fully deserve such a disgrace. If however, our propaganda work is conducted in a Bolshevik way the people will not let hostile persons slip into their supreme bodies."[13]

To legitimize his position Stalin quoted a 1919 speech of Lenin's, in which he stated that "the time was not far distant when the Soviet government would deem it useful to introduce universal suffrage without any restrictions."[14]

These remarks clearly indicate that Stalin regarded the removal of voting restrictions and allowing former *lishentsy* to run for public office as a demonstration of the Soviet Union's success in eradicating religion's influence over the Soviet people. As a preceding chapter notes, being branded a lishenets was a very serious matter. Not only could one not participate in political life, but one was also barred from certain jobs and even forbidden to live in certain areas. The threat of arrest was also very real. Many petitions to Kalinin and other members of the government consistently requested the return of their civil rights. The government was very liberal in branding someone a nonperson. In the city of Moscow alone, there were more than ninety thousand lishentsy.[15] Stalin was confident that Soviet society had evolved to the point that citizens would reject these former enemies of the state. President Kalinin seconded this plan, stating in an interview that "In giving the right to vote to our opponents . . . we are giving them the responsibility to participate in society."[16] The only way to prove to the world that the Soviet Union represented the most perfect form of government was to hold truly free elections.

The implications of these changes were enormous and caused great controversy both within the party and within the Church. Other members of the party were outraged when they heard of Stalin's plans not only to enfranchise clergy but also to allow them to run as candidates in local and national elections. There were also questions about how this would affect the current legal position of the Orthodox Church. Would this nullify the 1929 laws governing how church societies could operate?[17] In a surprisingly critical article, Emelian Yaroslavsky wrote against this idea of restoring political rights to clergy. He reminded the reader that the clergy are not workers but parasites and that they are "class enemies or agents of class enemies" and therefore do not deserve voting rights. He warned that the clergy could use the right to vote against the workers and peasants: "We don't need to give the church the ability to influence the government, business, or school." Although he did not believe that the new constitution would weaken the antireligious campaign, Yaroslavsky believed that it would interfere with antireligious propaganda and "strengthen religious fanaticism."[18] Kalinin himself also expressed concern that even though the constitution did not protect the rights of religious societies, it satisfied the demands of believers and alleviated the work of the clergy.

He also warned that the article allowing religious societies to meet without the permission of the authorities deprived the government of the legal right to control those societies' activities.[19]

Another interesting aspect of this voting amendment is that it appeared to go against the wishes of many of the Soviet citizenry. As J. Arch Getty observes, the majority of the proposals that citizens had submitted to the committee were in favor of retaining the clause in the constitution depriving certain classes of the right to vote. When the idea of restoring the lishentsy's political rights was discussed, the majority of the Soviet people's response was decidedly negative, especially in rural areas.[20] According to this interpretation then, by adopting this amendment, Stalin was not retreating from Marxist ideology in the face of hostile public opinion, as the government had done in the past. Rather, he was going against the prevailing current of public opinion. However, one must use caution when reading the supposed results of these surveys. Soviet pollsters were notorious for supplying the answers that the authorities wanted to hear or for omitting any responses that went against the party line. The reason for restoring the lishentsy's voting privileges lay in Stalin's desire to demonstrate to the outside world his commitment to democracy.

The Church experienced mixed reaction to the news of the clergy's reenfranchisement. Some clergy believed that Stalin was sincere in his actions and that this decision heralded a new era in Church-state relations. They also welcomed the opportunity to participate in politics and hopefully reinstate the power of the Orthodox Church. Other members of the clergy expressed reservations and feared that this was a precursor to a renewed wave of persecution. Still others refused to participate in the electoral process, believing that as long as the regime remained atheistic, voting and serving in a political office were akin to cooperating with the devil.

Although many people in the Church and in the Communist Party realized that Stalin's "liberal" gesture of restoring the rights of the clergy was principally for show, numerous members of the antireligious movement feared that religious organizations as well as ordinary believers would misinterpret the constitution and begin making demands for real religious freedom. As evidence, they cited letters to Kalinin and VTsIK demanding the reopening of churches.[21] The number of complaints from believers also rose, from 8,229 in 1934 to 9,646 in 1936.[22] One letter from the head of the Kuznetskii Raion political committee in Moscow province claimed that the agreement with a collective of believers allowing them to use a church was "a deep political mistake" and needed to be annulled.[23] One letter from Iosif Lyubimov of Saratov complained that despite the constitution's guarantee of freedom of religion, the churches in Saratov were still closed, whereas in Moscow, many churches were still open. He asked if the laws in Saratov were different from those in the rest of the country.[24] Another letter from a priest praised Stalin for the constitution and declared his loyalty to him.[25]

Nevertheless, despite the disapproval emanating from some quarters, the constitution was officially approved on December 5, 1936, and became the law of the land.[26] Article 124 reiterated the separation of Church and state and school from Church and guaranteed freedom of religious worship and antireligious propaganda. This article was not as controversial, as it merely restated those clauses that were mentioned in the 1918 and 1924 constitutions. The most contentious article concerning religion was article 136, which stated that "every citizen has the right to elect and be elected irrespective of race or nationality, religion, standard of education, domicile, social origin, property status, or past activities." However, despite the reinstatement of the clergy's political rights, there was still cause for concern. Article 135 stated that every citizen over eighteen years of age had the right to vote except the insane and those people deprived of electoral rights by sentence of court.[27] This latter category could include those clergy arrested on charges of "counterrevolutionary activities."

Additionally, despite their newly restored voting rights, clergy were still barred from participating in the economic life of the country. Priests and monastics were prohibited from working on a kolkhoz, although certain evidence indicates that many villages ignored this ban. It was also not uncommon for priests and monastics to participate in factory life. The social impact of the priests and monastics remained substantial, as various accounts testify to priests and the local party heads working together to ensure a good harvest or to resolve problems on the kolkhoz or in the factory.[28]

What then was the practical effect of the constitution on the Orthodox Church and, more specifically on monasteries? A report by the cult commission on the effect of the 1936 constitution on religion provides detailed statistics on various aspects of religious life during the period from 1934 to 1937.

The first question that the commission examined is the number of functioning "prayer buildings" in the Soviet Union in 1936.[29] According to the commission's calculations, before the 1917 revolution, there were

TABLE 1. Number of Functioning Prayer Buildings, 1936

Oblast	*Number of Functioning Prayer Buildings pre-1917*	*Number of Functioning Churches, 1936*
Moscow	3,731	1,993
Western oblast (including Smolensk and Kaluga oblasts)	2,048	871
Total in Russian federation	39,530	14,090
Total in USSR	68,383	19,090

SOURCE: GARF, f. 5263, op. 1, d. 832, 1.3.

39,530 prayer buildings in the Russian federation alone. By 1936, 20,318 of those had been closed, leaving 19,212 open. Of those remaining prayer buildings, 14,090 were still functioning. Within the entire Soviet Union, before the 1917 revolution there had been 68,393 prayer buildings, out of which 28,772 were still open and 19,090 were still functioning. By law, each of these parishes had to have a minimum of twenty members to be officially registered. Therefore, assuming that the number of parish members was twenty-five, approximately 750,000 "militant" Christians were working legally among the masses and contributing to the upkeep of religious life. Although the true number of monastics during this time can never be known, the commission stated that there were 250–300 "former" monastics and elders who were registered with the government in Voronezh province alone. In comparison to the national figures, the Russian federation had a higher percentage of functioning prayer buildings (35.6 percent) than the Soviet Union (28.5 percent) (see Table 1).[30] The survey further broke down the number of functioning prayer buildings by oblast. Within Russia, Moscow had 1,993 functioning buildings out of a prerevolutionary count of 3,731 (53.4 percent). In the western oblasts (which include Smolensk and Kaluga), the figures were 871 from 2,048 (42 percent).[31] Reports from the local party officials in Smolensk indicate an especially persistent remnant of religiosity. Although there were only four Orthodox churches functioning in the city of Smolensk, officials reported an increase in church attendance, especially among young people.[32]

These figures indicate that despite the intensity of the antireligious campaign of the late 1920s and early 1930s, a significant number of houses of worship remained open and functioning as such. However, in 1936 alone, the government closed 4,680 churches, synagogues, and other houses of worship, proving that reenfranchising the clergy did not translate into a real relaxation of religious policy. Additionally, the Soviet tribunals condemned 102 clergy to death and arrested more than 8,000 clergy, monks, nuns, rabbis, and other religious workers.[33] Other figures provided by the Warsaw Catholic Press Agency state that a total of 42,800 Orthodox priests were liquidated during the first half of 1936.[34] These instances of repression are in direct contrast to some of the rulings of the cult commission and highlight a lack of agreement within the party over the issue of religion. Indeed, the previous chapter discusses the commission's occasional resolutions in favor of believers. After the promulgation of the constitution, P. A. Krasikov, the head of the commission after 1935, demanded that those churches that had been illegally closed be returned to believers.[35]

Despite the hardship and the poverty that the church suffered, it seemed in many ways to appeal more to the average layperson. An article in the British Jesuit periodical *Blackfriars* reported that "All the sumptuousness of the Orthodox rite has disappeared in the agony. It has given way to surroundings which recall those of the primitive Christian communities. . . . The priest lives on alms and dwells in a tumbled down ruin or hides in the woods. Perhaps he is a young man who has been secretly ordained, or an old monk rendered homeless by persecution. In any case, he is very different from the big-bellied pope which the antireligious propaganda represents with guns and bags of gold holding out his hand to the capitalist."[36]

Yaroslavsky warned that despite the continuation of church closings, religion was still a real presence in the Soviet Union. These "new" priests who were active locally and inspired devotion among the public caused real anxiety to many Soviet leaders. According to official figures, the number of believers constituted thirty percent of the population of the towns, and among the rural population, two-thirds professed themselves believers. Regarding the antireligious campaign, Yaroslavsky stated, "There are some people who take comfort from the thought that a great number of churches are closed, and think that that means the end of religion. That is a great mistake. The danger consists precisely in the fact that, although the churches have been closed, our work has not been seriously effective among the masses. The priests are without their churches, but they are surrounded by their faithful. They have simply become 'traveling priests.' . . . Though the churches have been shut, the priests continue to be necessary in the eyes of the people."[37]

The 1937 Census

The first real test for the constitution came with the census of 1937. The government decided to undertake this project on the eve of the general elections to the Supreme Soviet for several reasons. For one thing, there existed a genuine need for information about the population, as the last census had taken place in 1926. Another reason involved the need for the government to prove that Communism was successful in the Soviet Union. One question appeared on the 1937 census that had not appeared on earlier ones. Question number five simply read "religion" and left a blank for participants to fill in. The original draft of the census did not include a question on religion; it was added later at Stalin's insistence.

This question provoked the most controversy both among the census officials and among the population. The census officials initially were not provided any instructions as to how to administer the census and how to interpret the religious question. Later, booklets were issued giving examples of forms and how to interpret replies. For question five, the explanation read: "An answer to this question should be given only for people aged 16 and above. The question is not about the faith to which the person asked or his parents belonged officially in past times. If the person asked considers himself a nonbeliever, write 'nonbeliever.' If the person asked considers himself a believer, write 'believer' and for persons holding a particular dogma, write the name of the religion (for example, Orthodox, Jew, Buddhist, etc.)"[38]

The purpose of the religious question on the census was to demonstrate the effectiveness of the antireligious campaign over the past ten years and also to alleviate fears that the Stalin constitution would enable clergy to infiltrate the government and undermine Communism. So confident was the government of the results of the census that the media ran stories predicting the responses to the religious question. On the day of the census (which, not coincidentally, was scheduled for January 6, Orthodox Christmas), *Pravda* ran an article stating that "The question of religion is special. The number of religious people recorded by the census officials among the general masses is, as one would expect, very insignificant. This attests that one of the strongest survivals of capitalism in people's consciousness is being rooted out."[39] *Komsomolskaia Pravda* reported that "[the results of the census] will demonstrate how great our successes are in the struggle against religious prejudices, where this work is proceeding and where it is standing still."[40]

When the census officials approached people with this question, they met with a variety of reactions. Many people were uncomfortable with this question, and either did not answer it or gave false answers. There were many rumors that circulated about the consequences of answering the religious question, which the newspapers reported and countered. In Moscow, one old woman asked whether it was true that all of the believers would be moved out of Moscow. Another rumor spread at a Moscow factory that "the census will take place at night and those who are for religion will be stamped with . . . the mark of the Anti-Christ."[41] Many people opted to run away or hide during the census. Many people who refused to answer the religious question were reported to the NKVD for "further measures."

Not all of the rumors had a negative connotation. One census official reported that believers told him that "People told them that if a lot of believers are recorded during the census then they'll build churches."[42] The head of the census, I. A. Kraval', told the central committee of rumors that said that "everyone should be registered as a believer, then they will open a church for them, as the census will be sent for scrutiny by the League of Nations, and the League of Nations will ask comrade Litvinov [commissar for foreign affairs] why we closed the churches when we have so many believers."[43]

The results of the census did not live up to the expectations of the Soviet officials. Fifty-six percent of the respondents declared themselves to be believers, and just under forty-three percent declared themselves to be nonbelievers (see Table 2).

The accuracy of these numbers is questionable, as many did not respond to the question out of fear or unclear understanding of the question. Nevertheless, these figures so unnerved the authorities that they suppressed the results and immediately began trying to place blame for the unexpected conclusion. They also called for a new census two years later, in 1939. The census officials were the first targets of retribution. One common criticism was that the questions were poorly worded and the guidelines given to the census workers were inadequate. Kraval', the census organizer, defended the census in a report to Stalin and Molotov and

TABLE 2. Religious Believers according to the 1937 Census

Total Adult Population	*Total Adult Believers*	*Orthodox*	*Adult Nonbelievers*	*Other Christians*
98,411,132	55,277,049	41,621,572	42,243,214	1,477,654

SOURCE: RGAE, f. 1562, op. 329, d. 143, ll.114–16.

blamed "class-hostile elements" for obstructing the census. With regard to the religious question, Kraval' admitted that the numbers were accurate and "the number of believers turned out to be greater than expected." However, he claimed that the responsibility for these unwanted results lay in the poor state of the antireligious propaganda.[44] Nevertheless, Kraval' and other census officials were purged, and the census officially was annulled. Despite the annulment, there was pressure from local authorities to release the data. They released information on other areas of the census, such as literacy and population growth, but refused to provide information on the religious question.[45] However, Yaroslavsky publicly estimated that in towns about two-thirds of adults identified themselves as atheists and in rural areas between one-half and two-thirds believed in God. Although this contradicted earlier official claims, these figures were later published in Soviet newspapers as factual.[46]

The shocking results of the 1937 census had repercussions on a wide segment of the Soviet population. Besides the census office, the antireligious movement was also subjected to purges. Another casualty was the cult commission, which was disbanded in April, 1938. This action as well as the confirmation of religion as an enduring force in the "progressive" Soviet Union signaled a renewed persecution of religion. As the professed religion of the majority of believers, the Orthodox Church became the main target of the government's wrath.

Comparing the 1937 census with the census conducted in 1939, some interesting similarities emerge. Although the 1939 census had no question on religion, it remained an issue in the minds of most people surveyed. Many viewed the question of nationality as an attempt to discover the respondent's religious affiliation. The same suspicion of the motives for the census remained, coming so soon after the suppression of the results of the 1937 census. As with the previous census, many people refused to participate. Many monastics encouraged people not to take part. In Tambov guberniia, officials reported that a nun "conducted agitation against the census."[47] Mordovia in particular had a high level of monastic involvement, all from nuns or former nuns. One former nun, Anna Andronovna, gave a particularly bold response to a census official. Anna had served a prison sentence for "anti-Soviet agitation" and refused to answer any questions during the census. She replied that she couldn't give any information about herself because she feared only God and in the census "you will mix up the believers with the atheists." She also criticized the government for closing the churches. Another former nun, Anna Kosenkova, specifically linked church closures with participating in the census. She told an official, "You closed the church. Open the church, and we'll take part."[48]

The 1937 Elections

The census was not the only unpleasant surprise for the Soviet officials. The elections for the Supreme Soviet were also designed to be a test of the new constitution and its guarantee of voting rights to clergy. Many Communists feared the results of the participation by the clergy. The Church was very politically active in the elections, sending priests to public reading rooms to spread propaganda. The Red Army newspaper *Krasnaia Zvezda* reported that "priests are everywhere, organizing courses of lectures on our constitution; and what is more provoking is that these courses are better attended than the official meetings."[49] In another article *Krasnaia Zvezda* complained about the enduring religious feelings among the soldiers and officers. According to several letters to the editor, some Red Army personnel "regarded the authority of the church higher than the laws."[50]

Indeed, the Orthodox Church proved very active in educating the citizens about the importance of voting and explained the electoral process. In their educational work, priests and monastics stressed loyalty to the regime, and except for requesting the reopening of churches, their speeches were not directly anti-Soviet in character. It was this emphasis on cooperation between Church and state and the efficiency of the Church's electoral campaign that disturbed the Soviet authorities. The prospect of having real participation from the Orthodox Church was not something that Stalin and the Soviet leadership either envisioned or desired. The prospect of "religious elements" undermining the election so unnerved the central committee that in a secret meeting in October, it decided to ban contested elections in the upcoming voting. Instead, only one candidate would run for each position.[51] Ironically, the Church's success in mobilizing the electorate eventually led to renewed persecution.

The Purges

The purge trials, known in the west as the "Great Terror," have been one of the most-written-about subjects in Russian history.[52] Studies of the purges are commonly divided into two periods. The first purge began in 1934 with the murder of Sergei Kirov, the popular Leningrad party chief. During this initial phase, the focus was mainly on cleansing the Communist Party of Stalin's political enemies, the so-called left and right oppositions. By 1937 it had expanded to include every segment of Soviet society. Any comments that could be construed as being against the Soviet government or against Stalin warranted an arrest from the NKVD and, at best, ten years in a labor camp. As with the collectivization campaign, the intensity of the purges varied depending on the geographical area. The Western oblast, which included Smolensk, suffered particular hardship. From 1933 until 1938, the Smolensk Communist Party experienced an almost continuous purge. Reasons for expulsion were numerous and included "religious ties." Figures for early 1936 show that the number of party members had declined to 42,000.[53]

Although the Communist Party was the primary target of the purges, other groups soon came under scrutiny. The former lishentsy consisting of kulaks and the clergy were targeted as "enemies of the people," sentenced to hard labor and often executed.[54] The number of people who perished during this time remains a subject of debate, ranging from 500,000 to 7 million. The most recent figures derived from archival sources suggests the relatively conservative estimate of people killed in the entire decade of the 1930s to be around 1.5 million people.[55] The exact number of clergy and monastics has also remained unknown. However, Alexander Yakovlev, the head of the Commission for Rehabilitating Victims of Political Repression, recently revealed that the number of priests, monks, and nuns killed in the purges is more than 200,000.[56]

Realizing that the clergy and believers took the promises of religious freedom seriously, in 1938 the regime issued new instructions regarding the regulation of churches. Under the new rules, churches were forbidden to help their members financially. Churches were also prohibited from creating associations for cultural and financial purposes; establishing sports associations, hospitals, or libraries; and holding services outside, including funerals. Priests were not allowed to visit church members privately whenever they knew that not all of the members of a family were believers. If churches were closed, all articles made of precious metals or stones were to be deposited in the state bank, and articles that possessed a historical value had to be turned over to the commissariat of education.[57] Another portent of renewed persecution was a decree published on August 1, 1938, by the people's commissariat of the interior, which ordered a census of all churches, synagogues, and mosques, together with a detailed description of religious objects of value. More ominously, each house of worship was now required to report the number of people who visited it.[58] These decrees were reminiscent of the famine of 1921–1922, when the monasteries and churches were forced to give up their sacred objects.

Despite the threat of arrest and execution, the Church managed to continue its activities. Perhaps the biggest threat to the Church was the loss of priests. The closure of the seminaries in the 1920s ensured that there would be no more replacements. However, the Church proved resourceful and continued to recruit new candidates for the priesthood. Many monasteries played a key role in this endeavor. One émigré periodical reported that in the Ural mountains, hidden monasteries served as secret seminaries. The students came from all parts of society and included former Red Army soldiers. One such former soldier became a bishop, who was later exiled to Turkestan. The paper also reported on the division that existed between the older and the younger clergy. The younger generation wore more modern clothes, wore their hair short, and criticized the older priests for their "backward" ways. The older generation adhered to the traditional dress and long hair and referred to the younger priests as "worldly popes." However, each side recognized that it needed the support of the other.[59]

The Persistence of Monasticism

Since the purges forced Orthodoxy to go even further underground, the exact numbers of monks and nuns during this period is extremely difficult to determine. The only official mention of monasteries and monastics occurred when a "secret" monastery was discovered, such as the Petrovski-Tor women's monastery in Moscow. In 1939 the Serbian newspaper *Lerkovnoje Obozrenie* published what it claimed was information from Russian sources. According to the report, Soviet authorities discovered a secret monastery that had existed since 1932 under the direction of Bishop Bartholomew. The nuns were described as "ordinary workers" in Soviet mills, and a few attended a university. Although the monastery was liquidated, some of the sisters managed to escape.[60]

There were many other "underground" monasteries functioning during this period, such as the one that Archimandrite Pimen formed together with ten monks in the city of Dnepropetrovsk. In Slavianskie Donetsk, dispossessed monks from Sviatogorski monastery found refuge among the inhabitants of the city, until in 1939 they were evicted from the city and "sternly dealt with."[61] In 1937 the Godless journal *Bezbozhnik* printed an article detailing the discovery and liquidation of an underground women's monastery in Smolensk.[62] That same year, another secret monastery was discovered in Nizhni Novgorod. The shocking revelation about this particular monastery was that it was allegedly run by a government official.[63]

The arrests and trials of clergy and monastics were also reported in the press. During the trials, the most common reasons given for arresting clergy were charges of spying or being "anticommunist." Unfortunately, some of these arrests arose out of information provided by members of the "community" close to the clergy, even from fellow clergymen. Father Arseny learned that a deacon was one of the ones who informed on him and who were responsible for his arrest in 1939. The deacon rose in the patriarchate, by 1960 becoming a high-ranking member.[64] Many of those accused clergy were executed immediately or exiled to labor camps. One well-known case involved a married priest named M. Ye. Yedlinsky. In October, 1937, he was arrested and charged with counterrevolutionary activities. One of these alleged crimes was passing information on the closure of monasteries in Kiev to a member of the True Orthodox Church. He was executed a month later.[65] According to one source on February 17, 1938, in Moscow alone, four monks and four nuns were shot for being "enemies of the people."[66] Another account states that in Arzamasskoi prison in Sarov alone, there were two thousand nuns from different monasteries in the Kazan province.[67] Even people close to Metropolitan Sergei, the acting patriarch, were not immune from persecution; in 1937 the NKVD arrested and shot Hieromonk Afanasi, Metropolitan Sergei's cell attendant. That same year the NKVD also shot the metropolitan's sister, Alexandra, who was also a nun.[68]

It was not only monastics and clergy who were the targets of this renewed antireligious campaign. Laypeople who were thought to have close connections to clergy and monastics were arrested and interrogated in hopes of obtaining damning evidence against them to use in a trial. The transcripts of these interrogations reveal the methods that the NKVD used to extract information from people as well as the types of evidence they hoped to obtain. They arrested men and women as young as fourteen and asked about their connections with monks and nuns and what their activities were. The most common question the NKVD asked involved monks' and nuns' involvement with "counterrevolutionary activities." In one case when the person being questioned stated that he never knew the priests and nuns to engage in counterrevolutionary activities, the interrogator claimed that because the nuns and priests were involved in running a monastery kolkhoz, that was proof enough of their counterrevolutionary behavior.[69]

Reliable reports of religious conditions in the Soviet Union were difficult to obtain because of the veil of secrecy that surrounded every aspect of Soviet life. The Soviet government routinely assured the West that its citizens had freedom of religious worship, as guaranteed in the constitution, and pointed to the few churches that were kept open for publicity purposes. However, branches of the Russian Orthodox Church in Western European countries such as France, Britain, and Germany published periodic reports on the true situation that their compatriots faced. They received their information from other recent exiles or émigrés who smuggled reports from priests, bishops, monastics, and other clergy and laity from the Soviet Union. These emigre periodicals provide a great source of contemporary information about conditions in the Soviet Union during the 1930s, although as with any source they must be used with caution. However, emigre bishops rendered a great service to their Orthodox brethren in the Soviet Union by holding conferences and dispelling the propaganda that the Soviet authorities disseminated. For example, Bishop Seraphim of the Russian Church in Germany stated that the belief that freedom of religion and conscience existed in Russia was false. As evidence, he claimed that in May, 1938, at least 250 priests were shot, and at Easter of that same year, more than one hundred priests were exiled.[70]

Another service that the emigre periodicals fulfilled was in describing the lives of many clergy and monastics who had either been executed or still languished in labor camps inside the Soviet Union. The accounts humanized the purges and reminded readers that behind the numbers lay human beings. It is from these accounts that latter-day readers and scholars obtain detailed accounts of prison and camp life that monastics endured.[71]

As with the previous round of arrests in 1932, the monastics who endured the labor camps discovered ways of preserving their monastic life and often engaged in passive resistance to the regime by refusing to answer the camp guards' questions about themselves, refusing to work in the camps, and adhering to the monastic prayer rule. These monks and nuns often not only incurred the wrath of the camp guards, but also frequently earned the enmity of other prisoners.[72] Although camp officials were far less tolerant than they had been about allowing services, priests and monastics continued to secretly serve well-attended liturgies, especially on Easter and Christmas. In camps where monastics and clergy were commonly sent, such as Solovki and Zhitomir, maintaining a semblance of monastic life was easier than for those monks and nuns who were more isolated. One of the most brutal camps was Butova, located outside of Moscow. Shrouded in secrecy, it is believed that between 40,000 and 200,000 people were executed there, the majority clergy and monastics. Accounts from monastics who experienced Butova described the hardship. However, Bishop Bartholomew from Vysoko-Petrovski monastery in Moscow was still able to communicate with nuns outside of Butova. His letters described not only the horrible conditions of the camp, but also his devotion to monasticism and Christ. His letters were meant to serve as inspiration to the other nuns and monks. At the close of one letter, he wrote: "Despite the fact that I am deprived of everything, I feel that Christ is near. . . . This is the one thing that I am not deprived of."[73]

Archbishop Leonty of Kiev described his experiences in various labor camps after his arrest in 1937. There he met many monks and nuns, some secretly tonsured and some who had been displaced from their monasteries. He also stated that many believers continued to assist imprisoned monastics by bringing or sending food and other necessities that they were allowed to receive in the camps. If it had not been for that assistance, many would not have survived.[74] Some monastics (almost always nuns) made the ultimate sacrifice for their spiritual fathers. They voluntarily accompanied them to the labor camps or into exile so that the elderly bishops would not be alone. Mother Evpraksia was one of the nuns who accompanied Bishop Bartholomew to Butova. She served as a correspondent to the other sisters.[75] Some of these nuns did not survive the camps.

Some monks in the camps met the very people responsible for placing them there. Father Arseny, a hieromonk who was first arrested in 1933 and again in 1939, spent almost twenty years in the "special" camps, where the harshest punishments were given out. While in the camps, he came to know Alexander Pavlovich Avsenkov. Avsenkov became close to Father Arseny, and although he was an atheist, he admired Father Arseny for his kindness and piety. During one conversation, Father Arseny remarked that the two men had a history together: "Oh yes, you know me, Alexander Pavlovich. In 1933 when Communism was trying to eradicate religion, hundreds of thousands of believers were exiled . . . and this is when for the first time I was sent away to camp on your instructions. In 1939 . . . you arrested me again and convicted me to be shot. But, thank you—you commuted the sentence to exile in camp. . . . All along I've been expecting to see you. So finally we meet."[76]

Despite the toll that the purges took on the infrastructure of the Church, monastics were still able to assist their fellow clergy through various secret networks that they had established. Abbess Juliana of Moscow in particular played an active role in helping persecuted clergy. She was a leading member of the Myrrh-Bearing Sisterhood of the Church of Christ the Savior in Moscow. This group formed a network throughout the Soviet Union and kept the leading bishops informed of the whereabouts of other hierarchs. Even after she was imprisoned in Solovki, Abbess Juliana was still able to remain in contact with and provide assistance to other imprisoned clergy. After World War II, she moved to California.[77]

Although exile and prison were the fate of many monastics and clergy, some managed to elude imprisonment. Mother Anatolia from Diveevo monastery was one of these fortunate ones. In 1937 she bought a house in the village of Murom, on the bank of the Oka river. Two of her fellow nuns lived nearby, and many pious laypeople came to visit her for spiritual counsel. She lived in this house until her death in 1949. Another nun, Agna, was the abbess of an unnamed monastery in central Russia. Although the Bolsheviks closed the monastery in 1918, the nuns returned and rebuilt it. When it was destroyed for good in the 1930s, Mother Agna fled into the surrounding forest, where she lived quietly until her death in 1953. Although she lived in hiding, those Orthodox who were searching for spiritual guidance knew where to find her.[78] Mother Serafima of Moscow, a secret nun, also managed to survive the Great Purges unscathed, mainly due to her self-imposed isolation. She continued to live her secular life as a doctor, avoided associating with other monastics, and told no one of her "other life" as a secret nun.[79]

Another monk from Optina Pustyn monastery, Father Sebastian, managed to provide for his flock even in exile. In 1933 he was exiled to Karaganda in Kazakhstan. Many nuns from all over the Soviet Union came to the village of Michailovka in Karaganda to be close to him, and within a few years, the community grew into an unofficial monastery. The nuns found work either as nurses or on local collective farms. This community thrived well into the 1960s.[80]

The danger of the current social situation prompted a curious but interesting reversal of Russian monasticism. As the introductory chapter points out, monasticism in Russia began as idiorythmic, with many people who desired the monastic life living as hermits. With the monastic revival and reforms in the eighteenth century, more monasteries became cenobitic, or communal. By the middle of the nineteenth century, the old idiorythmic ideal had disappeared. However, the renewed persecution of monasticism in the 1930s had the effect of reviving the old model. The monasteries were closed, and efforts to maintain the physical sense of community increased the chances of discovery and arrest. Those monastics who eluded capture tended to be those who returned to the hermit lifestyle. They also formed the nuclei of unofficial monasteries and churches. This illustrates another striking comparison with early Orthodox monasticism. In the early centuries before the advent of organized communities, Christians had gone to holy people for guidance. The popularity of the desert fathers, such as St. Anthony of Egypt, is perhaps the greatest example of this. As secret nun Galina Alexandrovna explained, with the churches and monasteries denied as places of pilgrimage, these "holy people" themselves became the objects of pilgrimage. In other words, what took place during the purges was that monasticism ceased to be objectified and became more personified.[81]

The purges also renewed the phenomenon of "wandering" monks and nuns. A common figure in Russian Orthodox life in the imperial period, wanderers typically were monks or nuns who left their monastery either temporarily or permanently to make a pilgrimage or to spread Christianity throughout the countryside. Wanderers also included laypeople who desired to retreat from society and find their spirituality. During the purges, being a wanderer was not so much a lifestyle choice as a necessity. To avoid detection, monks and nuns necessarily had to be constantly on the move. Although this type of existence seems well-nigh impossible during the rigid system of internal passports, according to personal accounts there were many ways for a person to elude authorities, especially with the help of a network of cooperative persons. Despite the oppressive presence of the internal police, there was no possible way for the authorities to have total control over everyone. This is not to deny the tyrannical nature of Soviet society in the 1930s; however, the conception of an omnipresent and omnipotent government is simply not an accurate portrayal of the situation and the times.

Another change in monasticism that occurred involved the living arrangements of the monastics. The closure of the monasteries beginning in the late 1920s forced many monks and nuns to find lodging wherever they could. Many monks and nuns simply moved to other monasteries that were still open. As mentioned earlier, although there were more nuns in Russia, there were fewer women's monasteries. As a result, it was not uncommon for displaced nuns to take refuge in men's monasteries. After all of the monasteries were officially closed, it was also common for monks and nuns to form "unofficial" monasteries consisting of both men and women. Such mixed societies would have been scandalous in prerevolutionary times, but the current circumstances made concerns over such superficial appearances unimportant.

Russian Monasteries outside of the Soviet Union

The situation of the monasteries in the Soviet Union had an effect on Russian-run monasteries located in other countries, especially Palestine, Mount Athos in Greece, and the islands of Lake Ladoga, which belonged to Finland during the interwar period. The Bolshevik revolution ruptured the ties between the Patriarchal Church and its monasteries in other countries. In Palestine the lack of monetary support for the ecclesiastical land belonging to the now-defunct Imperial Russian Orthodox Palestine Society left the monks and nuns in destitute conditions. Additionally, the British, who were administering Palestine under the League of Nations mandate given in 1922, were engaged in a struggle with the Soviet government and wanted the Russian ecclesiastical land turned over to them. This issue was not resolved during the interwar period; in the meantime, the Russian monks and nuns depended on the charity of British relief organizations as well as Russian émigrés and other Orthodox national churches.

The Russian monks of Mount Athos also suffered after the Bolshevik takeover. Like their brethren in Palestine, they suffered from lack of monetary support and also from the lack of new monks from Russia. The exodus from Mount Athos began in 1912, when the Russian government ordered Russian nationals living abroad to return home. By 1914 only 2,584 Russians remained on Mount Athos; by 1925 the number had dwindled to 560. Compared to the late-nineteenth-century population of 3,496, this was indeed a dramatic decline. Most of the remaining monks lived at the monastery of St. Panteleimon. Although St. Panteleimon had vegetable gardens and orchards to provide for their basic needs, many of the smaller sketes and monasteries had no such advantages and depended entirely on outside assistance. Between the years 1914 and 1937, no new Russian monks were allowed on Mount Athos.[82]

The disappearance of a Russian presence on Mount Athos greatly alarmed Russian Orthodox everywhere. Mount Athos is the most important site for monasticism in all of Orthodoxy. A monk's greatest aspiration is to visit if not live in one of the dozens of monasteries on the island. The loss of a Russian presence on the island would be a devastating setback to the power and prestige of Russian Orthodoxy. Russian émigrés, the Orthodox Church Abroad, and the Patriarchal Church in Moscow all contributed to the financial upkeep of the Russian monasteries on Mount Athos. However, not until 1987 could the beginning of a revival of Russian monasticism on Mount Athos be discerned.[83]

Not all monasteries outside of the Soviet Union suffered such extreme hardship during the interwar period. The monasteries of Valaam and Konevets belonged to Finland between the wars and came under the jurisdiction of the Patriarchate of Constantinople. In 1937 Valaam had about two hundred monks, out of which 170 were more than fifty years old. The monastery at Konevets had about forty monks. After the Declaration of 1927, many monks left these two monasteries and joined the Church Abroad. Aside from the problems of loss of contact with other Russian monks in the Soviet Union, the Valaam and Konevets monasteries did not suffer closure and eviction until after the Soviet-Finnish war in 1939, when all of the Lake Ladoga territory became Soviet.[84]

Until its closure, Valaam served as a source of spirituality for believers from a wide geographical area. One person who was greatly influenced by Valaam was the future patriarch Alexeii II. A native of Estonia, he spoke of a year-long pilgrimage that he made with his parents in 1938, before the monastery was closed. The monastery made a lasting impression on him, especially the contact he had with the spiritual elders of Valaam.[85]

Two other monasteries that escaped closure due to their geographic location were Piuhtitsai women's monastery and Pskov-Pecherskaia monastery, both located in Free Estonia. Piuhtitsai monastery is located between the Gulf of Finland and Lake Chudskoye on Piuhtitsai hill. In 1920 the Soviet Union formally granted Estonia independence. The monastery received the status of a women's labor society, with the majority of the original nuns remaining. In 1935 the Estonian Orthodox Church granted the monastery its original status of monastery, and the newly independent Estonian government allotted it 102 hectares of land.[86]

One of only two of the unique "cave" monasteries in the Soviet Union, Pskov-Pecherskaia is also the only monastery to have remained continuously open throughout the Soviet period, although it experienced hardship. Because it was incorporated into the free Republic of Estonia in 1918, it escaped closure. However, many monks left, leaving just fifty-six inhabitants in 1927.[87] The ones who stayed continued to work in the artisan shops making icons and candles and also in agriculture.

The Monasteries of the Russian Orthodox Church Abroad

The Russian Orthodox Church Abroad, the group that broke relations with Metropolitan Sergei after the Declaration of 1927, established its own monasteries both within and outside of the Soviet Union. The affiliated monasteries that existed in the Soviet Union referred to themselves as the "catacomb monasteries." The monks and nuns who joined these secret monasteries faced many hardships. Not only were they considered illegal by the Soviet government, but they were also regarded by the "official" Orthodox church of Russia as illegitimate and schismatic. They could not rely on the cooperation of the metropolitan or other members of the official church. Although this made their survival more tenuous, in some ways the situation may have worked to their advantage in that it fostered a closer sense of community among members. The "catacomb monasteries" also received aid from the Russian Orthodox Church Abroad whenever it could gain access to its members in the Soviet Union.

Aside from providing support to the catacomb monasteries inside the Soviet Union, the Church Abroad also set up monasteries in other countries. The purpose of establishing these institutions outside of Russia was "to build a foundation for new monasteries in a liberated Russia."[88] A total of 180 monks, 40 novices, and 450 nuns belonged to Orthodox Abroad monastic communities in various countries (see Table 3).

Aside from these monasteries under the jurisdiction of the Church Abroad, several other Russian monasteries were also founded in France, the Netherlands, and Germany under the auspices of the Russian Ortho-

TABLE 3. Monasteries of the Orthodox Church Abroad before World War II

Country	*Number of Monasteries*	*Number of Monks*	*Number of Women's Monasteries*	*Number of Nuns*
Palestine	1	20	2	300
Serbia	1	25	1	70
Bulgaria	1	10	1	10
China	1	26	1	40
Manchuria	1	70	1	30
United States	1	40	—	—

SOURCE: Georg Seide. *Monasteries and Convents of the Orthodox Church Abroad.* Munich: Monastery of Saint Job of Pochaev, 1990.

dox Archdiocese of Western Europe. Although referred to as "monasteries," in reality many were little more than settlements. Some had as few as two or three members. One of the most important "Church Abroad" monasteries is Holy Trinity Monastery in Jordanville, New York. Started by two Russian emigre monks in 1928, it became a magnet for Russian monks fleeing post–World War II Europe and later served as the center of the Russian Orthodox Church Abroad.

The largest enclave of the Russian Orthodox Church Abroad in the United States is in northern California, particularly around the San Francisco area. St. Tikhon's, the oldest Russian Orthodox monastery on American soil, was established as early as 1905 and also housed a theological seminary. In the 1930s between twenty and thirty monks belonged to the brotherhood.[89] Archbishop John established a community there comprised mainly of Russian Orthodox who had emigrated to Shanghai, China, in the 1920s. As the situation in China became more unstable in the 1930s, many monks and nuns left for California and established monasteries there. Unlike some of the other Russian Abroad monasteries, who focused on preserving the Old Slavonic language and the customs of prerevolutionary Russia, the monasteries in California made a conscious effort to reach out to non-Orthodox Americans. One monastery in particular, the Monastery of St. Herman of Alaska in

Platina, California, led the way in making monasticism and Orthodoxy accessible to Americans. Its key contribution was in translating religious literature from Russian into English and also providing translations of contemporary Russian emigre periodicals from France and Yugoslavia.

The monks and nuns always regarded their residence in these countries as temporary. When Communism was eventually destroyed, then they would return to re-Christianize Russia. In a 1938 address to members of the second pan-diaspora council of the Russian Orthodox Church Abroad, Archimandrite Seraphim laid out his plan for how the monastics of the Russian diaspora would "bring to a resurrected Russia the still-burning lamp of holy cenobitic Russian monasticism." The first priority was to live a strict monastic life. A second concern was to establish more monasteries and to attract new members. The most important challenge facing the Church Abroad monasteries lay in preparing what Archimandrite Seraphim termed "monastic reconstructionists." These monks and nuns would be responsible for reconstructing traditional monasticism in Russia when the time came. They divided the duties of the Church Abroad monasteries and convents into four categories: (1) missions with missionary courses and monastic schools; (2) establishments with printing presses and ecclesiastical concerns; (3) institutions with social and charitable activities, such as orphanages, hospitals, and clinics; and (4) monasteries and convents for a purely contemplative life.[90] Already many of the Church Abroad monasteries operated these institutions in their adopted countries in preparation for the return to the homeland. Aside from providing these services, Archimandrite Seraphim stressed that the monasteries must be self-supporting. They therefore engaged in farming and selling icons and other religious items, and some operated small independent publishing houses. As mentioned earlier, these Abroad monasteries played a role in disseminating information about the situation of the Church in the Soviet Union and made the rest of the world aware of the persecution to which the Soviets subjected the Russian Church.

The Church Abroad monasteries were quite successful in their endeavors to restore the character of Russian monasticism. Many of these new monasteries erected in foreign countries prompted a monastic revival. This was particularly true in Serbia and China, where Russian nuns became the abbesses of many new communities. Although these monasteries initially were established for and run by Russian émigrés, they also attracted many people from the native population who were previously not Orthodox. However, this success among the non-Orthodox raised questions among the Russian emigre monastics about the true mission of the monasteries abroad. Should the Church Abroad concentrate solely on the preservation of *Russian* Orthodoxy? Or did it have a larger mission to spread Orthodoxy to the non-Orthodox world? Evidence of this debate may be found in the different approaches used by monasteries. Some monasteries such as Holy Trinity in Jordanville, New York, focus on preserving the old Church Slavonic language. The monks and seminarians are Russian or Russian American. Instruction in the seminary is given in Russian, and most of the publications are in Russian. In contrast, the St. Herman of Alaska Brotherhood in California comprises mainly converts. Its printing press is almost exclusively in English, and the focus is on missionizing to the non-Orthodox world.

Examining the goals and programs of the Church Abroad monasteries invites comparison to the earlier monastic reforms and revivals of the early twentieth century. In his aforementioned speech, Archimandrite Seraphim stated that in the "resurrected" Russia, monastics should live industrious lives and not be wealthy landowners as in the past. In keeping with the previous monastic reforms of 1917, he also advocated strict adherence to the monastic rule and frequent confession. He stressed that the Church had a role in assisting the monasteries in their work of rebuilding Russia through establishing brotherhoods and other lay societies.[91] His proposition of having monasteries "specialize" prompted others to accuse him of remaking the Russian monasticism along the lines of the Roman Catholic monastic orders. He admitted that there would be some similarities and defended borrowing from the Catholics: "Concerning the practicality and efficiency of means of organization there is much to be learned from the Catholics."[92] However, he stressed that, internally, Orthodox monasticism would adhere to the traditions established in the fourth century by Basil the Great. Again it appears that the mode of adaptation that Russian monastics used during this period derived neither from previous Russian models nor from foreign religions. Rather, they hearkened back to the early Christian church of the fourth and fifth centuries.

In sum, the latter part of the 1930s provided both benefits and drawbacks for Russian monasticism. The 1936 constitution offered the hope that the Soviet Union was altering its stance on religion and that monasteries could once again establish some kind of *modus vivendi* with the atheistic Soviet government. However, the results of the 1937 census threatened the government and caused a renewal of persecution. The resulting wave of terror that engulfed the entire nation again threatened to destroy monasticism. However, as they had during the civil war and collectivization, monks and nuns found ways to not only endure, but also even to thrive. Those in prisons and labor camps continued to preserve their communities and provide inspiration to others. Others managed to remain underground and undetected and also served as spiritual guides for Orthodox laypeople.

Those Russian Orthodox who emigrated established printing presses and provided moral and monetary support to those monks and nuns left behind in the Soviet Union. The Church Abroad contributed to the survival of monasticism by establishing monasteries in other countries. All of these examples prove that although the monastic institutions had largely been destroyed, monasticism's spirit had not. In many ways the adversity served to make it stronger. One might even refer to this period as a revival of Russian monasticism. In contrast to previous revivals, which focused on political and administrative reforms, what occurred in the 1930s was more personal. No one knew how long this period of persecution would last. This led to an apocalyptic mood throughout Russian Orthodox society and contributed to the deep desire for monasticism. As noted earlier, many laity were attracted to the monastic way of life and looked to monks and nuns for spiritual guidance in time of uncertainty. In a time and place when the Soviet government proved morally inept, many laypeople saw the persecuted monks and nuns as offering something deeper.

Epilogue

When Germany invaded Poland in 1939, it plunged the world into the second world war of the twentieth century. Because of the nonaggression pact signed with Nazi Germany, the Soviet Union remained relatively unaffected until Germany attacked in 1941. Ironically, the German invasion and occupation, which almost destroyed the Soviet Union, served to temporarily improve the position of the Russian Orthodox Church.[93] On June 22, 1941, the same day that the Nazis invaded the Soviet Union, Metropolitan Sergei issued a declaration urging Russians to defend the "fatherland." Stalin quickly recognized the propaganda value of the Orthodox Church and used it to his full advantage. The government officially disbanded the League of the Militant Godless in 1941. Many churches were reopened, and Stalin restored the institution of the patri-

TABLE 4. Monasteries in the Soviet Union by Republic as of 1945

Republic	*Number of Functioning Monasteries (Both Men's and Women's)*
Russia	2 (Kursk and Pskov)
Ukraine	68
Moldavia	24
Byelorussia	3
Lithuania	2
Latvia	1
Estonia	1

SOURCE: GARF, f. 6991s, op. 2, vol. 1, dd. 206, 263.

archate, appointing Sergei to serve in that position. The government also allowed the patriarchate to publish its own journal and to reopen several seminaries. Sergei served Stalin well, organizing collections for the war effort and publishing a book for Western consumption titled "The Truth about Religion in Russia," a propaganda piece designed to demonstrate that the Soviet Union encouraged religious freedom.

The fate of the monasteries also improved during the war. As a result of the annexations of 1939 and 1940, the USSR received sixty-four functioning men's and women's monasteries, and the Germans reopened many monasteries in their occupied territory. This brought the total number of monasteries in the Soviet Union to 101 by 1945. For a breakdown of monasteries in the Soviet Union, see Table 4.

Despite this numerical increase in functioning monasteries, the result cannot be construed as a true renaissance of monasticism. The closures and the purges in the 1930s had taken a heavy toll on monasticism and made the process of rebuilding very difficult. Monks and nuns were not immune from arrest and murder, as illustrated by the murder of several nuns in Kaluga.[94] Nevertheless, monastics took full advantage of this "breathing space" to resume their activities, to openly declare themselves as monastics, and to recover their property when possible.

In spite of this apparent relaxation on the part of the Soviet government, the improvement did not last very long. After the Soviet victory in the war, Stalin reinstituted total control over Soviet society and once again closed monasteries and arrested monks and nuns. However, the years of persecution in the 1930s had prepared the monastics for an underground life, which they resumed. As the past two decades of Soviet rule had emphasized, being a monk or nun did not depend on whether one lived in a monastery; rather, it depended on one's lifestyle and dedication to the monastic rule.

Conclusion

DURING THE INTERWAR period, Russian Orthodox monasticism strove to survive the onslaught of the atheistic Bolshevik regime. Despite persecution, monks and nuns succeeded in their efforts to preserve the essence of monasticism. Proof of their achievements lies in recent evidence indicating a revival of interest in monasticism, particularly among young people. Statistics for 1998 cite a total of 478 monasteries in the former Soviet Union, out of which 299 are in the Russian Federation.[1] As of March, 1997, the Moscow diocese had 30 functioning monasteries, 12 women's and 18 men's. Smolensk diocese reported 3 monasteries, 2 men's and 1 women's, and Kaluga diocese has 8, 4 men's and 4 women's.[2] The exact number of monastics is unknown and does not include those men and women who have taken monastic vows but do not live in a monastery.

However positive it may appear, the post-Communist period also poses its challenges. The first is the physical rebuilding of the monasteries. Like most houses of worship, many monasteries were turned into factories, garbage dumps, insane asylums, or other secular facilities. In 1988, when the government began to formally return monasteries to the Orthodox Church,[3] much work had to be done to restore the buildings to livable conditions. The task was compounded due to lack of money and labor. The few monks and nuns that remained were elderly and incapable of doing hard physical labor. As in the past, the monks and nuns needed to rely on the assistance of the local people.

The outpouring of donations of money and labor from the people has been a testament to the feelings that monasteries aroused among the local population. People who themselves did not have much donated time, labor, and materials to rebuild the churches and buildings surrounding the monastery. Some people such as Vladimir Bubaev, an artist in

Moscow, have donated their talents to restoring monasteries. Bubaev has dedicated most of his time to restoring the icons at the Alekseev monastery, where he also serves on the parish council. Another example may be seen in Optina Pustyn monastery located outside the town of Kozelsk. On a visit in 1996, the author was present at the canonization of the Optina elders. The monks were also getting ready for the reconsecration of the Annunciation church. For months, the monks and the surrounding villagers had been working to rebuild the church. The defining moment came when the cross was raised once again to the top of the church. Father Melchizeldek, the abbot of the monastery, came out to bless the cross as it was solemnly raised. Everyone stopped what they were doing to witness this historic event. Many monks and local villagers openly wept. For them, it was a symbol of triumph over the decades of destruction and neglect under the Soviet regime.

Legal issues still remain a challenge for the monasteries. When the Bolsheviks nationalized them, they turned many buildings over to local villagers. As previously discussed, throughout the 1920s many monasteries were divided, with some of the buildings occupied by government departments and some occupied by monks and nuns. The same situation exists at the present time. The question of ownership and the fate of the villagers is an ongoing legal issue. One such case is in Optina Pusytn. In the late nineteenth century, at the height of the monastery's popularity, several of the elders decided that the number of pilgrims threatened to disturb their meditation. They therefore built a small community, known as a skete, about a mile away from the main monastery. The skete consisted of a small church, several modest homes where two or three elders lived, and a small library. People still came to see them there, but the activity did not disturb the other monks at the main monastery. After the closure of the monastery, the authorities gave the homes to local villagers. Although technically all of the buildings in the skete belong to the monastery, the villagers have sued to remain there or have the monastery pay them to relocate. The issue is still being debated in the local courts as of this writing. In the meantime, the villagers and the monks remain in an uneasy coexistence. Some of the villagers are not Christians, and occasional outbreaks of violence have occurred. The most tragic was the murder of three monks on Easter Sunday in 1993, allegedly by a mentally disturbed local man.

The phenomenon of "monasteries without walls" remains, although it is not fear of persecution that keeps monks and nuns in the world, but

Placing the cross on top of the restored church, Optina Pustyn

rather mundane reasons. They may not live near a functioning men's or women's monastery, or they may have family members who depend on them financially. Such men and women work in various secular jobs but remain celibate and follow the monastic rule.

The main purpose in writing this work was to illustrate how monastics adapted to the challenges of the atheist Bolshevik regime. Although monasteries differed in their methods depending on geography and individual cases, several clear patterns emerge. Nearly all monasteries initially put up physical resistance to attempted Bolshevik takeover. When it became apparent that the Bolshevik government was not going to disappear, tactics changed from open resistance to adaptation. Monasteries were quick to realize the economic potential they had and sought to use it to their advantage. The conversion to monastery communes and the effective public relations campaign they launched to persuade the authorities to keep them open is the best example of monasteries using a hostile ideology to their benefit. After the closure of the monasteries in 1930, monks and nuns continued to preserve their communities through secret meetings at people's homes, in graveyards, and in labor camps and prisons. As the risks of being a monastic increased, secret monasticism became the norm.

Grave of Elder Makarii, Optina Pustyn

This examination of monasticism illustrates the often-complex interaction between state and society in the Soviet Union, particularly during the interwar period. Preconceived Western notions of a totalitarian society have had to be revised as the totalitarian model has come under attack.[4] As the Soviet archives have opened, historians have uncovered evidence that the people in the Soviet Union were not passive actors but on the contrary actively participated in the political process. This participation occurred in the form of active resistance, strikes, and riots as well as letter- writing campaigns and petitions. This was a time when the Bolsheviks were still adjusting to their new status as rulers as opposed to rev-

Patriarch Alexei II at canonization of Optina Elders

olutionaries. As the issue of the monastery communes revealed, many authorities were responsive to petitions as well as arguments from their own party members to keep the communes open.

The method of coopting Communist ideology to preserve monasticism has incited many Orthodox to charge that monastery communes collaborated with the Bolsheviks. This is an accusation that the Patriarchal Church also faces.[5] These critics point to petitions using Communist rhetoric as evidence that the monasteries betrayed Orthodoxy and Christianity. On a superficial level, these accusations appear valid. However, before passing judgment, it is necessary to discuss the meanings of

Procession at canonization of Optina Elders

the words "collaboration," "resistance," and "adaptation." Even though interpretations of these words are highly subjective, it is nonetheless possible to apply some level of objectivity to their meaning.

First, Webster's dictionary defines the word "collaborate" as "1) to work together on a project and 2) [to] assist the invaders of one's country." Applying this to the monasteries in the Soviet Union, it appears that neither definition completely fits. One could argue that monastery communes cooperated with the Bolsheviks in an economic sense. Both sides benefited from the monastery communes' productivity. The Bolsheviks reaped economic rewards, and the monasteries were allowed to

The author with three Russian nuns

preserve their communities and institutions. The second definition is also problematic. The monasteries certainly did not assist the Bolsheviks in establishing a power base; on the contrary, most monastics supported the White cause during the Civil War. However, an argument can be made that by later supplying the Soviet government with produce from the monastery communes, they were aiding the atheist government's cause.

The term "resistance" also has multiple layers of meaning. The word inspires visions of violent protest to someone or something. Monasteries engaged in this type of resistance to nationalization and again during collectivization. It soon became clear that these acts of violence accomplished little except the creation of more martyrs for the Church. However, resistance does not have to be violent. It does not even have to be overt. In his book *Domination and the Arts of Resistance,* James C. Scott discusses the phenomenon of "hidden versus public transcripts" between the dominant and subordinate groups. He defines "public transcript" as "the open interaction between subordinates and those who dominate."[6] In other words, the subordinates say what they know their masters want to hear and vice versa. The purpose of these public transcripts is to "create the appearance of unanimity among ruling groups and the appearance of consent among the subordinates."[7] Examples of public transcripts in the case of the Soviet Union and the war on religion is the use of language in the constitutions, guaranteeing freedom of religion, and the use of euphemism for arrest and execution.

The monasteries' petitions to the authorities claiming that they were "run along Communist principles" is another such example. The hidden transcript, by contrast, is what is said behind closed doors and can include acts of passive resistance. In the Soviet Union, where the personal was also political, the very act of praying could be interpreted as an act of resistance. The fact that many people embraced secret monasticism during this time is a sign that people regarded their decision to become a monk or nun not only as a personal choice, but also as an act of quiet rebellion. An internal prayer life was one area of life that the Soviet authorities could not legislate or control.

The term "accommodate" according to Webster's means "to adjust to existing conditions." It appears that this word best summarizes what the monasteries did during the interwar period. Adaptation to one's surroundings—whether by an individual or an institution—is not synonymous with active support of that environment. The fact that a monastery converted itself into a collective farm does not necessarily mean that it accepted the ideals of collectivization. Adaptation can also be a temporary condition. Indeed, the Church always believed that the Bolshevik regime would not last forever and that whatever concessions they made would not be for an extended period of time. Monastics also rationalized their decisions to adapt to collectivization by claiming that monasticism is inherently a collective institution. Therefore, they were not compromising their principles but merely adhering to the traditional cenobitic lifestyle.

The question of whether monasteries collaborated with the Soviet regime is not an empty one but has significant importance for the current status of monasticism in Russia. Many Russians became disillusioned with the Russian Orthodox Church because of revelations of KGB collaboration among priests and bishops. Although monks and nuns are included in some of these accusations, they are generally exempt from popular condemnation of the Church. The prerevolutionary conception of monastics as embodying the true ideals of Christianity appears to still exist. However, if believers harbor doubts about a monastery's association with the Soviet regime, financial contributions to the institution could suffer.

The field of Russian religious history during the Soviet period has emerged as a new and exiting focus of current research, and as more archives are opened, the possibilities for a deeper understanding of the period increase. This work is an attempt to contribute to the historiography and provide a basis for further research and discussion.

APPENDIX A

Decree on Land Nationalization, November 8, 1917

1. Landed proprietorship is abolished forthwith without compensation.[1]

2. The landed estates, as well as all appanages, the monasterial and church lands, with all their livestock, implements, farm buildings, and everything pertaining thereto, shall be placed under the control of the volost Land Committees and the uezd Soviets of Peasants' Deputies pending the meeting of the Constituent Assembly.

3. All damage to the confiscated property, which henceforth belongs to the whole people, is declared a felony, punishable by the revolutionary courts. The uezd Soviets of Peasants' Deputies shall take all necessary measures for the preservation of the strictest order during the confiscation of the estates of the landlords, for determining which particular estates shall be subject to confiscation, for drawing up inventories of all property confiscated, and for the strictest revolutionary protection of all land transferred to the people and all structures, implements, cattle, supplies, etc.

4. The following peasant Instructions, compiled by the *Izvestiia* of All Russian Soviet of Peasants' Deputies from 242 local peasant Instructions and published in no. 88 of the *Izvestiia* (Petrograd, September 1, 1917) are everywhere to serve as a guide in carrying out the great land reforms until a final decision on the latter is taken by the Constituent Assembly.

5. The land of ordinary peasants and ordinary Cossacks shall not be confiscated.

APPENDIX B

Decree of the Soviet Commissars Concerning the Separation of Church and State and of Schools and Church, January 23, 1918

1. The Church is separated from the State.[1]
2. Within the confines of the Republic it shall be prohibited to issue any local by-laws or regulations restricting or limiting freedom of any kind based on the religious creed of citizens.
3. Every citizen may profess any religious belief or profess no belief at all. All restrictions of rights, involved by professing one or another belief, or by professing no belief at all, are null and void.
4. State or other public functions binding in law shall not be accompanied by the performance of religious rites or ceremonies.
5. Free performances of religious rites is permissible as long as it does not disturb public order or interfere with the rights of the citizens of the Soviet Republic. The local authorities shall be entitled in such cases to adopt all necessary measures for maintenance of public order and safety.
6. Nobody is entitled to refuse to perform his duties as a citizen on the basis of his religious belief. Exceptions to this rule, on condition that one civic be replaced by another, may be granted in each individual case by the verdict of the People's Court.
7. The official taking or administering of religious oaths is abolished. In necessary cases, merely a solemn promise may be given.
8. Births, marriages, and deaths are to be registered and solemnized solely by civic (secular) authorities: the marriage and birth registration offices.
9. The School is separated from the Church. Instructions in any religious creed or belief shall be prohibited in all State, public, and also private educational establishments in which general instruction is given. Citizens may give or receive religious instruction in a private manner.
10. All Church and religious associations are subject to the ordinary legislation concerning private associations and unions. They shall not enjoy special privileges, nor receive any subsidies from the State or from local autonomous or self-governing institutions.

11. Compulsory collection of imposts and taxes in favor of church and religious associations, also measures of compulsion or punishment adopted by such associations in respect to their members shall not be permitted.

12. No church or religious associations have the right to own property. They do not possess the rights of juridical persons.

13. The property of all church and religious associations existing in Russia is pronounced the property of the people. Buildings and objects especially used for the purpose of worship shall be let, free of charge, to the respective religious associations, by resolution of the local or central authorities.

APPENDIX C

Sample of Agreement between Believers and Soviet of Workmen-Peasant Deputies

We, the undersigned citizens of ________________, residing in such locality, have concluded the present agreement with the ________________ Soviet of Workmen-Peasant Deputies, represented by its plenipotentiary (office, name, and surname. to the effect that on this . . . day of the month of . . . in the year . . . we have taken over for use, for an indefinite period and free of charge, the (description of church or religious building) situated ________________ with property required for ritual purposes in accordance with a special list, undersigned by ourselves, on the following conditions:[1]

1. We, the undersigned citizens, undertake to maintain and keep the national property entrusted to us, and to use it solely for the purpose it is intended for, assuming all responsibility for the integrity and safety of such property entrusted to us, and also for the fulfillment of other obligations devolving on us under this agreement.

2. We undertake to use, and to permit our co-religionists to use, the churches and ritual articles in them solely for the purpose of satisfying religious needs.

3. We undertake to make sure that the property entrusted to us is made no other use of than mentioned in Articles 1 and 2 of this agreement.

More particularly, we undertake to prohibit in religious buildings and premises taken over by ourselves:

a. political meetings hostile to the Soviet regime
b. the spreading or selling of books, pamphlets, and other literature hostile to the Soviet regime or its individual representatives, and
c. delivering sermons and speeches hostile to the Soviet regime or its individual representatives
d. the ringing of alarm bells for the purpose of calling up the population and inciting it against the Soviet regime, in view of which we undertake to

fulfill all regulations and orders of the local Soviet of Workmen-Peasant Deputies in regard to the rules for using belfries and bell towers.

4. We undertake to cover from our own sources all current expenses in connection with the maintenance of the Church (or other buildings for religious purposes. and articles, or objects in it, such as: keeping it in a state of repair, heating, insurance, guarding, payment of debts, taxes, local imposts, etc.

5. We undertake to keep an inventory of the entire ritual property in which we shall enter all articles newly required for ritual purposes, unless they are the private property of individual citizens.

6. We undertake to admit without restriction, at times when no divine liturgy is going on, persons authorized by the Soviet of Workmen-Peasant Deputies to inspect and check the property.

7. For loss of, or damage to, articles entrusted to us we assume civil liability conjointly, to the extent of the actual loss or damage sustained.

8. In case of return of property entrusted to us, we undertake to return it in the same shape and condition in which we received it for use and for keeping.

9. In cemetery churches and in graveyards we undertake to bury co-religionists, in case persons interested desire it, with observance of religious rites which in all cases must be at equal fees for all citizens, the amount of such fee to be brought by ourselves to public notice every day.

10. In the event we fail to adopt all measures in our power in order to fulfill all our obligations under this agreement, we shall be criminally liable and shall be dealt with with all severity of revolutionary law; and in such contingencies the Soviet of Workmen-Peasant Deputies shall have the right to cancel this agreement.

11. In case we desire to terminate this agreement, we undertake to give notice in writing to the Soviet of Workmen-Peasant Deputies, the provision of this agreement shall continue binding on us, and we shall continue to be responsible for its execution; we also undertake to return within this space of time the property taken over by us.

12. Every one of us who has signed this agreement shall have the right to withdraw from it, giving notice in writing to the Soviet of Workmen-Peasant Deputies; this, however, shall not relieve the given persons of liability for losses and damage sustained by the respective national property during the time the given persons participated in the use of and administration of such property, prior to giving the Soviet of Workmen-Peasant Deputies notice of his intention to withdraw.

13. None of us, nor all of us taken together, shall have the right to refuse

any citizen, who is our co-religionist and not disqualified by verdict of court, to sign after his date the present agreement, and to participate in the administration and management of the property mentioned in this agreement, on identical conditions with all other persons who have signed it.

The original of this agreement shall be kept by the . . . Soviet of Workmen-Peasant Deputies, and a duly certified copy shall be issued to the group of citizens who have signed this agreement, and who have taken over for religious uses the church and the ritual articles in it, as specified in the inventory.

Notes

Preface

1. I have used the term "monastery" to denote both male and female institutions. I decided to use this term because Russian does not have a different word such as "convent" to distinguish a women's monastic community.

2. Examples include John Curtiss, *The Russian Church and the Soviet State, 1917–1950;* George Kline, *Religious and Antireligious Thought in Russia* (Chicago: University of Chicago Press, 1968); David E. Powell, *Antireligious Propaganda in the Soviet Union: A Study of Mass Persuasion* (Cambridge, Mass.: MIT Press, 1975); and James Thrower, *Marxist-Leninist "Scientific Atheism" and the Study of Religion and Atheism in the USSR* (Berlin and Amsterdam: Mouton, 1983).

3. On the eve of the 1917 Russian Revolution, there were 1,242 total monasteries and convents in the Russian Empire. By 1922, the Bolshevik government nationalized 722 of these, leaving 520. By 1929 no monasteries remained open. Cited in V. F. Zybkovets, *Natsionalizatsiia monastyrskikh imushchestv v Sovetskoi Rossii, 1917–1921,* pp. 77, 113; and Jane Ellis, *The Russian Orthodox Church: A Contemporary History,* 125.

4. Glennys Young, "Rural Religion and Soviet Power, 1921–1932," 278.

5. William Husband, *"Godless Communists": Atheism and Society in Soviet Russia, 1917–1932.*

6. William Husband, "Soviet Atheism and Russian Orthodox Strategies of Resistance, 1917–1932," *Journal of Modern History* 70, no. 1 (Mar., 1998): 107.

7. League of the Godless, "Stenograficheskii otchet vtorogo s"ezda soiuza bezbozhnikov," 1929; see also *Antireligioznik* 26 (1926): 40.

8. The only monastery that remained open throughout the twenties and thirties was Pskov-Pecherskaia, on the Russian-Estonian border. Techni-

cally it was a part of Free Estonia and beyond the jurisdiction of the Bolsheviks.

9. See William Fletcher, *A Study in Survival: The Church in Russia, 1927–1943,* and I. A. Andreev, *Russia's Catacomb Saints.*

10. For works on Soviet labor in the Soviet Union, see Isaac Deutscher, *Soviet Trade Unions: Their Place in Soviet Labor Policy* (London: Royal Institute of International Affairs, 1950); William Chase, *Workers, Society, and the Soviet State: Labor and Life in Moscow, 1918–1929* (Urbana: University of Illinois Press, 1987); and Jeffrey Rossman, "Worker Resistance under Stalin: Class and Gender in the Textile Mills of the Ivanovo Industrial Region, 1926–1941" (Ph.D. diss., University of California at Berkeley, forthcoming). For recent Western research on peasant resistance, see Sheila Fitzpatrick, *Stalin's Peasants: Resistance and Survival in the Russian Village after Collectivization,* (New York: Oxford University Press, 1994), and Lynne Viola, *Peasant Rebels under Stalin: Collectivization and the Culture of Peasant Resistance.* For recent work on popular opinion in the Soviet Union, see Sarah Davies's *Popular Opinion in Stalin's Russia: Terror, Propaganda, and Dissent, 1934–1941,* (Cambridge: Cambridge University Press, 1997). For examples of Russian scholarly work on this subject, see V. P. Danilov and N. A. Ivnitskii, eds. *Dokumenty svidetel'stvuiut: Iz istorii derevni nakanune I v khode kollektivizatsii, 1927–1932,* (Moscow: F2d-vo-polit. lit-ry, 1989), and I. E. Zelenin, "O nekatorykh belykh piatnakh zavershaiushchego etapa sploshnoi kollektivizatsii," *Istoriia SSSR* 2 (1989).

11. See Dimitry Pospielovsky, *A History of Marxist-Leninist Atheism and Soviet Anti-Religious Policies.*

12. See Orlando Figes, *Peasant Russia, Civil War: The Volga Countryside in Revolution, 1917–1921,* (Oxford: Clarendon Press, 1991).

13. Lev Denisov, *Pravoslavnie Monastyri Rossiiskoi Imperii.*

14. Merle Fainsod, *Smolensk under Soviet Rule,* 17–18.

15. See ibid. and, more recently, Glennys Young's dissertation. Archives in the State Archives of the Smolensk oblast focusing on religious issues include Smolensk church-diocese council, f. 1232, and the Council of Smolensk and Dorogobuzhskogo diocese, f. 47.

16. For examples of this model, see Dimitry Pospielovsky, *A History of Marxist-Leninist Atheism;* Ivan Andreev, *Russia's Catacomb Saints;* and virtually anything published by presses affiliated with the Russian Orthodox Church Abroad.

17. Recently, RTsKhIDNI has changed its name to RGASPI (Rossiiskii Gosudarstvennyi Arkhiv sotsial'no-politicheskoi istorii—the Russian Center for the Preservation and Study of Records of Modern History). For consistency, I have used the former name when citing this archive.

Chapter 1. The Church on the Eve of the 1917 Revolution

1. For more information about the Orthodox Church and its history and practices, see Timothy Ware, *The Orthodox Church;* Anthony Coniaris, *Basic Orthodoxy: Key Words of the Faith,* vol. 1 (Minneapolis, Minn.: Light and Life Press, 1989); Thomas Hopko, *The Orthodox Faith,* vols. 1–4 (New York: Department of Religious Education, Orthodox Church of America, 1971–1976); and Daniel B. Clendenin, *Eastern Orthodox Christianity: A Western* Perspective (Grand Rapids, Mich.: Baker Books, 1995).

2. The word *lavra* originally referred to a large community of monks. The term is now used to denote a large monastery of any kind. In the Russian empire, there are four lavras—the Kievo-Pecherskaia Lavra in Kiev, Alexander Nevsky in St. Petersburg, Holy Trinity in Sergeev Posad, and Pochaev Pecherskaia in Volhynia. Such monasteries usually have a seminary attached and continue to serve as educational and cultural centers.

3. Paul Johnson, *A History of Christianity* (New York: Antheneum, 1979), 141.

4. Steven Runciman, *The Great Church in Captivity,* 38.

5. G. P. Fedotov, *Svyatye drevnei Rusi (10–17 stoletiya)* (Paris, 1985), 235–36.

6. Vladimir Kotelnikov, "The Primacy of Monastic Spirituality," in Giuseppe Alberigo and Oscar Beozzo, eds, *The Holy Russian Church and Western Christianity* (London: SCM Press, 1996), 27.

7. The amount of material written about Optina Pustyn monastery is voluminous. Some good accounts are those of Sergei Chetvernikov, *Optina Pustyn* (Paris, YMCA Press, 1988); A. P., "Optina Pustyn: Istoricheskoe Opisanie," *Pravoslavnaia Rus* 17 (1989): 7–9; I. M. Kontsevitch, *Optina Pustyn i eia vremia* (Jordanville, N.Y.: Holy Trinity Monastery, 1975); and Leonard Stanton, *Optina Pustyn in the Russian Literary Imagination: Iconic Vision in Works by Dostoevsky, Gogol, Tolstoy, and Others.* Additionally, there is a series of biographies of individual elders published by St. Herman of Alaska Press. Some titles include Fr. Clement Sederholm, *Elder Leonid of Optina* (Platina, Calif.: St. Herman of Alaska Press, 1990), and *Elder Nektarii* (Platina, Calif.: St. Herman of Alaska Press, 1990).

8. Stanton, 45–46.

9. Runciman, *The Great Church,* 59. For more information about the Byzantine period, see John Julius Norwich, *A Short History of Byzantium* (New York: Alfred A. Knopf, 1997); Michael Angold, *Church and Society in Byzantium under the Comneni, 1081–1261* (Cambridge/New York: Cambridge University Press, 1995).

10. Michael T. Florinsky, *Russia: A History and an Interpretation,* vol. 1 (New York: Macmillan, 1953), 139–40.

11. See Fundamental Laws, Apr. 23, 1906, Chapter 5, art. 57; *Svod zakonov* 1, part 1.
12. James Billington, *The Icon and the Axe: An Interpretive History of Russian Culture,* 101.
13. The best example of hesychasm may be found in the classic of Russian spirituality, *The Way of a Pilgrim* trans. R. M. French (Pasadena, Calif.: Hope Publishing House, 1993). This anonymous journal written in the nineteenth century describes one pilgrim's quest to learn how to "pray without ceasing."
14. A *skete* is a small house where two or three monks or nuns live together. The exclusivity allows the monks and nuns to focus on prayer without the distractions of a larger monastery.
15. Stanton, 132.
16. Brenda Meehan-Waters, *Holy Women of Russia,* 12.
17. Dimitry Pospielovsky, *The Orthodox Church in the History of Russia,* 108.
18. For more information on Peter I's Reglament, see James Cracraft, *The Church Reforms of Peter the Great* (Stanford, Calif.: Stanford University Press, 1971); Alexander Muller, ed, *The Spiritual Regulation of Peter the Great* (Seattle: University of Washington Press, 1972).
19. Pospielovsky, 119.
20. V. V. Zverinskii, *Material dlia istoriko-topograficheskogo issledovaniia o pravoslavnykh monastyriakh v rossiiskoi imperii,* vol. 1 (St. Petersburg, 1890), xi.
21. A. D. Denisov, *Pravoslavnye Monastyri Rossiiskoi Emperii.*
22. Brenda Meehan-Waters, "Metropolitan Filaret and the Reform of Women's Monastic Communities," *Russian Review* 50 (1991): 321.
23. Abbot Herman, "Bishop Theofan the Recluse: Instructor of Monastic Women." *The Orthodox Word* 23, no. 2 (Mar.–Apr., 1987): 83.
24. Denisov, xii.
25. For more on Orthodox monasticism, see Fr. Sergii Chetverikov, *Starets Paisii Velichovskii* (Belmont, Mass: Nordland, 1980); Monakhina Taisia Sosshavila, *Russkoe Pravoslavnoe Zhenskoe Monashestvo,* vols. 18–20 (Sergeev Posad, Russia: Holy Trinity Monastery, 1992); and N. F. Robinson, *Monasticism in the Orthodox Churches.*
26. Christopher Read, *Religion, Revolution, and the Russian Intelligentsia, 1900–1912* (London: Macmillan, 1979), 38.
27. Ibid., 65. For more about Sergei Bulgakov, see his autobiography, *Avtobiograficheskie zametki* (Paris: YMCA, 1991). Some examples of his political and religious writing may be found in *Ot Marksisma k idealizmu: Sbornik statei 1896–1903* (Petersburg: 1903) and *Intelligentsiya i religiia: O protivorechivosti sovremennogo bexreligioznogo mirovozreniya* (Moscow: 1908). For more on Nicholas

Berdyaev, see his autobiography, *Dream and Reality,* (New York: Macmillan, 1951). Some of his best-known works include *The Russian Idea* (1947), *Freedom and the Spirit* (New York: A Scribner's Song, 1935), *The Meaning of Creativity* (1916), and *Slavery and Freedom* (New York: A Scribner's Song, 1944).

28. Stanton, 79.

29. Ibid., 213.

30. Konstantin Leont'ev, *Otets Kliment Zedergol'm: Ieromonakh Optinoi Pustyni,* 2d ed. (Moscow, 1882), 87.

31. Paul R. Vallière, "The Idea of a Council in Russian Orthodoxy, 1905," printed in Robert Nichols and Theofanis Stavrou, *Russian Orthodoxy under the Old Regime,* 185.

32. James Cunningham, *A Vanquished Hope,* 115.

33. Ibid., 98–99. For more detailed information on the church reform movement, see Alexander Bogolepov, *Church Reforms in Russia, 1905–1918;* Fr. John Meyndorff, "Russian Bishops and Church Reform in 1905," in Robert Nichols and Theofanis Stavrou, eds., *Russian Orthodoxy under the Old Regime;* Paul R. Vallière, "The Idea of a Council in Russian Orthodoxy in 1905," in Nichols and Stavrou; and John Curtiss, *Church and State in Russia, 1900–1917* (New York: Octagon Books, 1965). For a Russian interpretation, see P. N. Zyrianov, *Pravslavnaia Tserkov v borbe s revoliutsie, 1905–1907* (Moscow: Nauka, 1984); E. E. Golubinskii, *O Reforme v byte Russkoi Tserkvi* (Moscow, 1913); Vasilii Myshtyn, *Po Tserkovno-ocshchestvennym Voprosom* (Sergeev Posad, Russia, 1905–1906).

34. Cunningham, 107.

35. "Memorandum of Petersburg Priests." Materials from 1905 on parish clergy and seminarians in the 1905 revolution, in a 1995 seminar conducted by Gregory Freeze at Brandeis University.

36. Cunningham, 208.

37. Walter Laquer, *Black Hundred: The Rise of the Extreme Right in Russia* (New York: Harper Collins, 1993), 52.

38. Cunningham, 198 99.

39. For examples of scholars who view government interference as the reason for church failure, see James Cunningham, *A Vanquished Hope* (New York: St. Vladimir's Press, 1981); John Meyendorff, "Russian Bishops and Church Reform in 1905," in Robert Nichols and Theofanis Stavrou, eds., *Russian Orthodoxy under the Old Regime* (Minneapolis: University of Minnesota Press, 1978); and Nicholas Zernov, *The Russian Religious Renaissance of the Twentieth Century* (New York, 1963). For the view that the church shared more of the blame, see Gregory Freeze, "Going to the Intelligentsia: The Church and Its Urban Mission in Post-Reform Russia," in Edith Clowes

and James West, eds., *Between Tsar and People* (Princeton, N.J.: Princeton University Press, 1991).

40. Berdyaev, 176–77.

41. A. S. Khomyakov, "Tserkov odna," in *William Palmer, ed., A Classic of Russian Orthodoxy: The Church Is One* (London: Fellowship of St. Alban and St. Sergius, 1968).

42. Bogolepov, 54.

43. Freeze, 224.

44. Ibid., 225.

45. *Tserkovnyia Vedomosti,* Dec. 21, 1906, 3173.

46. Cunningham, 281–82.

47. Curtiss, 315.

48. *Tserkovnyia Vedomosti,* May 20, 1912, pp. 820–21.

49. Curtiss, 316.

50. One desiatina was equal to about 2.7 acres.

51. Ibid., 95.

52. Ibid.

53. Ibid., 318.

54. For accounts of the 1917 sobor, besides Bogoleopv and Curtiss, see James Cunningham, "The Russian Patriarchate and the Attempt to Recover Symphonia," *Canadian-American Slavic Studies* 26, nos. 1–3 (1992): 272–92; Catherine Evtuhov, "The Church in the Russian Revolution: Arguments for and against Restoring the Patriarchate at the Church Council of 1917–1918," *Slavic Review* 50, no. 3 (Fall, 1991); Fr. Vladislav Tsipin, *Istoriia Russkoi Pravoslavnoi Tserkvi, 1917–1990* (Moskva: Khronika, 1994); and A. N. Kasherov, *Gosudarstvo I Tserkov 1917–1945* (Sankt Petersburg, 1995). For a firsthand account, see Frs. Georgii Golubtsov and Nikolai Liubimov, *Rossiiskaia Tserkov v godi revoliutsi, 1917–1918 (sobornik).* This is part of the diaries of two of the participants. Reprinted in Moscow, 1995).

55. *Tserkovni Vedomosti,* 1917 no. 22–23, 148a.

56. *Postanovlenia Vserusskago s"ezda predstavitelei ot monastyrei, byvshago v Sviato-Troitskoi Lavre, s 16 do 23 iulia 1917g,* 3–4.

57. Ibid., 4–5.

58. Ibid., 8.

59. Vladislav Tsipin, *Istoria Pravoslavnaia Tserkvi, 1917–1990* (Moskva: Khronika, 1994), 25.

60. *Postanovlenie,* 8–10.

61. John Curtiss, *Church and State,* 316.

62. For more information on monasteries as prisons, see A. S. Prugavin, *Monastyrskiia Tiurmyi v borbe s sektantstvom* (The Hague: Mouton, 1970).

63. Ibid., 22.
64. James Cunningham, "The Russian Patriarchate and the Attempt to Recover Symphonia," 279.
65. Ibid., 275–76.
66. Ibid., 279.
67. *Postanovlenie,* 34.
68. Ibid.
69. GARF f. 3431, op. 1, d. 277, l. 3, "National Sobor of the All-Russian Orthodox Church: Department of the Situation of the Church and the State," session 2, Sept. 5, 1917.
70. Ibid., 10.
71. Ibid., 145, "Report of the legal situation of the church in the government."
72. The second article states that "The Orthodox Church in Russia in matters of doctrine of the faith and morals, liturgy, internal church discipline is completely independent *(nezavisima)* of the government, but in matters of church legislation, government, courts, and relations with other autocephalous churches, [the Church] is directed by its dogmatic-canonical principles, using the rights of self-government *(samoupravlenie)* and self-determination *(samoopredelenie)*."
73. Ibid., "Special opinion of member of the All-Russian Sobor A. F. Odarchenko of the 6th department," 157.
74. Catherine Evtuhov, "The Church in the Russian Revolution: Arguments for and against Restoring the Patriarchate at the Church Council of 1917–1918," *Slavic Review* 50, no. 3 (Fall, 1991), 506–507.
75. For a good biography of Tikhon, see Mikhail Vostryshev, *Patriarch Tikhon* (Moscow: Molodaia Gvardiia, 1995).

Chapter 2. Revolution, Civil War, and Famine, 1917–1922

1. In Yuri Lotman and B. A. Uspenskii, *The Semiotics of Russian Culture,* 5.
2. Ibid., 10.
3. Delos B. McKown, *The Classical Marxist Critiques of Religion: Marx, Engels, Lenin, Kautsky* (The Hague: Martinus Nijhoff, 1975), 10–12.
4. Ibid., 112.
5. Robert Williams, *The Other Bolsheviks: Lenin and His Critics, 1904–1914* (Bloomington, Ind.: Indiana University Press, 1986), 57. The best example of Gorky's conception of self-sacrifice can be found in Gorky's novel *Mother.* The hero embodies both Christian and socialist virtues, and the novel is full of Christian imagery of martyrdom and immortality.

6. Sheila Fitzpatrick, *The Commissariat of Enlightenment* (Cambridge: Cambridge University Press, 1970), 5–6.

7. Ibid., 14.

8. For Lunacharskii's views on religion, see *Ob ateizme i religii* (Moscow: Mys'l, 1972); *Khristianstvoi ili kommunizm: Disputi mitrA Vvedenskim* (Leningrad, 1926); *Religii i veshchenie* (Moscow: Sovietskaia Rossia, 1985); and *Religiia i sotsializm*, 2 vols. (St. Petersburg, 1911).

9. V. I. Lenin, *Collected Works*, 5th ed., vol. 4 (Moscow: Foreign Languages Publishing House, 1962), 83–84.

10. Martin McCauley, ed., *The Russian Revolution and the Soviet State, 1917–1921: Documents* (London: Macmillan, 1975), 184.

11. Boleslaw Szczesniak, ed., *The Russian Revolution and Religion: A Collection of Documents concerning the Suppression of Religion by the Communists, 1917–1925*, 28. Numerous other books give a general overview of the Bolsheviks' religious policy. John Curtiss's *Russian Church and the Soviet State, 1917–1950* remains the authoritative work. A more recent monograph is from the Finnish scholar Arto Luukkanen, *The Party of Unbelief: The Religious Policy of the Bolshevik Party, 1917–1929* (Helsinki: Suomen Historiallinen Seura, 1994).

12. For more on the Bolsheviks' inconsistencies, see William Husband's *Godless Communists: Atheism and Society in Soviet Russia, 1917–1932*.

13. Orlando Figes, *Peasant Russia, Civil War*, 148.

14. GARF, f. 353, op. 2, d. 694, l. 200–201.

15. Baruch Knei-Paz, *The Social and Political Thought of Leon Trotsky* (Oxford: Clarendon Press, 1978), 285.

16. The "Marriage, Children, and Regulation of Civil Status" law does not, as commonly supposed, prohibit church marriages; however, it does state that the only marriages that the state will recognize are those that occur at city hall. It also requires all religious institutions to transfer all records of births, deaths, and marriages to the proper civil authorities. Szczesniak, 31–33.

17. Ibid., 34.

18. See article 4, Appendix B: "State or other public functions binding in law shall not be accompanied by the performance of religious rites or ceremonies."

19. Szczesniak, 35.

20. For more on the Orthodox understanding of sainthood, see Vladimir Demshuk, *Russian Sainthood and Canonization* (Minneapolis, Minn.: Light and Life Publishing, 1978).

21. See the letter of Mar. 8, 1919, from the NARKOMIUST to the Yaroslavskii Liquidation Committee outlining conditions under which ex-

humations should take place. The letter stresses the presence of doctors, party members, and worker and peasant organizations and warns that the "uncoverings" must not occur during services. GARF, f. A-353, op. 2, d. 690, l. 22.

22. F. Kovalev, "Documents and Evidence about Relics," *Bezbozhnik* 7 (Apr., 1926), 7.

23. GARF, f. A-353, op. 4, d. 384, l. 24–25.

24. GARF, f. A-353, op. 4, d. 392, l. 70–70ob.

25. For more on cases of relic exposure in early modern Russia, see Eve Levin, "False Miracles and Unattested Dead Bodies: Investigations into Popular Cults in Early Modern Russia," in *Official Religion and Lived Religion in the Early Modern World,* ed. James Tracy, forthcoming, Cambridge University Press.

26. Sergei Volkov, *Poslednie u Troitse* (Moscow, 1995), 212–13.

27. Statement of Patriarch Tikhon, Aug. 28, 1920, in M. E. Gubonin, *Aktyi Sviateishego Tikhona, Patriarkha Moskovskogo i vsia Rossia,* 167.

28. *Russkaia Vedomosti,* Jan. 25, 1918.

29. Luukkanen, *The Party of Unbelief,* 70.

30. *Russkaia Vedomosti,* Jan. 23, 1918.

31. The city of St. Petersburg has undergone several name changes throughout the twentieth century. In Aug., 1914, it was christened Petrograd in a patriotic reaction against the "Germanic" name of St. Petersburg. In 1924, shortly after V. I. Lenin's death, the city was renamed Leningrad in his honor. In 1991, after the breakup of the Soviet Union, the original name was restored.

32. A. N. Kashevarov, *Gosudarstvo i Tserkov: Iz istorii vzaimootnoshenii sovietskoi vlasti i russkoi pravoslavnoi tserkvi,* 73, 80.

33. Message of Patriarch Tikhon, Anathematizing the Soviet Regime, Jan. 19–Feb. 1, 1918. Printed in M. E. Gubonin, *Aktyi Sviateishego Tikhona,* 82–83.

34. *Russkaia Vedomosti,* Jan. 21, 1918.

35. John Curtiss, *The Russian Church and the Soviet State,* 57.

36. GARF, f. 353, op. 3, d. 731, l. 63–65ob.

37. G. P. Fedotoff, *The Russian Church since the Revolution,* 39.

38. *Pravda,* no. 188, 23, VIII, 1922.

39. Metropolitan Vitaly, "Saint Jonah, Bishop of Hankow," in *Living Orthodoxy* 17 (Sept.–Oct., 1996): 3.

40. Sosshavila, *Russkaia Pravoslavnoe Zhenskoe Monashestvo,* 271.

41. M. Enisherlov, ed., *Voinstvuishchee Bezbozhie v SSSR za 15 let* (Moscow, 1932), 320.

42. Sosshavila, *Russkaia Pravoslavnoe Zhenskoe Monashestvo,* 259.

43. Curtiss, 94.
44. Szczesniak, 49.
45. Curtiss, 89.
46. Nikolai Bukharin and E. Preobrazhensky, *The ABC of Communism* (London: The Communist Party of Great Britain, 1922), 255.
47. Ibid.
48. "Contemporary Ascetics of Piety: Elder Sampson, Patron of the Orthodox Convert Movement." *The Orthodox Word* 30 (July–Aug., 1994): 201.
49. The terms "Cheka" and "GPU" both refer to the secret police. The All-Russian Extraordinary Commission for Struggle against Counter-Revolution, Sabotage, and Speculation (referred to as the "Cheka") was formed in Dec., 1917. During the civil war, it assumed the broader functions of security police and became an organ of terror. After the civil war, the Chief Political Administration (GPU) replaced the Cheka. Although the GPU did not come into existence until after the civil war, many Russians use the two terms interchangeably. Therefore, in this example, I use the terms that Nun Taisia used in her narrative.
50. "Little mother," a term of affection used for priests' wives and abbesses.
51. Sosshavila, 261.
52. Ibid., 262.
53. *Revolutsiia i Tserkov* no. 9–12 (1920): 83.
54. R. S. F. S. R., Narodnyi Kommissariat Iustisii, *Otchet IX Vserossiskomu S'ezdu Sovetov*, 48–49.
55. *Revoliutsiia i Tserkov* nos. 3–5 (1919): 12–13.
56. Ibid., no. 2 (1919): 37; nos. 9–12 (1920): 64–66.
57. Alexander Solzhenitsyn, *The Gulag Archipelago*, part 2 (New York: Harper and Row, 1975), 19.
58. Ibid., 31n.
59. Ibid., 30–31.
60. *Deianiia Sviashchennago Sobora Pravoslavnoi Rossiskoi Tserkvi*, kniga 9, vypusk 2, 25–29.
61. Szczesniak, 43.
62. Ibid., 44.
63. GARF, f. 353 op. 2, d. 690 l. 18.
64. A *sovkhoz* is a state-owner farm that practiced large-scale agriculture. The agricultural workers worked for wages and were supervised by appointed managers.
65. GARF, f. 353, op. 2, d. 690, l. 20.
66. Gosudarstvenny Arkhiv Kalugoi Oblasti (GAKO) f. R-1498, op.1, d. 651, l. 90.

67. GAKO, f. 109, op. 1, d. 98, l. 13.
68. GAKO, f. R-1498, op. 1, d. 651, ll. 90–91.
69. GAKO, f. 1267, op. 29, d. 10, l. 4.
70. P. N. Miliukov, *Outlines of Russian Culture,* (Philadelphia: University of Pennsylvania Press, 1942), I, 165.
71. Gosudarstvenny Arkhiv Moskovskogo Oblasti (GAMO), f. 66, op. 17, d. 118, l. 28, 90, 124.
72. GAMO, f. 66, op. 1, d. 117, l. 24.
73. GAKO, f. 1267, op. 29, d. 10, ll. 3–4.
74. Zybkovets, 102.
75. An *artel* is a cooperative system in which the communal element is confined to marketing and does not extend to production. An artel can be devoted to either agricultural work or light industry.
76. Ibid., 105.
77. Volkov, 195.
78. Ibid., 220.
79. *Zhizn Hieromonakha Nikona, Poslednyi Starets Optina Pustyna,* 141–42.
80. Zybkovets, 104.
81. Telegram 17/2/19 RTsKhIDNI, f. 2, op. 1, d. 10937.
82. Letter from Archimandrite John to Patriarch Tikhon, Mar. 20, 1918, GARF f. A-353, op. 4, d. 384, l. 6.
83. GARF, f. A-353, op. 2, d. 697, l. 30; GARF, f. A-353, op. 2, d. 671, l. 33.
84. Zybkovets, 99.
85. *Tserkovnyia Vedomosti Izdavaemyia pri Vysshem Russkom Tserkovnom Upravlenii Zagranitsei,* nos. 6–7 (June, 1922), 3–5.
86. A. I. Vvedenski, *Tserkov i Gosudarstvo* (Moscow, 1923), 219.
87. *Tserkovnia Vedomosti . . . Zagranitsei,* nos. 6–7 (1922): 2–3.
88. This decree is different from the earlier Jan., 1918, decree of separation of church and state. It discusses the rules by which the monasteries and clergy may use land.
89. Letter from NARKOMIUST to all zemotdels, Oct. 30, 1919, GARF f. 353, op. 4, d. 372, l. 2.
90. Vladimir Rusak, 217–18.
91. GARF, f. A-353, op. 2, d. 671, l. 120.
92. Ibid.
93. Ibid., 121 ob.
94. Letter from citizens of Nr'ev village, May 13, 1920, GAMO f. 4997, op. 1, d. 486, l. 4.
95. Ibid., l. 16.
96. In 1919 Florensky published an essay titled "The Trinity-St. Sergius

Lavra and Russia," in which he outlined the history of the monastery and its significance in Russian culture and argued for its preservation. For the English translation, see Pavel Florensky, "The Trinity-St. Sergius Lavra and Russia," in *Variable Readings in Russian Philosophy,* No. 1 (New Haven, Conn.: The Variable Press, 1995).

97. Abbot Herman, "St. Paul Florensky." *The Orthodox Word* 23, no. 4 (July–Aug., 1987): 227, 230.

98. GARF, f. 353, op. 4, d. 376, l. 5, 79.

99. Fainsod, 39.

100. GARF, f. A-353, op. 4, d. 317, l. 25.

101. Figes, 149.

102. Interview with Mother Serafima, All Saints Church, Moscow, Aug. 26, 1996.

103. Curtiss, 82.

104. Szczesniak, 62.

105. Lotman, pp. 13, 16, 28.

106. Curtiss, 107.

107. Ibid., 110.

108. Ibid., 111.

109. Ibid., 112.

110. Ibid., 113.

111. Richard Pipes, *The Unknown Lenin* (New Haven, Conn.: Yale University Press, 1996), 150–53.

112. Frank Golder, American Relief Association, personal papers at Hoover Institute, Box 24, folder 6, 7.

113. Ibid., 6.

114. Ibid., 5.

115. Szczesniak, 61.

Chapter 3. The New Economic Policy Years, 1912–1928

1. Sheila Fitzpatrick, Alexander Rabinowitch, and Richard Stites, eds., *Russia in the Era of NEP: Explorations in Soviet Society and Culture,* 3. For other accounts of the New Economic Policy, see Alan Ball, *Russia's Last Capitalists: The Nepmen, 1921–1929* (Berkeley, Calif.: University of California Press, 1988); E. H. Carr, *The Bolshevik Revolution,* 3 vols. (New York: Macmillan, 1951–1953); Sheila Fitzpatrick, ed., *Cultural Revolution in Russia, 1928–1931* (Bloomington, Ind.: Indiana University Press, 1978); and Lewis Siegelbaum, *Soviet State and Society between Revolutions, 1918–1929.* For a Soviet interpretation, see E. B. Genkina, *Perekhod sovetskogo gosudarstvo k novoi ekonomicheskoi politike, 1921–1922 gg*

(Moscow, 1954); K. P. Kim, *Kulturnaia revoliutsia v SSSR, 1917–1965* (Moscow, 1967); Institute of History of USSR, Academy of the Sciences of the USSR, *Kulturnoe stroitelstvo v SSSR, 1917–1927: razrabotka edinoi gosudarstvennoi politiki v oblasti kultury* (Moscow, 1989).

2. Fitzpatrick, Rabinowitch, and Stites, 4.

3. RTsKhIDNI, f. 89, op. 3, d. 1, "Vserossiiskoe soveshchanie zavediuishikh agitotdelami gubkomov i oblastkomov RKP," May 7–11, 1921.

4. No. 86.

5. Dimitry Pospielovsky, *Soviet Antireligious Campaigns and Persecutions,* vol. 2 (New York: St. Martin's Press, 1988), 55–56.

6. A. I. Vvedenski, *Tserkov i Gosudarstvo,* 109–10.

7. Philip Walters, "The Renovationist Coup: Personalities and Programmes." In *Church, Nation, and State in Russia and Ukraine,* ed. G. Hosking, 252 (New York: St. Martin's Press, 1991).

8. Ibid., 41.

9. Walters, 252.

10. *Izvestia,* Mar. 26, 1922.

11. Curtis, 121.

12. Luukkanen, *The Party of Unbelief,* 115.

13. John Curtiss, *The Russian Church and the Soviet State, 1917–1950,* 131.

14. "Vremennoe samoustranenie sv.patriarkha Tikhona ot upravleniia," *Zhivaia Tserkov* (May 23, 1922), no. 2, 1.

15. RTsKhIDNI, f. 5 op. 1, d. 120, ll. 12, 13. Telegram from Lunacharsky to Lenin, May 9, 1921.

16. Edward Roslof, "The Renovationist Movement in the Russian Orthodox Church, 1922–1946," 1.

17. Curtiss, 135.

18. I. N. Nikodimov, *Vospominanie o Kievo-Pecherskoi Lavra,* 131.

19. Roslof, 108.

20. *Vestnik sviashennogo sinoda pravoslavnoi rossiskoi tserkvi,* 18.

21. Ibid., 19.

22. Ibid., 20.

23. Fainsod, 430.

24. B. V. Titlinov, *Tserkov vo vremya revoliutsiia* (Moscow, 1924), 181.

25. Father Boris, "Monk Boris of Valaam." *Orthodox Word* 4 (1991): 237–76.

26. Elder Michael, "Elder Michael the First of Valaam." *Orthodox Word* 2, no. 4 (July–Aug., 1996): 196.

27. Curtiss, 142.

28. Smolensk Party Archive (henceforth referred to as WKP) 458, 58–60.

29. The parish council is a group of laypeople who are responsible for the

daily running of the church. They are usually elected by their fellow parishioners or sometimes appointed by the priest. Parish council duties include paying the priest's salary, paying for repairs to the buildings, and raising money for various church and charitable activities.

30. Edward Roslof, "The Heresy of Bolshevik Christianity: Orthodox Rejection of Religious Reform during NEP." *Slavic Review* 55, no. 3 (Fall, 1996): 617.

31. Curtiss, 144.

32. Ibid.

33. Roslof, 618.

34. *Akty . . . Patriarkha Tikhona,* 344.

35. For a full copy of Patriarch Tikhon's statement, see *Akty . . . Patriarkha Tikhona,* 280. For an English translation, see Boleslaw Szczesniak, *The Russian Revolution and Religion,* 177–78.

36. *Akty . . . Patriarkha Tikhona,* 285.

37. Gregory Freeze, "Counter-Reformation in Russian Orthodoxy: Popular Response to Religious Innovation, 1922–1925," pp. 305–306.

38. *Akty . . . Patriarkha Tikhona,* 348.

39. Ibid., 339.

40. Ibid., 350.

41. Roslof, "The Heresy of Bolshevik Christianity," 617.

42. Freeze, 306.

43. *Tserkovnyia Vedomosti Izdavaemyia pri Vysshem Russkom Tserkovnom Upravlenii Zagranitsei,* nos. 3–4 (Feb., 1924): 8; nos. 5–6 (Mar., 1924): 10.

44. GARF, f. 353, op. 3, d. 766.

45. See GAMO, f. 66, op. 11, d. 2099, for a report on giving the property of Sretenski monastery in Moscow to an Evangelist group, 1925–1926.

46. Fainsod, 431.

47. RTsKhIDNI, f. 89, op. 4, d. 158. Unfortunately, the figures provided do not specify what the term "religious organizations" means. It is not known whether this refers to a specific denomination such as the Orthodox Church, the Catholic Church, or Protestant churches or whether the numbers refer to any religious affiliation.

48. RTsKhIDNI, f. 89, op. 4, d. 184.

49. Oct. 3, 1923. RTsKhIDNI, f. 17, op. 3, d. 385, l. 37.

50. Luukkanen, 179.

51. Curtiss, 206.

52. Daniel Peris, "Commissars in Red Cassocks," 342. For a more in-depth treatment of the League, see Daniel Peris, *Storming the Heavens: The Soviet League of the Militant Godless.*

53. See the letter from Georgian party member Gogoberidze to Yaroslavky requesting that a former Georgian Orthodox priest be restored his rights and used in antireligious work. RtsKhIDNI, f. 89, op. 4, d. 135.
54. Peris, 363–64. For more information on Communism as religion, see Arthur Jay Klinghoffer, *Red Apocalypse: The Religious Evolution of Soviet Communism* (Lanham, Md.: University Press of America, 1996).
55. *Antireligioznik* 6 (1926): 40.
56. Ibid., 41–42.
57. Glennys Young, 12.
58. Ibid., 183–85; 37–44.
59. WKP 458; 52.
60. WKP 458, 58–60.
61. Lewis Siegelbaum, *Soviet State and Society between Revolutions, 1918–1929*, 163.
62. Pospielovsky, 112.
63. For one example, see the letter from Moscow sovdep, Sept., 1925, about the need to close down the artel of nuns in Borvikha village, Moscow oblast. GAMO, f. 19, op. 1, d. 177, l. 117.
64. GAMO, f. 66, op. 11, d. 864.
65. Ibid.
66. GAMO, f. 66, op. 11, d.864, l. 15.
67. Optina Pustyn's golden age occurred roughly from the 1820s until its closure in 1923. During this time pilgrims from all over Russia came to the monastery to talk with the elders. See Chapter 1 for further discussion of Optina Pustyn and the intelligentsia.
68. Tatiana Vladimirovna, "Optina Elder Sebastian," *Orthodox Word* 26, no. 3 (May–June, 1990), 144. For a detailed description of the life of Elder Nektary, see I. M. Kontzevitch, *Elder Nektary of Optina* (Platina, Calif.: St. Herman of Alaska Brotherhood, 1998).
69. *Zhizhneopisanie hieromonakha Nikona, Posledny Starets Optinoi Pustyn*, 156–57.
70. Ibid., 157–59.
71. Ibid., 159.
72. From the unpublished letters of Archbishop Leonty, held at St. Paisius Abbey, Forrestville, Calif.
73. Ibid.
74. Ibid.
75. Monakhina Ignatia, "Vysoko-Petrovskii monastyr v 20–30 gody," *Alfa i Omega* 7, no. 4 (Moscow, 1996): 116.
76. Ibid., 115.
77. Mother Ignatia's memoirs have recently been published in their entirety. *Monashestvo poslednix vremen* (*Monasticism of Times Past*, Moscow, 1998) tells her

life story and focuses mainly on her experiences in the Vysoko-Petrovsky monastery.

78. Ibid.

79. Ibid., 114, 128–29.

80. *Akty . . . Patriarkha Tikhona,* 361.

81. Ibid., 182.

82. The Unified State Political Administration, successor to the GPU and predecessor of the NKVD.

83. *Akty . . . Patriarkha Tikhona,* 509.

84. For more on Metropolitan Sergei and the declaration, see William C. Fletcher, *The Russian Orthodox Church Underground, 1917–1970;* Arfved Gustavson, *The Catacomb Church* (Jordanville, N.Y.: Holy Trinity Monastery, 1960); and I. Andreev, *Notes concerning the Catacomb Church* (Jordanville, N.Y.: Holy Trinity Monastery, 1947).

85. The Declaration of 1927 continues to be a litmus test for Orthodox Christians; members of the Russian Orthodox Church Abroad (the successor of the Karlovatskii synod) and the Catacomb and True Orthodox Churches (internal schismatics) insist that the Patriarchal Church betrayed Orthodoxy by affirming loyalty to the regime. Historical treatment of this period is often colored by the authors' political views of Metropolitan Sergei; Russian émigré authors such as Fr. Mikhail Pol'skii and I. Andreev have been the most vociferously anti-Sergian, whereas Abbot Innokenty and Metropolitan Ioann and the Canadian historian Dmitry Pospielovsky defend Sergei and his actions. No resolution of the schism appears imminent.

86. Abbot Herman, "A Silent Giant," *The Orthodox Word,* no. 169(1993): 138.

87. Dimitry Pospielovsky, *Russkaia Pravoslavnaia Tserkov v XX veka* (Moscow, 1995), 166. By this time, the term "renovationist" (*obnovlentsy* in Russian) was often used to characterize any dissenters from the Patriarchal Church.

88. Gustavson, 85–86.

89. Ibid.

90. Irina Reznikova, *Pravoslavie na Solovkakh,* 29.

91. These lectures have recently been compiled into two volumes, titled *Monastyr' v Miru (Monastery in the World)* (Moscow, 1995).

92. Fr. Valentin Sventitsky, *Monastyr' v Miru,* 8, 12.

93. Abbot Herman, "New Russian Confessor Archpriest Valentin Sventitsky." *The Orthodox Word* 18, no. 4 (July–Aug., 1983): 133.

94. For the proceedings of the Fifteenth Party Congress, see *K itogi XV S'ezda VKP* (Leningrad, 1927) and *Rezoliutsii i postanovleniia XV s"ezda VKP* (Moscow, 1929).

Chapter 4. The Good Friday of Russian Monasticism, 1928–1934

1. I. Stalin, *Vosprosi leninizma,* (Moscow: Foreign Language Publishing House, 1937), 192–93.

2. Robert Conquest, *Harvest of Sorrow* (New York: Oxford University Press, 1986), 87.

3. Moshe Levin, *The Making of the Soviet System* (New York: The New Press, 1985), 209.

4. Much research has been done on collectivization and its consequences. For more in-depth discussion, see R. W. Davies, *The Socialist Offensive: The Collectivization of Soviet Agriculture, 1929–1930* (Cambridge, Mass.: Harvard University Press, 1980); Lynne Viola, *The Best Sons of the Fatherland: Workers in the Vanguard of Soviet Collectivization* (New York: Oxford University Press, 1987); Lynne Viola, *Peasant Rebels under Stalin: Collectivization and the Culture of Peasant Resistance;* Viktor Danilov, *Dokumenty svidetel'stvuiut: Iz istorii derevni nakanune i v gody kollektivizatsii, 1927–1932;* and N. L. Rogalina, *Kollektivizatsiia: itogi pro idennogo puti* (Moscow, 1989).

5. The word *kulak* in Russian literally means "fist." It was originally used to describe rich peasants. However, none of the Soviet ideologues agreed on who exactly is a kulak. At the height of the collectivization campaign, a kulak became anyone who opposed collectivization. Eventually, a kulak was thought of more as having a certain state of mind rather than a specific social class.

6. The Komsomol was the acronym for the All-Union Leninist Communist Union of Youth. Founded in 1918, it was the youth arm of the Communist Party. Although technically a separate organization, it has worked closely with the party and was viewed as a training ground for future party leaders. Prior to collectivization, Stalin purged the Komsomol to rid it of potential class enemies so it could be a more effective tool in the collectivization struggle.

7. "Kto My? Kulaki ili sredniaki? I chto nam dal'she delat'?" [Who are we? Kulaks or sredniaks? And what are we to do next?] Letter to *Krestianskaia gazeta,* Apr. 4, 1928, quoted in Danilov, *Dokumenty svidetel'stvuiut,* 118.

8. Conquest, 95.

9. Fainsod, 240.

10. Lewin, 127.

11. RTsKhIDNI, f. 89, op. 4, d. 69, l. 12.

12. RTsKhIDNI, f. 17, op. 60, d. 509, pp. 96–99.

13. Letter from Sir Esmond Ovey to Mr. A. Henderson, Mar. 3, 1931, *British Documents on Foreign Affairs,* part 2, series A, "The Soviet Union, 1917–1939," vol. 10, "The Soviet Union, May 1930–Dec. 1931," 226, document 148.

14. GARF, f. 5407, op. 2, d. 143, l. 4, "Letters to the Editor of *Bezbozhnik.*"

15. One desiatin was equal to 2.7 acres.
16. GARF, f. 5407, op. 2, d. 143, l. 13.
17. Fr. Vladislav Tsipin, *Istorii Russkoi Tserkvi, 1917–1997,* vol. 9, 187.
18. The central standing commission of religious questions was a new permanent commission created in 1929 by the VTsIK that would deal exclusively with matters concerning religious questions.
19. Arto Luukkanen, *The Religious Policy of the Communist State* (Helsinki: Finnish Historical Society, 1997), 87.
20. Ibid., 101.
21. For example, see B. Kandidiv, "Kontrrevoliutsionaia rabota popov sredi zhenshin," in *Sbornik materialov po antireligioznoi propaganda,* 116–17. See also *Bezbozhnik,* Aug. 24, 1924; ibid., 1925, no. 5, 4.
22. Daniel Peris, *Storming the Heavens: The Soviet League of the Militant Godless,* 118.
23. Letter from Semion Pylankin, Tambov guberniia, 1927. RTsKhIDNI, f. 78, op. 1, d. 282, ll. 87–88.
24. Anonymous letter to Mikhail Kalinin, June 23, 1929, RTsKhIDNI, f. 78 op. 1, d. 356, ll. 4–6.
25. Letter to Kalinin from Ivana Federovna Vasileva, July, 1928. RTsKhIDNI, f. 78, op. 1, d. 312, l. 8.
26. Ibid., 152.
27. RTsKhIDNI, f. 89, op. 4, d. 125, l. 4–5.
28. Letter from Anna F. Biberdeeva, Aug., 1928. RTsKhIDNI, f. 78, op. 1, d. 312, l. 3.
29. *Pravda,* Mar. 15, 1930.
30. GARF, f. R-5407, op. 1, d. 49, l. 6.
31. Conquest, 101.
32. "Report on eviction and resettlement of kulaks," July 12 and 14, 1931, Library of Congress, *Revelations from the Russian Archives,* 384, 387.
33. Conquest, 103.
34. RTsKhIDNI, f. 17, op. 85, d. 355, l. 1.
35. Ibid.
36. Ibid.
37. Letter from P. I. Velichenko to Stalin, Sept. 3, 1926. RTsKhIDNI, f. 17, op. 85, d. 494, l. 143.
38. See the letter from the commander of the Siberian Military District, Apr. 30, 1930, regarding directives forbidding the use of the military in operations against the kulaks, RGVA, f. 4, op. 1, d. 142, l. 21.
39. Although Reese discusses several instances of remaining religious feelings within the Red Army, his primary focus is on collectivization. There is little archival evidence indicating how widespread religion was in the army.

Much more scholarship in this area is needed before drawing any definite conclusions about the level of religious feeling in the Red Army.

40. Roger Reese, *Stalin's Reluctant Soldiers: A Social History of the Red Army, 1925–1941* (Lawrence: University Press of Kansas, 1996), 89. For works specifically focusing on atheistic propaganda in the Red Army during this period, see Kapiton A. Paisusov, *Ateisticheskoe vospitanie sovetskhikh voinov* (Moscow: Voenizdat, 1963); and F. Rodinova, *Krasnoarmeiskii antureligioiznyi uchebnik*, 2d ed. (Moscow: *Bezbozhnik*, 1931).

41. RTsKhIDNI, f. 89, op. 4, d. 78, l. 7.

42. Reese, 83.

43. Some examples can be found in Kalinin's *lichnyi* (personal) fond in RTsKhIDNI, f. 78 op. 1.

44. Monakhina Anna Tepliakova, *Vospominanie*, 12.

45. Ibid., 46.

46. This was the one in Leningrad, not the one in Moscow.

47. Levitin-Krasnov, *Likhie gody, 1925–1941: Vospominanie*, 194.

48. Mother Serafmina, interview, All Saints Church, Moscow, Aug. 26, 1996.

49. Monakhina Anna, 75.

50. Monakhina Ignatii, 61.

51. Mother Serafima, interview. All Saints Church, Moscow, Aug. 26, 1996.

52. Ibid.

53. Monakhina Taisia, 262.

54. Ibid., 275.

55. Viktor Korolev, ed. *Dushu ne Pogiblyu: Ispovedniki i osvedomiteli v dokumentakh i o metodakh agenturnoi*, 51.

56. Mother Serafima, interview, All Saints Church, Moscow, Aug. 26, 1996.

57. Monakhina Taisia, 201.

58. Levitin-Krasnov, 222. See also Aleksandr Solzhenitsyn, *The Gulag Archipelago*, 51.

59. *Istorii Russkoi Tserkvi*, 198.

60. Monakhina Taisia, 222.

61. *Istoriia Russkoi Tserkvi*, 197.

62. Ibid.

63. Korolev, 34.

64. *Istoriia Russkoi Tservki*, 197.

65. Monakhina Anna, 19.

66. Ibid., 6, 14.

67. Monakhina Serafima, *Zhizenopisanie Mat'ia schemamonakhinin Fomary* (Moscow, 1991), 6.

68. Irina Reznikova, *Pravoslavie na Solovkakh*, 39.

69. Alexander Solzhenitsyn, *The Gulag Archipelago,* vol. 2, 420–21.
70. Ibid., 309.
71. Reznikova, 41.
72. Ibid., 16.
73. Ibid., 14.
74. Ibid., 43–47.
75. Ibid., 61.
76. Ibid., 66.
77. Ibid., 78.
78. Ibid., 18.
79. Dimitry Pospielovsky, "The Survival of the Russian Orthodox Church in Her Millennial Century: Faith as Martyria in an Atheistic State," in Geoffrey Hosking, ed. *Church, Nation, and State in Russia and Ukraine,* 278.

Chapter 5. The Descent into Hell, 1934–1939

1. See N. S. Timasheff, *The Great Retreat* (New York: E. P. Dutton & Co., Inc., 1946).
2. For a full account of the various strictures imposed on the NKVD, see "On the Procedure for Executing Arrests," June 17, 1935, RTsKhIDNI, f. 17, op. 3, d. 965, l. 75.
3. For an excellent study of this commission, see Arto Luukkanen, *The Religious Policy of the Stalinist State: A Case Study: The Standing Commission on Religious Questions, 1929–1938.*
4. Sarah Davies, *Popular Opinion in Stalin's Russia: Terror, Propaganda, and Dissent, 1934–1941,* 78.
5. Letter, Jan. 31, 1934. GARF, f. 5263, op. 1, d. 1398, l. 40.
6. Stephen Kotkin, *Magnetic Mountain: Stalinism as a Civilization* (Berkeley:University of California Press, 1995).
7. Luukkanen, 113.
8. Luukkanen, 110–11.
9. "Religioznyie perezhitki v kolkhoznoi derevne." *Pod Znamenem Marksisma* no. 4 (1936): 79–89.
10. Luukkanen, 110.
11. I. V. Stalin, *On the Draft Constitution of the USSR: Report Delivered at the Extraordinary Eighth Congress of the Soviets of the USSR.* Nov. 25, 1936, Moscow, pp. 15, 17.
12. For documents from the draft commission, see GARF, f. 6982, op. 1, and RTsKhIDNI, f. 17, op. 120, d. 232 ll. 36–52, "Dokladnaia zapiska o xode vsenarodnogo obsuzhdeniia proekta Konstitutsii SSSR na 15/X-1936g."
13. Ibid., 40.

14. Ibid., 41.
15. V. I. Tikhonov, *Lishenie izbiratel'nykh prav v Moskve v 1920–1930 gody*, 125.
16. Kalinin, quoted in article in *Izvestiia*, June 7, 1936.
17. For discussions on this issue, see Kalinin's file, RTsKhIDNI, f. 78, op. 1, d. 559.
18. Emelian Yaroslavsky, "The New Constitution and the Question of Religion," *Antireligioznik*, June 10, 1936. However, in Jan., 1937, Yaroslavsky wrote another article in *Bezbozhnik*, defending the constitution and stressing the need to work harder for antireligious propaganda. "Nado rabotat' a ne khnykat," *Bezbozhnik*, 12.
19. Letter from Kalinin to the politburo, Sept. 15, 1937. RTsKhIDNI, f. 78, op. 7, d. 209, l. 3.
20. J. Arch Getty, "State and Society under Stalin: Constitutions and Elections in the 1930s." *Slavic Review* 50, no. 1 (Spring, 1991): 25. In Smolensk, seventeen percent of the letters that the government received protested granting clergy and other dispossessed people the right to vote.
21. Yaroslavsky, *Bezbozhnik* 4 (1937): 35.
22. Report from the cult commission, GARF, f. 5263, op. 1, d. 48, l. 6.
23. Letter from A. Milovanov to the cult commission, Apr. 23, 1937. GARF, f. 5263, op. 1, d. 48, l. 43.
24. Letter from Iosif G. Lyubimov, Apr. 2, 1937, to Kalinin. RTsKhIDNI, f. 78, op. 1, d. 593, l. 155. See also a letter from Voronezh complaining of local soviet officials denying believers entry to their churches, RTsKhIDNI, f. 78, op. 1, d. 592, l. 13.
25. RTsKhIDNI, f. 17, op. 120, d. 256, ll. 42–44.
26. Much has been written about the constitution of 1936. For a full English translation of the constitution, see "The New Soviet Constitution" (New York: Soviet Russia Today, 1936). For the text in Russian, see *Istoriia sovetskoi konstitutsii v dokumentakh, 1917–1956* (Moscow, 1957), 345–59; for a full text of Stalin's speech, see I. V. Stalin, *On the Draft Constitution of the U.S.S. R.* For Western contemporary commentary, see Kathleen Barnes, "The Soviet Constitution of 1936," in *Research Bulletin on the Soviet Union* 1, no. 9 (Sept. 30, 1936); J. R. Starr, "New Constitution of the Soviet Union," *American Political Science Review* 4 *(1936): 1143–52; Beatrice and Sidney Webb, Soviet Communism: A New Civilization?* (New York: Scribner's Sons, 1936); and Anna Louise Strong, *The New Soviet Constitution: A Study in Socialist Democracy* (New York: H. Holt, 1937). For other scholarly works see Aryeh L. Unger, *Constitutional Development in the U.S.S. R.* (New York: Pica Press, 1981); J. Arch Getty, "State and Society under Stalin: Constitutions and Elections in the 1930s," *Slavic Review* 50, no. 1 (1991): 18–35; and Ellen Wimberg, "Socialism, Democratism and Criticism: The Soviet Press and the

National Discussion of the 1936 Draft Constitution," *Soviet Studies* 44, no. 2 (1992): 313–32. For works in Russian, see S. I. Iakubovskaia, *Razvitie SSSR kak soiuznogo gosudartstva, 1922–1936* (Moscow: Nauka, 1972); A. N. Kositsyn, *Istoriia sovetskogo gosudarstva i prava v 3-x knigakh* (Moscow: Nauka, 1968–1985); G. S. Kalinin, *Istoriia gosudarstva i prava* (Moscow: Iurid Lit, 1972); and V. V. Kabanov, "Iz istorii sozdaniya konstitutsii SSSR 1936 goda," *Istoriia SSSR* 6 (1976): 126.

27. *The New Soviet Constitution,* 30.

28. *Blackfriars* (Sept., 1938).

29. This term could be used to designate a number of buildings used for religious practices, including churches of various denomination, monasteries, synagogues, mosques, chapels, and so on.

30. GARF, f. 5263, op. 1, d. 832, l. 3.

31. GARF, f. 5263, op. 1, d. 832, l. 4.

32. WPK 499, 295–97.

33. *Blackfriars* (July 17, 1937): 95.

34. *The Tablet* (Apr. 30, 1938): 566.

35. Odintsov, 68.

36. *Blackfriars,* Sept., 1938.

37. From *Les Dernières Nouvelles,* cited in *Eastern Churches Quarterly* 3, no. 5 (1938–1939): 324–26.

38. *Blanki i posobiia dlya shchetchika v gorodskikh poseleniyakh* (Tsentral'noe upravlenie narodnokhozaistvennogo ucheta Gosplana SSSR, Moscow, 1936) issued instructions for the census in urban areas. There was a separate booklet for census takers in the countryside.

39. *Komsomolskaia Pravda,* Jan. 6, 1937.

40. Ibid.

41. Ibid.

42. Ibid.

43. RGAE, f. 1562, op. 329, d. 143, ll. 114–16.

44. O predvaritel'nikh itogakh vsesoyuznoi perepisi naseleniya, RGAE, f. 1, ll. 148–60.

45. Only recently has information about the 1937 census become available to scholars. For a full account of the 1937 census in English, see I. A. Poliakov, V. B. Zhiromskaia, and I. N. Kiselev, "A Half-Century of Silence: The 1937 Census," *Russian Studies in History.* For a more general guide to the methodology of Russian and Soviet censuses, see Ralph Clem, ed., *Research Guide to the Russian and Soviet Censuses.* For works in Russian, see I. A. Poliakov and E. Vodarskii, eds. *Vsesoiuznaia perepis' naseleniia 1937: Kratkie itogi.*

46. E. M. Yaroslavsky, *Ob antireligioznoi propagande.*

47. RGAE, f. 1562, op. 329, d. 278, ll. 12–15.

48. RGAE, f. 1562, op. 329, d. 285, l. 62.
49. *Krasnaia Zvezda,* Oct. 13, 1937.
50. *Krasnaia Zvezda,* no. 163, June 17, 1937.
51. Getty, "State and Society under Stalin," 31.
52. The historiography of the purges is too extensive to mention in detail. Some important works on the subject in English are Roy Medvedev, *Let History Judge: The Origins and Consequences of Stalinism;* Robert Conquest, *The Great Terror: A Reassessment* (New York: Oxford University Press, 1990); Conquest, *Inside Stalin's Secret Police: NKVD Politics 1936–1939* (Stanford, Calif.: Hoover Institution Press, 1985); Arkady Vaksberg, *Stalin's Prosecutor: The Life of Andrei Vyshinsky* (New York: Grove Weidenfeld, 1990); Robert Tucker and Stephen Cohen, eds., *The Great Purge Trial* (New York: Grosset and Dunlap, 1965); J. Arch Getty and Roberta Manning, *Stalinist Terror: New Perspectives* (Cambridge: Cambridge University Press, 1993); and J. Arch Getty, *Origins of the Great Purges: The Soviet Communist Party Reconsidered, 1933–1938* (New York: Cambridge University Press, 1985); in Russian, see Vadim Rogovin, *Partiia Rasstreliannyx* (Moscow, 1997); O. Kklevniuk, *1937-i Stalin, NKVD, i sovetskoe obshchestvo* (Moscow, 1992).
53. Fainsod, 55.
54. See report from Ezhov, July 30, 1937, about the need to repress former kulaks and religious workers, cited in D. Orlovskii, *Mucheniki, ispovedniki i podvizhniki blagochestiia Russkoi Pravoslavnoi Tserkvi XX stoletiia* book 2, 17–18.
55. J. Arch Getty and Olg Naumov, *The Road to Terror: Stalin and the Self-Destruction of the Bolsheviks, 1932–1939,* 591.
56. *The Tablet* (Dec. 23, 1995): 168.
57. *The Tablet* (Apr. 16, 1938): 504.
58. *The Tablet* (Aug. 20, 1938): 238.
59. *The Tablet* (May 28, 1938): 704.
60. Printed in *The Tablet* (July 1, 1939): 12.
61. Vladislav Tsipin, *Istorii Russkoi Tserkvi,* kn. 9 (Moscow, 1997), 258.
62. I. Sergeev, "Monastyr'-priton," *Bezbozhnik,* Feb., 1941, 7.
63. N. S. Timasheff, *Religion in Soviet Russia, 1917–1942* (New York: Sheed and Ward, 1942), 81.
64. Vera Bouteneff, *Father Arseny, 1893–1973: Priest, Prisoner, Spiritual Father,* 149.
65. Felix Corley, *Religion in the Soviet Union: An Archival Reader.*
66. Tsipin, 252.
67. Monakhina Serafima (Bulgakova), *Diveevo Predaniia* (Moscow, 1996), 53.
68. Tsipin, 255.
69. Korolev, 65.
70. *The Tablet* (July 29, 1939): 144.
71. For examples, see "Gruppa monakhin' v Solovetskom kontslagere,"

Pravoslavnaia Rus' (Paris) Aug. 16, 1947, no. 13, pp. 9–11; "Matushka Maria Gatchinskaia," *Pravoslavnaia Rus'* Feb. 1, 1952, no. 3, 10–12.
72. See Nina Gazen-Torn, "O verakh," excerpt from *Soprotivlenie v GULAGe* (Moscow: Vozvrashchenie, 1992), 228.
73. Monakhina Ignatiia, *Monashestvo poslednikh vremen* (Moscow, 1998), 162.
74. Archbiship Leonty of Chile, unpublished memoirs, 41.
75. Monakhina Ignatiia, 162.
76. Bouteneff, 15.
77. I. M. Andreev, *Russia's Catacomb Saints.*
78. Orlovskii, vols. 1, 13, 15.
79. Interview with Mother Serafima, Aug. 26, 1996, Moscow.
80. Tatiana Vladimirovna, "Optina Elder Sebastian: Schema-Archimandrite of Karaganda." *The Orthodox Word* 26, no. 4 (July–Aug., 1990): 235–36.
81. Interview with Galina Alexandrovna, Aug. 6, 1996, Moscow.
82. Georg Seide, *Monasteries and Convents of the Orthodox Church Abroad* (Munich: Monastery of Saint Job of Pochaev, 1990). For more on the Russian Orthodox Church Abroad, see Alexey Young, *The Russian Orthodox Church outside Russia: A History and Chronology* (San Bernadino, Calif.: St. Willibrord's Press, 1993); *A History of the Russian Orthodox Church Abroad, 1917–1971* (Seattle, Wash., 1972).
83. Ibid., 89.
84. Ibid., 93–95.
85. "Interview with the Most Holy Patriarch Alexis II of Moscow and All Rus," *Trud* 17 (Feb., 1999).
86. "Puhtitsa Women's Monastery of the Annunciation," brochure, publication information unknown, 33.
87. Prof. Vasilii Sinaiskii, *Pskov-Pecherskii monastyr'* (Riga, 1929), 49.
88. Seide, 36.
89. Ibid., 35.
90. Ibid., 37.
91. Ibid., 178.
92. Ibid., 175.
93. For more about the Russian Orthodox Church during World War II, see Harvey Fireside, *Icon and Swastika: The Russian Orthodox Church under Nazi and Soviet Control* (Cambridge, Mass.: Harvard University Press, 1971); Wassilij Alexeev and Thoefanis Stavrou, *The Great Revival: The Russian Orthodox Church under German Occupation* (Minneapolis, Minn.: Burgess, 1976); and M. I. Odintsov, comp. "Religioznye organizatsii v SSSR: Nakanune i v Pervye gody Velikoi Otchestvennoi Voiny (1938–1943)." *Otechestvennye Arkhivy* 2 (1995): 37–67.
94. Tsipin, 267.

Conclusion

1. Andrei Zolotov, "Patriarch Criticizes Rich Priests," *Moscow Times*, Dec. 25, 1998.

2. Vladimir Tsipin, *Istoriia Russkoi Tserkvi, 1917–1991*, 774–82.

3. The first monastery to be returned to the Church's control was Danilov monastery in Moscow, the official residence of the patriarchate. It was also the last to have been closed in 1930. It was turned into a prison camp for the children of "enemies of the people."

4. For the debate about the uses of the term "totalitarianism" see Ian Kershaw, *The Nazi Dictatorship: Problems and Perspectives of Interpretation*, 3d ed. (London: Edward Arnold, 1993); and Abbot Gleason, *Totalitarianism: The Inner History of the Cold War* (New York: Oxford University Press, 1995).

5. For more information about the Russian Orthodox Church and historical memory, see Jennifer Wynot, "The Persistence of Memory: The Russian Orthodox Church and the Problem of Historical Memory," *Modern Greek Studies Yearbook* 14–15 (Spring, 1999).

6. James C. Scott, *Domination and the Arts of Resistance*, 2.

7. Ibid., 52.

Appendix A

1. Boleslaw Szczesniak, *The Russian Revolution and Religion: A Collection of Documents concerning the Suppression of Religion by the Communists, 1917–1925* (Notre Dame, Ind.: University of Notre Dame Press, 1959), 28–29.

Appendix B

1. From Boleslaw Szczesniak, *The Russian Revolution and Religion: A Collection of Documents concerning the Suppression of Religion by the Communists, 1917–1925* (Notre Dame, Ind.: University of Notre Dame, 1959), 34–35.

Appendix C

1. Boleslaw Szczesniak, *The Russian Revolution and Religion: A Collection of Documents concerning the Suppression of Religion by the Communists, 1917–1925* (Notre Dame, Ind.: University of Notre Dame Press, 1959), 46–48.

Glossary

artel cooperative system in which the communal element is confined to marketing and does not extend to production. An artel can be devoted to either agricultural work or light industry.
bedniaks poor peasants
cenobitic communal model of the Egyptian ascetic Pachomius
chistka purge
desiatina land measurement equal to 2.7 acres
GAKO State Archive of Kaluga Oblast
GAMO State Archive of Moscow Oblast
GARF State Archive of the Russian Federation
GPU acronym for Chief Political Administration (the secret police agency formed after the civil war)
guberniia province
hesychasm prayer of the heart
igumen superior (of a monastery)
klobuk a hat with a veil attached given to a monastic
kolkhoz a communal farm where workers pooled their land and resourcesand marketed the produce collectively
Komsomol the All-Union Leninist Communist Union of Youth
krasnii ugol beautiful corner
krasnii red
krestian peasant
kulak See chapter 4, note 5, for discussion
lavra originally, a large community of monks. Now, a large monastery of any kind
lichnyi personal
lishenets (plural lishentsy) person deprived of citizenship
mera (plural meri) unit of agricultural measurement

NARKOMIUST People's Commissariat of Justice
narodniki those who demonstrated on behalf of the peasants
nastaitel dean
oblast region
obnovlentsy renovationist
obshchestvennost the emerging social identity of the educated, propertied, urban middle strata
Philokalia a collection of mystical, ascetic texts from ancient Christian tradition
podvorye diocesan inns
pud measure of weight approximately equal to 36 pounds or 16.38 kilograms
rassaphore second stage of Orthodox monasticism
schema final stage of entry into monasticism
skete a small community of from three to ten monks or nuns
skhod village assembly
sobor church council
sovdep Soviet of Workers', Soldiers', and Peasants' Deputies
soviet village council
sovkhoz a state-owned farm that practiced large-scale agriculture. The workers were paid wages by the state.
sredniaks middle peasants
starchestvo tradition of Othodox eldership
starets/staritsa an older monk or nun who is highly regarded for spiritual wisdom
symphonia partnership between church and state
trapeze refectory
uezd district
volost village district or county
VTsIK the all-Russian central executive committee
Zemotdel land department
zhenskie obshchiny women's communities

Bibliography

Archives, Libraries, and Other Sources in Russia and the United States

Center for the Preservation and Study of Documents on Recent History (RTsKhIDNI), fonds 2,5, 17, 78, 89
Central State Archive of Kaluga Oblast (GAKO) fonds r-1498, 109, 1267
Central State Archive of the Moscow Oblast (GAMO) fonds 19, 66, 4997
Central State Archives of the Russian Federation (GARF) fonds 353, 3431, 5407, 5263, 6982
Holy Trinity Monastery, Jordanville, N.Y.
Hoover Institute, Stanford University, Stanford, Calif.
Moscow Theological Academy, Zagorsk
Russian State Economic Archives (RGAE) fonds 1, 1562
Russian State Library
Russian State Military Archives (RGVA) fond 4
Smolensk Party Archives, Emory University, Atlanta, Ga.
St. Herman of Alaska Brotherhood, Platina, Calif.
St. Vladimir's Seminary, Crestwood, N.Y.
Tikhon Theological Institute, Moscow
University of Minnesota

Interviews

Galina Alexandrovna, interview by author, Moscow, August 5, 1996.
Mother Serafima, interview by author, All Saints Church, Moscow, August 26, 1996.

Journals and Newspapers

Antireligioznik (Moscow)
Bezbozhnik (Moscow)
Blackfriar (London)

Istoriia SSSR (Moscow)
Istoricheskii Voprosii
Izvestia (Moscow)
Krasnaia Zvezda
Krestianskaia Pravda (Leningrad, until 1938)
Novy Mir (Moscow)
Orthodox Word
Pravda (Moscow)
Pravoslavnaia Mysl (Paris)
Pravoslavnaia Rus (New York)
Revoliutsiia i Tserkov (Moscow)
Russkaia Vedomosti
Tserkovnaia Vedomosti
The Tablet (London)

Primary and Secondary Sources

Andreev, Ivan. *Russia's Catacomb Saints.* Platina, Calif.: St. Herman of Alaska Press, 1982.

Berdyaev, Nicholas. *The Russian Idea.* Hudson, N.Y.: Lindisfarne Press, 1992.

Berelowitch, A., and Victor Danilov, eds. *Sovetskaia Derevnia Glazami VCHK-OGPU-NKVD 1918–1939: Dokumenty i materialy v 4 tomakh,* vol. 1, 1918–1922. Moscow: Rosspen, 1998.

Billington, James. *The Icon and the Axe: An Interpretive History of Russian Culture.* New York: Vintage Books, 1970.

Bogolepov, Alexander. *Church Reforms in Russia, 1905–1918.* Bridgeport, Conn.: Metropolitan Council of the Russian Orthodox Church of America, 1966.

Bouteneff, Vera, ed. *Father Arseny, 1893–1973: Priest, Prisoner, Spiritual Father.* Crestwood, N.Y.: St. Vladimir's University Press, 2000.

Budovnits, I. U. *Monastyri na Rusi i borba s nimi krestian v XIV-XVI vekakh.* Moscow: Nauka, 1966.

Clem, Ralph, ed. *Research Guide to the Russian and Soviet Censuses.* Ithaca, N.Y.: Cornell University Press, 1986.

Cohen, Stephen. *Rethinking the Soviet Experience: Politics and History since 1917.* New York: Oxford University Press, 1985.

Conquest, Robert. *The Great Terror: A Reassessment.* New York: Oxford University Press, 1990.

Corley, Felix. *Religion in the Soviet Union: An Archival Reader.* New York: New York University Press, 1996.

Cunningham, James. *A Vanquished Hope.* New York: St. Vladimir's Press, 1991.

Curtiss, John. *The Russian Church and the Soviet State, 1917–1950*. Gloucester, Mass.: Peter Smith, 1965.
Danilov, Victor. *Central Problems of Russian and Soviet History: New Research and Approaches*. Moscow: Nauka, 1990.
———, and N. A. Ivnitskii, eds. *Dokumenty svidetel'stvuiut: Iz istorii derevni nakanune I v khode kollektivizatsii, 1927–1932*. Moscow: Izd-vo-polit. lit-ry, 1989.
———, and Roberta Manning, eds. *Tragediia Sovetskoi Derevni: Kollektivizatsiia i raskulachivanie Dokumenty i materiali*, vol. 1, May, 1927–November, 1929. Moscow: Rosspen, 1999.
Davies, Sarah. *Popular Opinion in Stalin's Russia: Terror, Propaganda, and Dissent, 1934– 1941*. Cambridge: Cambridge University Press, 1997.
Davis, Nathaniel. *A Long Walk to Church*. Boulder: Westview Press, 1995.
Deianaiia Sviashchennago Sobora Pravoslavnoi Russkoi Tserkvi, book 9, vypusk 2
Denisov, Lev. *Pravoslavnie Monastyrie Rossiskoi Empirii*. Moscow, 1908.
Ellis, Jane. *The Russian Orthodox Church: A Contemporary History*. Bloomington: Indiana University Press, 1986.
Fainsod, Merle. *Smolensk under Soviet Rule*. Cambridge: Cambridge University Press, 1958.
Fedotoff, G. P. *The Russian Church since the Revolution*. London: Society for Promoting Christian Knowledge, 1928.
Figes, Orlando. *Peasant Russia, Civil War: The Volga Countryside in Revolution 1917–1921*. Oxford: Clarendon Press, 1991.
Fitzpatrick, Sheila. *The Cultural Front: Power and Culture in Revolutionary Russia*. Ithaca, N.Y.: Cornell University Press, 1992.
———. *Stalin's Peasants: Resistance and Survival in the Russian Village after Collectivization*. New York: Oxford University Press, 1994.
———, Alexander Rabinowitch, and Richard Stites, eds. *Russia in the Era of NEP: Explorations in Soviet Society and Culture*. Bloomington: Indiana University Press, 1991.
Fletcher, William. *The Russian Orthodox Church Underground 1917–1970*. London: Oxford University Press, 1971.
———. *A Study in Survival: The Church in Russia 1927–1943*. New York: Macmillan, 1965.
Frank, Stephen, and Mark Steinberg, eds. *Cultures in Flux: Lower-Class Values, Practices, and Resistance in Late Imperial Russia*. Princeton: Princeton University Press, 1994.
Freeze, Gregory "Counter-Reformation in Russian Orthodoxy: Popular Response to Religious Innovation, 1922–1925." *Slavic Review* 54, no. 2 (Summer, 1995): 305–39
Georgievski, Evlogii, Metropolitan. *Put' Moei Zhizhni*. Moscow: Moskovskii Rabochii, 1994.

Getty, J. Arch, and Roberta Manning, eds. *Stalinist Terror: New Perspectives.* Cambridge: Cambridge University Press, 1993.

———, and Oleg Naumov, *The Road to Terror: Stalin and the Self-Destruction of the Bolsheviks, 1932–1939.* New Haven, Conn.: Yale University Press, 1999.

Golubtsov, Sergii. *Troitse-Sergeev Lavra za poslednie sto let.* Moscow, 1998.

Gubonin, M. E. *Aktyi Sviateishego Patriarkha Tikhona, Patriarkha Moskovskogo i vse Rossii.* Moscow: St. Tikhon Institute, 1994.

Husband, William. *Godless Communists: Atheism and Society in Soviet Russia, 1917–1932.* Dekalb, Ill.: Northern Illinois University Press, 2000.

———. "Soviet Atheism and Russian Orthodox Strategies of Resistance, 1917–1932."

Journal of Modern History 70, no. 1 (1998): 74–107.

Ioann, Metropolitan of St. Petersburg and Ladoga. *Tserkovnye raskoly v russkoi tserkvi 20-x i 30-x godov XX stoletiia: Grigorianskii, Iaroslavskii, Iosiflianskii, Viktorianskii i drugie, ikh osobennosti i istoriia.* Sortavala, Russia: Sortavalskoi knizhnoi tip., 1993.

Istorii Russkoi Pravoslavnaia Tserkvi v dokumentakh, vols. 1–2. Moscow, 1998.

Jakobson, Michael. *Origins of the GULAG: The Soviet Prison Camp System, 1917–1934.* Lexington: University Press of Kentucky, 1993.

Kartashev, A. V. *Ocherki po istorii russkoi tserkvi.* Paris: YMCA Press, 1959.

Kashevarov, A. N. *Gosudarstvo i Tserkov: Iz istorii vzaimootnoshenii sovetskoi vlastii i russkoi pravoslavnoi tserkvi.* St. Petersburg, 1995.

Korolev, Victor. *Dushu ne Pogiblyu: Ispovedniki i osvedomiteli v dokumentakh i o metodakh agenturnoi raboti.* Moscow, 2001.

Korzun, M. S. *Russkaia pravoslavnaia tserkov 1917–1945 gody: izmenenie sotsialno-politicheskoi orientatsii i nauchnaia nesostoiatelnost verouchenia.* Minsk, 1987.

Krasnaia Patriarkha: Volki v oveshei shkure sviashchestvo Tserkvi presviatoi Bogoroditsy. Moscow: Bogorodichnyi Tsentr, 1993.

Lebedeva, Monakhina Ignatiia. *Monashestvo poslednikh vremen.* Moscow, 1998.

Leonty, Archbishop of Chile. Unpublished letters, St. Herman of Alaska Brotherhood, Platina, Calif.

Levitin-Krasnov, A. E. *Likhie gody: 1925–1941: Vospominanie.* Paris: YMCA Press, 1977.

Lewin, Moshe. *Russian Peasants and Soviet Power: A Study of Collectivization.* New York: W. W. Norton and Co. 1968.

Livshin, A. Ia. *Pis'ma vo Vlast' 1928–1939.* Moscow: Rosspen, 2002

Lotman, Yuri, and B. A. Uspenskii. *The Semiotics of Russian Culture.* Ann Arbor: University of Michigan, 1984.

Luukanen, Arto. *The Party of Unbelief.* Helsinki: Suomen Historiallinen Seura, 1994.

———. *The Religious Policy of the Communist State: A Case Study: The Standing*

Commission on Religious Questions, 1929–1938. Helsinki: Finnish Historical Society, 1997.

Mat' Veronika. *Vospominanie Monakhini.* San Francisco, 1954.

Medvedev, Roy. *Let History Judge: The Origins and Consequences of Stalinism.* New York: Alfred A. Knopf, 1971.

Meehan-Waters, Brenda. *Holy Women of Russia.* San Francisco: Harper, 1993.

Nichols, Robert, and Theofanis Stavrou, eds. *Russian Orthodoxy under the Old Regime.* Minneapolis: University of Minnesota Press, 1978.

Nikodimov, I. N. *Vospominanie o Kievo-Pecherskoi Lavre.* Munich, 1960.

Orlovskii, Hieromonk Damaskin. *Mucheniki, ispovedniki, i podvizhniki blagochestiia Rossiskoi Pravoslavnoi Tserkvi XX stoletiia,* vols. 1–6. Tver, Russia: Bulat, 1996.

Pavlova, I. V., ed. *Vozvrashenie pamiati: Istoriko-arkhivny al'manakh.* Novosibirsk, Russia, 1997.

Peris, Daniel. "Commissars in Red Cassocks." *Slavic Review* 54, no. 4 (Summer, 1995): 340–64.

———. *Storming the Heavens: The Soviet League of the Militant Godless.* Ithaca, N.Y.: Cornell University Press, 1998.

———. "The 1929 Congress of the Godless." *Soviet Studies* 43, no. 4 (1991): 711–32.

Perits, M. M. *Deiateli Oktiabria o religii i Tserkvi.* Moscow: Mysl, 1968.

———. *Otdelenie Tserkvi ot gosudarstva i shkolyi ot tserkvi v SSSR.* Moscow: Nauka, 1958.

Poliakov, I. A., V. B. Zhiromskaia, and I. N. Kiselev. "A Half-Century of Silence: The 1937 Census." *Russian Studies in History* 31, no. 1 (1992): 3–98.

———, and E. Vodarskii, eds. *Vsesoiuznaia perepis' naselenie 1937: Kratkie itogi.* Moscow: Akademia Nauk, 1991.

Pospielovsky, Dimitry. *A History of Marxist-Leninist Atheism and Soviet Anti-Religious Policies,* vol. 2. New York: St. Martin's Press, 1987.

———. *A History of Soviet Atheism in Theory and Practice, and the Believer,* vol. 1. New York: Shmorting Press, 1987.

———. *The Orthodox Church in the History of Russia.* Crestwood, N.Y.: St. Vladimir's Seminary Press, 1998.

———. *The Russian Church under the Soviet Regime 1917–1982,* vols. 1–2. Crestwood, N.Y.: St. Vladimir's Seminary Press, 1984.

———. *Soviet Antireligious Campaigns and Persecutions.* New York: St. Martin's Press, 1988.

Postanovlenie Vrerusskago s"ezda predstavitelei ot monastyrei, byvshago v Sviato-Troitskoi Lavre, s 16 do 23 iulia 1917 g.

Proshin, G. *Chernoe voinstvo: Russkii pravoslavnyi monastyr: Legenda i byl.* Moscow: Izd-vo polit. lit-ry, 1988.

Pushkarev, Sergei, Vladimir Rusak, and Gleb Yakunin. *Christianity and Government in Russia and the Soviet Union.* Boulder: Westview Press, 1989.

Reznikova, Irina. *Pravoslavnie na Solovkakh.* St. Petersburg: Memorial, 1994.
Robinson, N. F. *Monasticism in the Orthodox Churches.* London: Cope and Fenwick, 1916.
Roslof, Edward. "The Renovationist Movement in the Russian Orthodox Church, 1922–1946." Ph.D. diss., University of North Carolina, Chapel Hill, 1994.
Runciman, Sir Steven. *The Great Church in Captivity.* New York: Cambridge, 1968.
Rusak, Vladimir. *Svidetel'stvo obvineniia: tserkov i gosudarstvo v Sovetskom Souize.* Valley Cottage, N.Y.: Multilingual Typesetting, 1987.
Russkaia Pravoslavnaia Tserkov i Kommunisticheskoe Gosudarstvo 1917–1941: Dokumenty i fotomaterialy. Moscow, 1996.
Russkaia Pravoslavnaia Tserkov. *The Call of the Russian Church: A Report of the General Council of the Russian Orthodox Church, January 31–February 2, 1945.* London: Soviet News, 1945.
Russkoe Proshloe Istoriko-dokumental'nyi al'monakh, book 5, St. Petersburg, 1994.
Sbornik materialov po antireligioznoi propagande. Leningrad, 1938.
Scott, James C. *Domination and the Art of Resistance.* New Haven, Conn.: Yale University Press, 1990.
Serafima, Monakhina. *Iz vospominanii o matushke skhiigumenii Famari.* Moscow, 1991.
Shishkin, A. A. *Sushchnost i kriticheskaia otsenka obnovlencheskogo raskola russkoi pravoslavnoi tserkvi.* Kazan, Russia: Kazan University, 1970.
Siegelbaum, Lewis. *Soviet State and Society between Revolutions, 1918–1929.* Cambridge, UK: Cambridge University Press, 1992.
Sinaiskyi, Vasilii. *Pskovo-Pecherskii Monastyr.* Riga, Latvia, 1929.
Smolich, I. K. *Russkoe Monashestvo.* Moscow: Tserkovno-nauchny tsentr pravoslavnaya entsiklopedia, 1999.
Sokolov, A. K., ed. *Obshchestvo i vlast' 1930-god: Povestvovanie v Dokumenty.* Moscow: Rosspen, 1998.
Solzhenitsyn, Alexander. *The Gulag Archipelago,* vols. 1–3. New York: Harper and Row, 1973; Part 2, 1975.
Sosshavila, Monakhina Taisia. *Russkoe Pravoslavnoe Zhenskoe Monashestvo,* vols. 18–20. Sergeev Posad, Russia: Holy Trinity Monastery, 1992.
Stalin, I. V. *On the Draft Constitution of the USSR: Report Delivered at the Extraordinary Eighth Congress of the Soviets of the USSR.* Moscow, November 25, 1936.
Stanton, Leonard. *Optina Pustyn in the Russian Literary Imagination: Iconic Vision in Works by Dostoevsky, Gogol, Tolstoy, and Others.* New York: Peter Lang, 1995.
Szczesniak, Boleslaw. *The Russian Revolution and Religion: A Collection of Documents concerning Repression of Religion by the Communists, 1917–1925.* Notre Dame, Ind.: University of Notre Dame Press, 1959.

Tepliakova, Monakhina Anna. *Vospominanie.* Moscow: Novaia Kniga, 1998.

Tikhonov, V. I. *Lishenie izbiratel'nykh prav v Moskve v 1920–1930 gody.* Moscow, 1998.

Timberlake, Charles. "The Fate of Russian Orthodox Monasteries and Convents since 1917." Published as part of the Donald Treadgold papers, no. 103, Jackson School of International Studies, University of Washington, Seattle. May, 1995.

Tsipin, Protoieri Vladislav. *Istoriia Russkoi Pravoslavnaia Tserkvi, 1917–1990: Uchebnik dlia pravoslavnykh dukhovnykh seminarii.* Moscow: Moskovskaia Patriarkhiia Izdatel'skii dom "Khronika," 1994.

———. *Istoriia Russkoi Tserkvi, 1917–1997,* vol. 9. Moscow: Moskovskaia Patriarkhiia Izdatel'skii dom "Khronika," 1997.

Tucker, Robert, and Stephen Cohen, eds. *The Great Purge Trial.* New York: Grosset and Dunlap, 1965.

Valentinov, A. A. *The Assault of Heaven.* London: Boswell Printing, 1925.

Vasileva, Olga. "Russkaia Pravoslavnaia Tserkov v 1927–1943 godakh." *Voprossii Istorii* 4 (1994): 35–46.

Vestnik sviashchennago sinoda pravoslavnoi Rossiskoi tserkvi, no. 5, 1926.

Viola, Lynne. *Peasant Rebels under Stalin: Collectivization and the Culture of Peasant Resistance.* New York: Oxford University Press, 1996.

Ware, Timothy. *The Orthodox Church.* Harmonsworth, Middlesex, UK: Penguin, 1980.

Warhola, James. *Russian Orthodoxy and Political Culture in Transformation.* Pittsburgh: Center for Russian and East European Studies, 1993.

Yaroslavsky, E. M. *Ob antireligioznoi propagande.* Moscow, 1937.

Young, Glennys. "Rural Religion and Soviet Power, 1921–1932." Ph.D. diss., University of California, Berkeley, 1989.

Za Khrista Postradavshie: goneniia na russkuiu pravoslavnuiu tserkov' 1917–1956, book 1. Moscow, 1997.

"Zashita Veri v SSSR: Rukopis privezennaia iz Sovetskoi Rossii." Paris, 1966.

Zhizn Hieromonakha Nikona, Poslednyi Starets Optina Pustyn. St. Petersburg: Satis, 1994.

Zhuravskii, Alexander. *Tragediia v Raifskom Monastyre.* Kazan, Russia, 1994.

Zybkovets, Vladimir Filatovich. *Natsionalizatsiia monastyrskikh imushchestv v Sovetskoi Rossii, 1917–1921.* Moscow: Nauka, 1975.

Index

Pages with photographs indicated by *italic* typeface.

The ABC of Communism (Bukharin), 52
adaptation vs. accommodation: communist ideology as adaptive method, 102, 141, 174–75; and émigré monastic communities, 163–67; and goals of monastic survival, 112–13; in patriarchate, 51, 57–60, 108–11; post-communist era analysis of, xiv, 172–77; and pre-revolutionary reform movement, 31; and renovationists, 86–87, 90; success of adaptation, 138–39; during WWII, 167–68
Agafangel, Metropolitan of Iaroslavl, 84
Agafon, Abbot of Vysoko-Petrovskii, 107
agriculture: collectivization, 115–21, 125–28, 140; monasteries as communes, 37, 58–59, 61–70, 89, 101, 175–76; as spiritual practice vs. economic profit, 30
Akatevski monastery, 101
Aleftina, Abbess of Paul Posad, 44
Alekseev monastery, 171
Aleksei, Bishop of Smolensk, 90
Aleksia, Abbess of St. Nikolas, 59–60, 62
Alexander Nevsky lavra, 46–47, 101–102
Alexander-Svirski monastery, 49
Alexei I, Patriarch, 53–54
Alexei II, Patriarch, 162, *174*
Alexeivski monastery, 70
All-Russian Congress of Representatives from Monasteries (1917), 25–32
All-Russian Sobor of 1917, 32–35
All Saints Church and Monastery, *132*
Amvrosii (Ambrose), Elder, 6, 16, 41
Anatole, Elder, 69
Andreev, G., 137–38
Andreev, I. M., 138
Andrei, Bishop of Ufimski and Meizelinski, 31
Andronovna, Anna, 153
antireligious campaigns: and census results, 150–53; early Bolshevik, 38–45, 49–57; émigré churches as information sources, 157–58; inconsistencies in, 67, 83–84, 124–25; increasingly restrictive laws, 121–25; laity as focus of, 156–57; Lenin's views, 37, 38; mass deportations to labor camps, 134–39; under NEP, 94–108; relaxation of restrictions, 144–45; short- vs. long-term goals, 112. *See also* resistance to antireligious campaigns

Antonievo-Siiski monastery, 90
Antoniev-Spiiskom monastery, 64
Antonii, Metropolitan of St. Petersburg, 24
Antonii of Volhynia, 19–20
Antonin, Bishop, 88
Antonina, Abbess of Kizliar monastery, 51, 54–55, 133, 134
April laws of 1929, 121–25
aristocracy, pre-revolutionary, 18–19, 38, 45
Arsenii, Bishop of Pskov, 22
Arseny, Fr., 156, 158–59
artels, 62–70, 101, 175–76, 197*n* 75. *See also* communes, monastic
atheism, 36–37, 36–38, 53, 86. *See also* antireligious campaigns; League of the Militant Godless
Augustine, Bishop, 136
Avsenkov, Alexander Pavlovich, 159

Bartholomew, Bishop, 106, 158
Basil the Great, 4
Batozsky, Fr. Tavrion, 138
bedniaks (poor peasants), 117, 126
bells, church, removal of, 122, *123*
Berdyaev, Nicholas, 15–16, 20–21
Bezbozhnik, 42, 97. *See also* League of the Militant Godless
bishops, hierarchical role of, 3, 4, 24. *See also* patriarchate
black clergy vs. white clergy, 4, 5, 17–19, 30, 34. *See also* monasticism
Black Hundreds, 19–20
"Bloody Sunday" in 1905, 18–19
Bogdanov, Alexander, 38
Bogolepov, Alexander, 21
Bogoliubski monastery, 65
Bogoroditsa Smolenskii travelers' society, 134
Bol'shakovoi, Alipii, 92
Bolsheviks: antireligious campaigns, 38–45, 49–57; Church accommodation of, 57–60; and famine, 72–79; initial impact on Church, 34–35; and monasteries as agricultural communes, 61–70; philosophical opposition to religion, 36–38; religious resistance to, 45–49, 60–61, 70–72; support for renovationist movement, 85–87. *See also* New Economic Policy (NEP); Soviet government
Bonch-Bruevich, V. D., 47
brotherhoods, lay, 31–32, 41, 60–61, 73
The Brothers Karamazov (Dostoevsky), 16
Bubaev, Vladimir, 170–71
Bukharin, Nikolai, 38, 52–53
Bulgakov, Sergei, 15
Butova labor camp, 158–59

calendar issue (Julian vs. Gregorian), 90, 91
California, émigré monasteries in, 164–65
capitalism in monasteries, 24, 30, 45
Catacomb Church, xiv. *See also* Karlovatskii synod
Catherine the Great, 9–10, 11
ceaseless prayer, 9, 13, 111–12
cenobitic monastic model, 4–5, 10, 12–14, 163–67. *See also* communes, monastic
censuses, 95, 150–53
charitable work, 14, 88, 89, 121
Cheka (All-Russian Extraordinary Commission for Struggle against Counter-Revolution, Sabotage, and Speculation), 52, 196*n* 49
Cheliabinskaia, Evgenia, 134
China, émigré monasteries in, 164
Christianity and socialism, 38, 57, 90. *See also* monasticism; religion; Russian Orthodox Church
churches, parish: closing of, 125, 127, 135, 141, 149; declines in numbers

and increase in usage, 147–49; monasteries as, 120; and nationalization of property, 58; renewed persecution of, 155
civil rights, xiii, 41, 66, 118, 143–47, 154
civil war, Russian (1918–1921): Bolshevik antireligious campaign, 49–57; Church accommodation to Bolsheviks, 57–60; and famine, 72–79; lay brotherhoods' defense of monasticism, 60–61; monasteries as agricultural communes, 61–70; persistence of religious faith during, 70–72
class, socioeconomic: Church's focus on certain classes, 15, 21–22; class struggle ideology and peasants, 117; and equality in monasteries, 5; intelligentsia, 15–17, 21–22, 91; and League of the Militant Godless, 97; and nationalization of property, 179; pre-revolutionary aristocracy, 18–19, 38, 45; and restrictions on voting rights, 146; and treatment by Soviet authorities, 44–45, 59, 61, 101, 116; working class and religion, 58–59, 61, 88–89, 100
clergy: black vs. white, 17–19, 30, 34; co-opting of ideology for survival, 102, 141, 174–75; economic marginalization of, 121, 147; influence of young, 149; re-enfranchisement of, 144, 145; resentment of state control, 11; resistance to Soviets, 56, 126–27; response to Great Retreat, 146; Soviet fears of political power, 150; Soviet inconsistencies in treatment of, 54–55. *See also* executions of clergy; monasticism; parish priests; patriarchate
closing of churches, 125, 127, 135, 141, 149
collectivization, 115–21, 125–28, 140
communes, monastic: as agricultural collectives, 37, 58–59, 61–70, 89, 101, 175–76; and *cenobitic* model, 4–5, 10, 12–14, 163–67; charitable work, 14, 88, 89, 121; and "cooperation" with Soviets, 175–76; and evangelization, 99; vs. other agricultural collectives, 119
communism: class struggle ideology and peasants, 117; clergy's co-opting of ideology for survival, 102, 141, 174–75; as compatible with religion, 123–24; in monastic social structure, 4–5, 61–70; as substitute religion, 98
Communist Party: controversy over clergy rights, 145; disunity on religion, 38, 80, 83–84, 149; pressure for monasteries to join, 59–60; purges within, 81, 142, 154; religious members of, 71; as sole legal party, 143. *See also* Soviet government
confession, 6, 11
Constantine the Great, 7
Constantinople, patriarch of, 3
constitution of 1936, 143–54
contemplative vs. charitable monasteries, 9, 14, 89
corruption in monasteries, 22–23. *See also* moral issues for monasteries
councils, church, 25–35, 85, 87–88
CSCRQ (Standing Committee on Religious Questions), 141–42, 147–48, 152
cult commission (CSCRQ), 141–42, 147–48, 152
culture, Russian: Bolshevik debate over value of, 38; destruction of old to make way for new, 36, 116; mistrust of capitalist philosophy, 45; religion as integral part of, 8, 40, 72, 79; renewal under NEP, 81
Cunningham, James, 15
Curtiss, John, 14–15, 51

Danilov monastery, *129*, 129–30, 211*n* 3
Davies, Sarah, xi, 142
Declaration of 1927, 109–10, 202*n* 85
Decree of Separation of Church and State in Russia, 40, 181–82
Denisov, Lev, xii
Deutscher, Isaac, xi
diocesan inns, reform of, 24
discipline, monastic, reform of, 10, 23. *See also* moral issues for monasteries
disunity within Church: and adaptation vs. accommodation, 108–13; prerevolutionary lack of, 20–21; renovationist movement, 82–94, 137, 202; as weakness against Bolsheviks, 34–35
Diveevo monastery, 131
Dnepropetrovsk, secret monastery in, 156
Domination and the Arts of Resistance (Scott), 176
Don monastery, *130*
Donskoi monastery, 69
Dostoevsky, Fyodor, 16

economic issues: collectivization, 115–21, 125–28, 140; marginalization of clergy, 121, 147; and monastery management, 24, 30, 50, 87; relaxation of strict communism, 81. *See also* New Economic Policy (NEP); property
education as tool in antireligious campaign, 83, 95, 98, 122–23
eldership tradition, 6–7, 102–103
elections under constitution of 1936, 145, 153–54
Elizabeth, Tsarina of Russia, 11
Elizabeth Society, 68–69
émigré Orthodox churches, xiv, 110–11, 157–58, 161–67
Estonia, surviving monasteries in, 119, 162–63
evangelization, monasteries as tools for, 88, 99
Evpraksia, Mother, 158
executions of clergy: by Bolsheviks, 53, 76; during civil war period, 82; during Great Retreat, 149; during Great Terror, 154, 156; increase under Stalin, 135; under NEP, 84
exile, internal, 56, 111, 126, 134–39, 158–59

famine, 72–79, 82, 83–84, 135
farming. *See* agriculture
fascism vs. communism, 144
Fedotov, G. P., 6
Filaret, Metropolitan of Moscow, 12
Finland, émigré monasteries in, 162
Fitzpatrick, Sheila, x, xi, 81
Flavian, Metropolitan of Kiev, 19–20
Fletcher, William, x
Florensky, Pavel, 69–70
Fomara, Mother, 136
forced-labor camps, 56, 111, 134–39, 158–59
Fourth All-Russian Missionary Congress, 23
freedom of religion, mixed record of Soviets on, 41, 144, 181
Freeze, Gregory, 15, 21
Frolovna, Nina, 133
Fudel, S. I., 112

Gapon, Fr. Georgii, 18–19
Gefimanski skete, 63, 102
Getty, J. Arch, 146
Gogol, Nikolai, 16
Golder, Frank, 76, 77
Goloseevski monastery, 106
Gorky, Maxim, 38
GPU (Chief Political Administration), 55, 84, 140, 196*n* 49
graveyards as religious meeting places, 134

Great Retreat (1933–1935), 140–43
Great Terror (1937–1938), 154–61
Gregorian vs. Julian calendars, 90
Griaznova, Vasilia, 44

hermetic life, 4, 133, 160
hesychasm (prayer of the heart), 9, 13, 111–12
hired workers and loss of monastic discipline, 24 25, 30
Holy Trinity St. Sergius lavra, 26, 41, 63, 69–70, 98
hospitality of monasteries, pilgrims' abuses of, 28
Husband, William, x6p1.259

Iaonno-Bogoslovski monastery, 50, 134
icons, religious, restoration of, 100, 171
identity, Russian ethnic, Church as integral part of, 8, 40
idiorhythmic tradition, 9–12, 160
Ignatia, Mother, 107, 133
individualism, proponents of, 15–16
industrialization and collectivization of agriculture, 115–16
intelligentsia and Church, 15–17, 21–22, 91
internal security organizations: Cheka, 52, 196*n* 49; GPU, 55, 84, 140, 196*n* 49; NKVD, 140, 156–57; "sabotage" investigation, 142
international opinion, Soviet concern over, 150
involuntary seclusion and moral abuses among monastics, 30
Ionniki, Abbot of Novo-Ierusalimski, 56
Iosif, Elder, 16
itinerant monastics, 120, 134, 160–61
Ivan IV of Russia, 8
Ivanovskii monastery, 61

Jonah, Fr., 50
judicial structure, changes in, 140
Juliana, Abbess, 159
Julian vs. Gregorian calendars, 90
juridical rights, Church's lack of, 110

Kalachevskii monastery, 63
Kalinin, Mikhail Ivanovich, 125, 145–46
Kalinovskii, Fr., 85
Karlovatskii synod: and Church politics, 77, 78, 110, 137; in forced-labor camps, 111, 137; patriarchal source for, 51
Kazanskii cathedral at Optina Pustyn, 103
Kerensky, Alexander, 31
Khomyakov, Aleksei Stepanovich, 21
Khrapovitskii, Antonii, Metropolitan of Kiev and Kharkov, 18, 19, 77
Kievo-Pecherskaia lavra, 87, 93, 104–106
Kirillo-Belozerskii monastery, 22
Kirov, Sergei, 143, 154
Kitaevski Pustyn monastery, 106
Kizliar monastery, 51
Kline, George, 14–15
kolkhozi (agricultural communes), 61–70, 101, 119
Kollontai, Alexandra, 46
Komsomol (Young Communist League), 95, 99, 116, 125, 203*n* 6
Konevets monastery, 162
Kosenkova, Anna, 153
Kotelnikov, Vladimir, 6
Kotkin, Stephen, 142
Kozelsk as center for informal monasticism, 103 104
Krasikov, P. A., 149
Kraval', I. A., 151–52
Kronid, Archimandrite, 45, 63
kulaks (rich peasants), 91, 116–18, 126, 127, 203*n* 5
Kuznetsov, Nikolai, 65

labor camps, 56, 111, 134–39, 158–59
labor communes, 62–70, 101, 175–76. *See also* communes, monastic
laity: appeal of persecuted church for, 149; brotherhoods, 31–32, 41, 60–61, 73; as focus of antireligious persecution, 156–57; lack of input into Church future, 18; monasteries as retreat houses for, 88, 89, 120; participation in 1917 *sobor*, 32; and prosecutions for relic fraud, 44; and renovationist movement, 91; restrictions on visitations to monasteries, 30; support for monastics, x–xi, 6, 60–61, 99, 158, 170–71; support for patriarchate, 19. *See also* peasants
Lake Ladoga, émigré monastery at, 162
land, monastic. *See* property
lavra (unofficial groups of monks), 4, 189*n* 2
League of the Militant Godless: and church closings, 135; disbanding of, 167–68; focus on soldier conversions, 128; ineffectiveness of, 122–25; rise and fall of, 97–100; and Yaroslavsky, 51, 83
Lenin, Vladimir Ilyich: death of, 108; relaxation of strict communism, 81; on religion, 37, 38, 39–40, 75–77; succession issue, 96; support for militant atheist society, 95
Leonid of Optina, 6
Leont'ev, Konstantin, 16
Leonty, Archbishop of Chile, 104–105, 106
Leonty, Archbishop of Kiev, 158
Leushinski monastery, 62
Levchenko, Fr. Lavrentii, 103
Levin, Moshe, x, 115
Levitin-Krasnov, A. E., 131
liberal clergy. *See* renovationist movement
lishentsy (rights-deprived persons), xiii, 118, 145, 154
Living Church movement, 18, 82–94, 110
local Soviet authorities: fears of peasant rebellion, 127; and inconsistencies in antireligious policies, 39, 54–55, 67; power of, xi; as scapegoats for unpopular central policies, 125
Lotman, Yuri, 36, 72
Lunacharskii, Anatoli, 38, 79, 83, 85–86, 95
Luukaanen, Arto, 96–97, 142
Lvov, V. N., 25

Marinskii labor camp, 135
marriage, parish priests vs. monastics, 4
Marriage, Children, and Registration of Civil Status, 40
Marx, Karl, 37
Marxism, shortcomings of vision, xi–xii
Maxim, Bishop of Serpukhov, 111
Mazinova, Olga, 44
McKown, Delos B., 37
Meehan-Waters, Brenda, 12
Melchizeldek, Abbot of Alekseev, 171
men's monasteries, disciplinary reforms, 13, 27–28. *See also* monasticism
middle class, Church's failure to court, 21–22
Mikhailovich, Alexei, 130
military, naval revolt after civil war, 80. *See also* Red Army/Red Guards
Miliukov, P. N., 60
Mitrofan, Bishop of Astrakhan, 34
monasteries in the world, 113, 129–34, 171–72
monasticism: appeal for intelligentsia, 16; black clergy vs. white clergy, 4, 17–19, 30, 34; Bolshevik compromise

treatment of, 57–60, 61; Bolshevik persecution of, 45–47, 49–50, 100–108, 134–39, 158–59; and census participation, 152–53; closing of monasteries, 55–56; and collectivization campaign, 118–21; daily life in, 14; early reform efforts, 12–14; flexibility vs. patriarchate, 78; land losses, 10–11, 56–59; lay support for, x–xi, 6, 60–61, 99, 158, 170–71; and League of the Militant Godless, 98; monasteries as sources of wealth, 9–12; monastery definition, 187*n* 1; moral behavior issues, 22–32, 35, 87, 101; in Moscow, xii–xiii; Orthodox vs. Catholic, 3–4; outside Soviet Union, 119, 161–67; overview, ix–x, 9–10; persistence of, 71–72, 155–61; post-Communist status of, 170–71; power in Church, 17–18, 83; prerevolution strength, 187*n* 3; and renovationist reforms, 87–90, 92; resistance to Soviet regime, xi, 78–79, 81–82, 112–34, 177; Soviet fear of, 65–66, 86; and *starchestvo* tradition, 6–7; urban underground, 128–34; Whites vs. Reds in treatment of, 49–51; WWII numbers, 168. *See also* adaptation vs. accommodation; communes, monastic; property

monetary assets of monasteries, Soviet confiscation of, 58

moral issues for monasteries, 22–32, 35, 87, 101, 138

Mount Athos, 13, 161–62

museums, monastery conversions into, 44, 69, 78–79, 98, 102

NARKOMIUST (People's Commissariat of Justice), 52, 55–56, 65–66, 72

nationalization: of Church property, 10–11, 37, 38–41, 47, 56–59; collectivization of agriculture, 115–21, 125–28, 140; and local government stewardship, 183–85; and social class, 179

national Orthodox churches, 3

Nazari, Bishop, 43–44

Nektaria, Mother, *17*

Nektary, Elder of Optina Pustyn, 102–103, 110

New Economic Policy (NEP): and Church schism, 108–13; compromises on religion, 82; ending of, 114–15; erosion of monasticism under, 100–108; Living Church movement, 82–94; as relaxation of war communism, 80–82; renewal of antireligious campaign, 94–100

New York, émigré monasteries in, 164, 166

Nicholas II, Tsar of Russia, 20, 78

Nikandr, Bishop, 72

Nikitskii monastery, 66

Nikolo-Babaevskii monastery, 64

Nikolo-Perevinski monastery, 64

Nikolski monastery, 63, 70

Nikon, Bishop of Vologda, 23

Nikon, Fr., 62, 64, 103, 104

Nizhni Novgorod, secret monastery in, 156

NKVD (People's Commissariat of Internal Affairs), 140, 156–57

non-Orthodox Christians in Russia, 18, 90, 93, 165–66

nonperson, designation as, 145

novitiate, 5, 28

Novodevichy monastery, 69, *131*

nuns. *See* monasticism; women

Ober-Procurator, 10

obshchestvennost (middle class), 21–22

Odarchenko, A. F., 33
OGPU (Chief Political Administration), 55, 84, 140, 196*n* 49
Okninsky, A., 71
Olsufiev, Count A., 48
Optina Pustyn monastery: as agricultural commune, 63–64; bells at, *123;* closing of, 102–104; craft work in, *29;* elder's house, *17;* relics of, 41; restoration of, *172, 173, 174–75, 176;* St. John's skete, *104, 105;* and *starchestvo* practice, 6, 16, 69, 102–103, 110
orders, monastic, Orthodox lack of, 4

Palestine, Russian Orthodox monasteries in, 161
parish churches. *See* churches, parish
parish priests: governmental role of, 5; local political power of, 99; and monastic discipline, 30, 111–12; vs. monastics, 4, 17–19, 30, 34; and renovationist movement, 83, 86, 91
passive resistance method, 126, 177
Patriarchal Church: adaptation vs. accommodation in, xiv, 51, 57–60, 108–11; Alexei I, 53–54; Alexei II, 162, *174;* vs. Karlovatskii synod, 110, 137; and renovationist movement, 82–83, 86. *See also* Russian Orthodox Church; Tikhon Belin, Metropolitan of Moscow
patriarchate: abolishment of, 10; restoration movement, 17–18, 19, 34; Stalin's wartime revival of, 168; and structure of Church, 3
peasants: Bolshevik conversion strategies, 86; Church's focus on support from, 21; collectivization and control of, 115–16; as defenders of faith, x, 56, 70–71, 117, 121; *kulaks,* 91, 116–18, 126, 127, 203*n* 5; resistance to Soviet policies, 80, 95, 125–26; Soviet concerns about antagonizing, 82, 101, 127
Peris, Daniel, 97
persecution: as inspiration to new monastics, 102, 106–108, 131, 133; of laity, 156–57; of monastics, 45–47, 49–50, 100–108, 134–39, 158–59; of parish churches, 155; persistence of faith under, 77; and personification of monasticism, 160. *See also* antireligious campaigns
Peter, Metropolitan, 109
Peter the Great, 10–11, 45
Philip, Metropolitan of Moscow, 8
Philokalia (Velichovsky), 13
pilgrims to monasteries, restrictions on visitation, 28
Pimen, Archimandrite, 156
Piuhtitsai monastery, 162–63
Pobedonostsev, Konstantin, 18
podvorye (diocesan inns), reform of, 24
politics: and Karlovatskii synod, 77, 78, 110, 137; and monasteries as sources of wealth, 9–12; parish priests vs. monastics, 4, 5, 17–19, 30, 34; and religion at village level, 91, 99, 126–27; Soviet fears of clergy power, 65–66, 86, 101, 150; traditional Orthodox role in, ix, 4, 13. *See also* Communist Party; state/Church relationship
Polozov, Y. A., 93
POMGOL (Central Committee for Aid to the Starving), 73
Popov, N., 87
Porfiri, Brother, 63
Pospielovsky, Dimitry, 82
post-Communist restoration of monasteries, 170–71
poverty as monastic ideal, 9. 30
prayer of the heart, 9, 13, 111–12
pre-sobor commissions, 20, 25–32

prisons, monastery conversions to, 56–57
Problems of Life (Trotsky), 40
Prokopii, Bishop, 46
property: Bolshevik inconsistencies in handling, 61–70; brotherhoods' role in preserving, 60–61; class considerations, 118, 179; communal use of, 10, 13; and difficulties in restoring monasteries, 171; dispossession of Church, 182; distribution to peasants, 56; richness of monastic holdings, 24–25; state vs. Church control, 20, 31. *See also* nationalization
Protestant churches, 90, 93
protests. *See* resistance to antireligious campaigns
Pskov-Pecherskaia monastery, 119, 162–63
public opinion and preservation of religion, 120, 146–47
purges (1934–1938), 143–44, 152, 154–61

Rabinowitch, Alexander, 81
Radonezh, Sergius, 9
Rasputin, 23
rassaphore level in monasteries, 5
Read, Christopher, 15
Red Army/Red Guards: inconsistency of indoctrination in, 71; mixed reactions to religious regiments, 50–51; reliability problems with soldiers, 127–28; religious feeling in, 46–47, 128, 204–205*n* 39; vandalism of monasteries by, 49, 50
Reese, Roger, 128
reform movements, Church, 12–17, 18, 82–94, 110
Regiments of Jesus, 50–51
relics, Soviet exposure campaign, 41–45
religion: Bolsheviks' philosophical opposition to, 36–38; communism as substitute for, 98; as compatible with communism, 123–24; evidence of survival, 150–53; freedom of, 41, 144, 181; inconsistency of Bolshevik policies, 66–67; as integral part of Russian culture, 8, 40, 72, 79; in labor camps, 135–37; monasteries as spiritual sources for laity, 120; non-Orthodox Christians in Russia, 18, 90, 93, 165–66; peasants as defenders of, x, 56, 70–71, 117, 121; people's attachment to, 45–49, 70–72, 95–96, 103–104, 106; persistence under persecution, 102, 106–108, 131, 133, 134; restoration of icons, 100; soldiers' attachment to, 46–47, 128, 204–205*n* 39; Soviet tolerance of, 59, 68–69, 82; village protection of, 99, 116, 126–27. *See also* monasticism; Russian Orthodox Church
religious processions as protests, 48, 92
renovationist movement, 18, 82–94, 110
resistance to antireligious campaigns: by clergy, 46, 56, 126–27; and focus of research, x; in forced-labor camps, 158; initial protest against Bolsheviks, 45–49; monastic, xi, 78, 81–82, 112–34, 177; nature of, 173–76; by peasants, 70–71, 80, 95, 125–26; and persistence of faith, 70–72; violent, 47–48, 85, 92, 99, 122, 176; written complaints to government, 124–25. *See also* adaptation vs. accommodation
Revolutionary Divorce Law, 40
rights, civil, xiii, 66, 118, 143–47, 154
Roman Catholic Church, 3–5, 89, 166
Roslof, Edward, 86
Rossman, Jeffrey, xi
Rufina, Abbess of Iaonno-Bogoslovski monastery, 50, 134

rural areas: antireligious campaign problems in, 125–28; and NEP policies, 81; opposition to Militant Godless, 98–99; persistence of religion in, 103–104, 106; rejection of renovationist movement in, 91; secret monasteries in, 133–34. *See also* agriculture; peasants
Russia in the Era of NEP (Fitzpatrick, Rabinowitch, and Stites), 81
The Russian Idea (Berdyaev), 15
Russian Orthodox Church: anti-Communism as focus for unity, 36; benefits of WWII for, 167–68; disillusionment over perceived collaboration, 177; disunity within, 82–94, 108–13, 137, 202; and famine, 72–79, 83–84; historical overview, 8–11; information difficulties during Great Terror, 157; initial Bolshevik impact on Church, 34–35; as last bastion against Bolsheviks, 48; nineteenth century reform movement, 14–17; overview, ix, xii; vs. Roman Catholic Church, 3–5, 89, 166; support for Whites during civil war, 50–51; and voter education, 153. *See also* monasticism; Patriarchal Church; patriarchate; state/Church relationship
Russian Orthodox Church Abroad, xiv, 163–67
Russian People's Church, 91

St. Amvrosii (Ambrose) of Optina Pustyn, 6, 16, 41
St. Daniel monastery, 61
St. Herman of Alaska monastery, 164–65, 166
St. John's skete, Optina Pustyn, *105*
St. Petersburg, 195*n* 31
St. Sergius of Radonezh, 41, 45–46
St. Tikhon's Monastery, California, 164
Sampson, Elder, 53–54
schema level of monastic life, 5
schism of 1927, 108–13, 137, 202
schools, separation from Church, 181
Scott, James C., 176
Sebastian, Fr., 159–60
secret monasticism: disciplinary basis for, 112; and émigré monasteries, 163; punishment for, 135; as resistance method, 177; underground system, 155–61; in urban areas, 132–34
sectarians in Russia, 94, 96–97, 99
secularization of rites of passage, 181, 194*n* 16
self-determination vs. separation of Church and state, 33, 193*n* 72
separation, Church/state: inconsistency of Bolshevik policies, 66, 69–70; maintenance of, 147; official declaration, 40, 181–82; pre-revolutionary positions, 32–35, 193*n* 72; Soviet insistence on, 57
Serafima, Abbess of Vladimir-Ekterina monastery, 43
Serafima, Mother, 71–72, 131, 133
Seraphim, Archimandrite, 165, 166
Sergei, Metropolitan of Iaroslavl, 94
Sergei, Metropolitan of Nizhni Novgorod, 109–10, 167–68
Serpukhovski Devichy monastery, 64–65
Shakhovski monastery, 68
Shamordino monastery, 6, 16, 59, 63, 103
Shishilenko, Michael A., 111
sketes, 9, 190*n* 14
skhod (village assembly), 99, 126–27
Slavianskie Donetsk, secret monasteries in, 156
Smolensk guberniia, xiii, 94, 99
sobornost, 20–21, 32
sobors (Church councils), 25–35, 85, 87–88

socialism and Christianity, 38, 57, 90
Sofia of Raiskii, Mother, 135
Solovki monastery, 56, 137–39
Solzhenitsyn, Alexander, 56, 136
Sorskii, Nils, 9
Soviet government: censuses, 95, 150–53; class consciousness of, 44–45, 59, 61, 101, 116, 179; elections (1937), 153–54; fear of clergy influence, 65–66, 86, 101, 150; Great Retreat (1933–1935), 140–43; interference in patriarchal succession, 109–10; new constitution (1936), 143–54; purges (1934–1938), 143–44, 152, 154–61; response to rural resistance, 127–28; shifts in historical view of, xi–xii, 173–74; support for monastery collectives, 89; support for renovationist movement, 93; WWII relaxation of religious restrictions, 167–69. *See also* antireligious campaigns; Bolsheviks; Communist Party; local Soviet authorities; nationalization
soviet (village council), 99, 126–27
sovkhozi (monastic agricultural communes), 59, 62, 65. *See also* communes, monastic
spiritual monasticism, 112
sredniaks (middle peasants), 117, 126
Stalin, Iosif V.: and characterizations of 1933–1935 period, 142; concern about international opinion, 146; and control of patriarchate, 109; and harder line on religion, 114, 119; initial moderate stance on religion, 96; public enfranchisement of clergy, 144; reputation for murder, 143; seminary training of, 97; use of Church for WWII propaganda, 167
Stalin Constitution (1936), 143–54
starchestvo (eldership tradition), 6–7, 102–103
state/Church relationship: autonomy movement for Church, 7, 17–22, 31; Church as first among denominations, 32–33; history of, 7–8; and need for Bolsheviks to destroy past, 36; subordination of Church to state, 10–11, 18. *See also* antireligious campaigns; New Economic Policy (NEP); separation, Church/state
Stites, Richard, 81
suffrage issue, 118, 144–45, 146
Sventitsky, Valentin, 111–12
Sviatgorski monastery, 156
symphonia (equal partnership), Church/state, 7, 11, 17–22
synod of bishops and church structure, 3, 60

Talgskii monastery, 124
Theofan the Recluse, Bishop, 12–13
Tikhon Belin, Metropolitan of Moscow: anathematizing of Bolshevik regime, 47–48; death of, 108; denial of support to Whites, 51; and disunity over patriarchate, 83; elevation to patriarchate, 34; and Karlovatskii synod, 77, 78; lay loyalty to, 91; powerlessness of, 65; and relic exposure campaign, 43–44, 46; vs. renovationists, 84, 92–93; response to famine, 73, 74–75; support for monastic labor communes, 62; support for resistance to Soviets, 56
Timasheff, Nicholas, 140, 142
Titlinov, Boris, 90
Tolstoy, Lev, 16
Tomskii, Mikhail, 100
tonsures, 5, 102, 133
totalitarian model of Soviet society, questioning of, 173–74
transfers of monks and moral behavior problems, 29–30

treasures, church. *See* valuables, church
trials of clergy and laity by Soviets, 82, 84, 106, 135. *See also* executions of clergy; forced-labor camps
Troitse-Sergeev lavra, 26, 41, 63, 69–70, 98
Trotsky, Leon, 38, 40, 83–84, 96, 100
Trubetskoi, E. N., 33
True Orthodox Church. *See* Karlovatskii synod
Tuchkov, Evgenyi Aleksandrovich, 84

Union of Russian People, 19, 20
United States, émigré monasteries in, 164–65
Ural mountains as refuge for monastics, 155
urban religious life: Church neglect of, 21–22, 34–35; Church's focus on middle class, 15; continuation during civil war, 72; as focus of research, xii–xiii; Militant Godless campaign in, 100; and origins of renovationist movement, 91; and revival at Vysoko-Petrovskii, 106; underground monasticism, 128–34
Uspenski monastery, 70

Vadkovskii, Metropolitan Antonii, 18
Valaam monastery, 90, 162
Valdaisky Korotsky monastery, 59–60
valuables, church, confiscation of, 73–77, 84, 85, 93, 106, 155
Vasiliev, A. V., 33
Velichovsky, Paisius, 13
Veniamin, Metropolitan of Petrograd, 48, 83
villages: protection of religion in, 91, 99, 116, 126–27; tension over land restoration to monasteries, 171. *See also* peasants
Viola, Lynne, xi
violence: bell-removal protests, 122; as ineffective resistance method, 176; over confiscation of church valuables, 85; and rejection of antireligious campaign, 47–48, 99; against renovationists, 92
Vladikavkaz, Caucasus, 51
Vladimir, Metropolitan of Kiev, 48
Vladimir of Kiev, Prince, 8
Volkova, Evdokia, 43
voting rights, 118, 144–45, 146
VTsIK (All-Russian Central Executive Committee of Soviets), 121
Vvedevenskii, Dean Alexander, 65, 83, 92
Vysoko-Petrovskii monastery, 106–108

wandering monastics, 120, 134, 160–61
war communism, revolt against strictures of, 80
Western Europe, émigré monasteries in, 163–64
Whites during civil war, 49–51, 77–78
White Sea monastery, 8
white vs. black clergy, 4, 5, 17–19, 30, 34. *See also* parish priests
Witte, Sergei, 18
women: disciplinary reforms in monasteries, 25, 27–28; in forced-labor camps, 136, 158; and immorality excuse for closure of monasteries, 101; Militant Godless focus on education of, 123; monastic attention to spiritual life of, 6; and protests against antireligious campaigns, 122; return of *cenobitic* model, 12–13; and social position of monasteries, ix
workers: criticism of monastics as, 88–89; monastics as proletarians, 58–59, 61; religiosity of urban, 100
World War I, Church's support for, 34–35

World War II and relaxation of religion prohibitions, xiv, 167–69
worship services, 121, 158, 181

Yakovlev, Alexander, 154
Yaroslavsky, Emelian: Communism as substitute religion, 98; on dangers of clergy influence, 119, 145, 149; on demise of renovationist movement, 93; educated vs. uneducated believers, 83; as education advocate, 123; moderation of antireligious policy, 82; on persistence of religion dangers, 142; and violence of peasants, 50–51
Yedlinsky, M. Ye., 156
Young, Glennys, x, 99
youth, return to monasticism under persecution, 133

Zagorsk monastery/museum, 69
zhenskie obshchiny (women's cenobitic communities), 12
Zhidkov, Hieromonk Dosifei, 43
Zhirnov, Br. Ilya, 64
Zosima Pustyn monastery, 107

ISBN 1-58544-332-8

90000

9 781585 443321